MASONIC FACTS AND FICTIONS

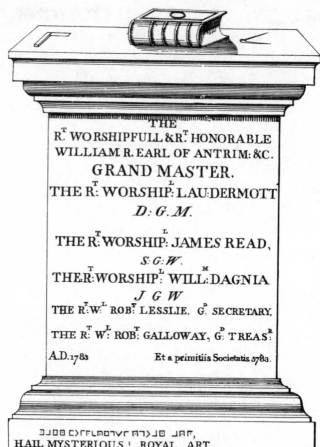

THE
R.^T WORSHIPFULL &R.^T HONORABLE
WILLIAM. R. EARL OF ANTRIM: &C.

GRAND MASTER.

THE R.^T WORSHIP:^L LAU:DERMOTT
D: G. M.

THE R.^T WORSHIP:^L JAMES READ,
S: G: W.

THE.R:WORSHIP:^L WILL:^M DAGNIA
J G W

THE R:W.^L ROB.^T LESSLIE. G.^D SECRETARY,

THE R:^T W:^L ROB.^T GALLOWAY, G.^D TREAS.^R.

A.D. 1783   Et a primitiis Societatis 5783.

HAIL MYSTERIOUS ! ROYAL ART,

WHAT WONDERS ! DOES, THY SONS IMPART:

WHO, WITH TWO SQUARES, CAN MAKE APPEAR,

THAT HANDS CAN SPEAK ! AND EYES CAN HEAR !!!

L. DERMOTT.

FROM A DRAWING BY LAU. DERMOTT IN THE
"H. R. A. GRAND .CHAPTER REGISTER" ("ANCIENTS")

MASONIC FACTS AND FICTIONS

Comprising

A New Theory of the Origin of the 'Antient' Grand Lodge

HENRY SADLER, P.M. and P.Z.

Formerly Grand Tyler and Sub-Librarian
of the Grand Lodge of England

Introduced by John Hamill

If circumstances lead me, I will find
Where truth is hid, though it were hid indeed
Within the centre.

Shakespeare

THE AQUARIAN PRESS

First published 1887
This Edition first published 1985

British Library Cataloguing in Publication Data

Sadler, Henry
Masonic facts and fictions.
1. Freemasons—Ancient Grand Lodge
(England)—History
I. Title
366.1′0942   HS596.A5

ISBN 0-85030-440-7

*The Aquarian Press is part of the
Thorsons Publishing Group, Wellingborough,
Northamptonshire, NN8 2RQ, England*

Printed in Great Britain by
Woolnough Bookbinding Limited, Irthlingborough,
Northamptonshire

3 5 7 9 10 8 6 4

To

The V.W. Thomas Fenn,

Past Grand Deacon of England,

President of the Board of General Purposes, &c.,

As a small acknowledgment of
many acts of brotherly kindness
received at his hands,

In humble admiration of his numerous and
important Masonic services
and his indefatigable zeal for the benefit of

The Fraternity in general
and
The Emulation Lodge of Improvement
in particular,

This Work is respectfully and fraternally
Dedicated by the Author.

London, 1887.

HENRY SADLER

INTRODUCTION

HENRY SADLER was born on 19 October 1840. Nothing is
known of his early life or education. He entered the
Merchant Marine at the age of fifteen and served until 1862,
when he returned to London and spent two years as a
commercial traveller. It was at this time that he began his
long connection with Freemasonry, when he was initiated
in 1862 in the Lodge of Justice No. 147, London. At the
same time Freemasons' Hall, which had stood since 1776,
was being greatly expanded and Sadler was taken on to the
Grand Secretary's staff as Assistant to the Grand Tyler in
1865. A full-time, paid official of the Grand Lodge, the
Grand Tyler's principal duty was to prepare for and assist
at the quarterly meetings of the United Grand Lodge and
Supreme Grand Chapter of England, the great ceremonial
occasions of both and at the Consecration of new lodges
and Chapters in London. In addition he acted as
housekeeper at the Hall and saw to the letting of the various
lodge and committee rooms, to do which he had living
accommodation in the Hall. Sadler was himself appointed
Grand Tyler in 1879 and was to hold the office for thirty-
one years, during which he assisted at over six hundred
Consecrations, regularly attended many of the lodges and
Chapters meeting in his domain, and became one of the best
known and most popular figures in London Freemasonry.
　Early in his Masonic career Sadler developed an interest
in the history of Freemasonry. His position and residence
in Freemasons' Hall gave him a unique opportunity to
search through all the cupboards and storerooms in the Hall

and to collect together and conserve the archives of the Grand Lodge and Grand Chapter. The publication of two new weekly Masonic newspapers, *The Freemason* (1869) and *The Freemasons' Chronicle* (1875) enabled him to share his discoveries with the Craft in general. These contributions to the Masonic press brought him to the attention of that select band of Masonic students, Gould, Hughan, Lane, Speth *et al.*, who were beginning to establish what has become known as the scientific or authentic school of Masonic history. The subject, from the first official history compiled by James Anderson for the *Constitutions* of 1723 to the multi-volumed effusions of the Revd. George Oliver (1782—1867), had been bedevilled by writers who made up for what they lacked in authentic detail by romantic speculations, who made no differentiation between established fact and informed, or more often than not uninformed, conjecture. Sadler's contributions to the Masonic press rapidly established him as an authority well within the authentic school.

His interest in preserving and disseminating the original records of the Craft and his growing reputation as a Masonic historian were crowned in 1887 by his being appointed the first Sub-Librarian of the Library and Museum of the United Grand Lodge of England, in addition to his duties as Grand Tyler. A more judicious choice could not have been made. The Library and Museum had been formed in 1837 from a collection of regalia, pottery and glass in a cupboard in the Grand Secretary's office. A Committee was set up, the Grand Secretary was to have the management of the collection and money was advanced for repairs and book-binding. The Committee met rarely, no Librarian was appointed and no provision was made for the purchase of items, the result being that the collection continued to languish in a cupboard.

Sadler changed all that. In the twenty-four years that the

Library and Museum were under his care he collected and sorted all the archives in Freemasons' Hall, though unfortunately he marred many documents by placing the Library stamp on them or writing on them in indelible blue pencil; he persuaded many members to donate items, actively sought out new publications, arranged for publication two catalogues of the printed and manuscript volumes in the Library, and changed a cupboard full of books into a working Library. So greatly did he increase the collection that in 1904 a building adjacent to the Hall was taken over and completely given over to the housing of the Library and Museum. On his giving up the office of Grand Tyler in 1910 Sadler was appointed the first Librarian and Curator to Grand Lodge.

The very firm foundations laid by Sadler were built upon by successive Librarians and Curators, to the extent that the Library and Museum are now regarded by Masonic scholars as the most important repositories of the history of English Freemasonry. Had the enquiring mind and collector's nature of Sadler not been channelled into this enterprise it is doubtful if the collections would have become so comprehensive. Much of what he found and preserved in the Hall, and much that was donated because he was there, would have been lost, as were a number of important collections before Sadler's appointment. The Grand Lodge Library and Museum are a living memorial to his dedicated work in establishing them.

As a Masonic historian Sadler was meticulous in his attention to detail and scrupulous in his attention to factual truth. His painstaking research is apparent in his two major works, the present reprint and his *Thomas Dunckerley: His Life, Labours and Letters* (1891). Both works, despite their age, still stand as landmarks in the historiography of English Freemasonry and are perfect examples of the *scientific* approach to Masonic history. In both works

Sadler lays all the ascertainable facts and evidence before his readers, reproducing all his evidence at length, microscopically examining each piece and building up his case from that critical examination. He begins with no preconceived ideas, he simply lets the evidence speak for itself; and, unlike his predecessors, he clearly states what *is* fact and what is his *interpretation* of those facts, assiduously pointing out that he is developing a theory that may be open to argument. His meticulous research earned him to accolade, in 1903, of full membership of Quatuor Coronati Lodge No. 2076, the most prestigious Lodge of Masonic research, which led him in 1910 to the blue ribband of Masonic scholarship, the Mastership of that Lodge. To the great sorrow of the Lodge and the world of Masonic letters he died on 15 October 1911 some three weeks before his year of office was completed. The many tributes to his memory praise his kindness, helpfulness and great willingness to share what he had learned from the treasures under his care. These tributes were well deserved, for there were few books, research papers or journalistic writings on the subject of Masonic history published from 1887—1910 that did not gratefully acknowledge the valuable assistance given by Henry Sadler in their preparation.

Masonic Facts and Fictions is a seminal work in the historiography of English Freemasonry. Although Sadler subtitled his work 'A new theory of the origin of the "Antient" Grand Lodge', so persuasive is his critical examination of the evidence that few, if any, today would question his conclusion that the Antient Grand Lodge did not develop from a schism in the premier Grand Lodge but had its beginnings in a group of unattached Masons of Irish origin who rejected the alterations that the premier Grand Lodge had made in the ritual as a result of the exposures of the late 1720s and, particularly, Prichard's *Masonry Dissected* of 1730. So acceptable has Sadler's theory become that it seems odd to present-day Masonic historians that the schism theory could ever have been accepted as other than a propaganda exercise by members of the premier Grand Lodge to discredit its junior rival. We forget, though, how bitter could be the rivalry between the two bodies, and how much the premier Grand Lodge resented both the existence and the popularity of its rival, particularly its close ties with the Grand Lodges of Ireland and Scotland and the predominance of its lodges in North America.

It says much for the power of *ideas oft expressed* and the power of the printed word that within a short space of time the schism theory should have become accepted as unquestioned fact and have gone unchallenged for so long. Sadler was spurred into researching the origins of the Antients by his rediscovery of *Morgan's Register*, the first Register and Minute Book of the Antients. This provided him with the missing evidence: the names of the prime movers and founder members of the Antient Grand Lodge. It seems remarkable to me that, even without *Morgan's Register*, no one before Sadler had questioned the schism theory, particularly as, as Sadler demonstrates, there is no indication in the records of the premier Grand Lodge of any major breakaway, the only evidence being in secondary printed sources such as Preston's *Illustrations*. It says little for the historians of the pre-authentic school era that they were prepared to accept secondary sources rather than examine the original records, or is this being too condemnatory of them? Perhaps it took the arrival of Sadler to make those records available to them.

Sadler was breaking new ground not just with his theory but by discussing the Antients at all. Snobbishly and derisively dismissed by the premier Grand Lodge as tradesmen and menials of little interest to anyone, the Antients continued to be ignored down to our time by all but Sadler. Whilst odd facets of their history and practices have been studied, it was not until 1981 that a full-scale account of their history was undertaken, by C. N. Batham in his Prestonian Lecture, *The Grand Lodge of England according to the Old Institutions* ....

The opening chapters of Sadler's study develop his theory of the two classes of Freemasons in early Grand Lodge days and the development of a 'class' struggle. This lead to the eclipse of the original simple intention of a fraternal charitable society and the gradual take over of the Society by a group of intellectuals who provided the foundations for a moral philosophy based not on one particular creed or set of political beliefs, but that was open to men of all faiths. It seems to me that for today's Masonic students this section of Sadler's book is the one to be studied and re-examined in the light of information that may have come to light since Sadler's day. The whole question of the origins of speculative Freemasonry is one that is periodically re-examined. The acceptable theory arising out of the researches begun by the original members of the authentic school is that there was an organization of operative stone masons practising primitive initiatory rites and having secret modes of recognition. Into this organization in the late sixteenth and early seventeenth centuries were introduced *gentlemen* masons who gradually took over the operative lodges (the transition theory) and transformed them into purely speculative lodges of Free and Accepted Masons. This theory is now undergoing re-evaluation, with a number of present-day historians believing that, unlike Sadler, their predecessors had made the evidence fit their theories rather than letting the theory develop from all the available evidence. The two latest hypotheses are that speculative Freemasonry arose in the late sixteenth century as a common meeting place for men of widely differing religious and political views in a period of religious and political turmoil, or that it was another manifestation of the seventeenth-century growth of self-help groups providing immediate assistance to members in time of need. To supporters of both groups I would recommend that they re-read Sadler's early chapters in *Masonic Facts and Fictions*.

Since Sadler's time nothing new has come to light to add to or subtract from the evidence from which he deduced his theory of the origin of the Antients, and as such his writing needs no correction. With his attention to detail and factual accuracy, he refers to the early meetings of the Antients not as Grand Lodge meetings but, as they were, meetings of a Grand Committee, resulting in his giving the starting date of the Antients Grand Lodge as 1753. Attitudes change and today we normally date the Antients Grand Lodge as existing from the first meeting in 1751. Not only has Sadler's theory stood the test of time but the book itself has much of use to present-day students. It contains a wealth of quotations from Grand Lodge and private lodge archives that are not readily available elsewhere. At the end of the volume he provides a transcript of the *Grand Lodge No. 1 MS* (1583) of the *MS Constitutions* or *Old Charges*. The transcriber was, unfortunately, not an expert in late sixteenth-century penmanship and the printed text contains many minor and some major errors of transcription, rendering it unsuitable as a guide for textual comparison with other versions of the *Old Charges*.

J. M. HAMILL

APPENDIX 1
SADLER'S MASONIC CAREER

Professional
1865 Appointed assistant to the Grand Tyler.
1879 Appointed Grand Tyler
1887 Appointed Sub-Librarian
1910 Appointed Librarian and Curator

Craft
1862 10 December: initiated Lodge of Justice No. 147. Master 1872-73.
1881 Founder Member Southgate Lodge No. 1950.
1886 Founder and 1st Master Walsingham Lodge No. 2148.
1890 Joined Strong Man Lodge No. 45.
1903 Elected a Full Member of Quatuor Coronati Lodge No. 2076. Master 1910-11.
1911 Founder Member Winchmore Hill Lodge No. 3523.

1879 Appointed Grand Tyler of the United Grand Lodge of England. Retired 1910.
1897 Appointed Provincial Grand Director of Ceremonies, Provincial Grand Lodge of Kent.
1910 Appointed Past Assistant Grand Director of Ceremonies of the United Grand Lodge of England.

Royal Arch
1869 21 December: exalted in Royal York Chapter of Perseverance No. 7.
1872 Joined Chapter of Temperance No. 169. First Principal 1880-81.

1893 Joined Domatic Chapter No. 177.

1895 Took the Scottish form of Royal Arch in St Andrew's Chapter No. 83, Edinburgh.

1879 Appointed Grand Janitor of Supreme Grand Chapter of England. Retired 1910.

Mark Masonry

1892 Advanced in New Era Lodge of Mark Master Masons No. 176. Master 1895. Treasurer 1896-1911.

1897 Grand Inner Guard, Grand Lodge of Mark Master Masons.

APPENDIX 2
BIBLIOGRAPHY OF
SADLER'S WRITINGS

Books

1887 *Masonic Facts and Fictions*, comprising a new theory of the origin of the 'Ancient' Grand Lodge. Founded on original records and recently discovered documents, London (Diprose & Bateman), xxi, 214pp., illustrated.

1889 *Notes on the Ceremony of Installation*, London (Kenning), x, 57pp., frontispiece.

1891 *Thomas Dunckerley, His Life, Labours and Letters*, including some Masonic and Naval memorials of the 18th century, London (Diprose & Bateman), xxiv, 316pp., frontispiece, illustrated.

1898 *Masonic Reprints and Historical Revelations*, including original notes and additions, London (Kenning), var. pag.

1904 *Illustrated History of the Emulation Lodge of Improvement, No. 256, 1823 to 1903*, with brief historical sketches of its branches and offshoots, London (Spencer), x, 217pp., frontispiece, illustrated.

1904 *Some Memorials of the Globe Lodge No. 23 of Ancient Free and Accepted Masons of England*, with a sketch of the origin and history of the Red Apron, London (Warrington), 92pp., frontispiece, illustrated.

1906 *History and Records of the Lodge of Emulation No. 21 of Ancient Free and Accepted Masons of England 1723-1906*, London (Warrington), x, 211pp., frontispiece, illustrated.

Papers and periodical contributions

Sadler was a regular ocrrespondent in the letter columns
of the *Freemason* and *Freemasons' Chronicle*, as well as a
regular contributor to the *Notes and Queries* columns of
those weekly papers. His major contributions were:

1886 'Thomas Dunckerley — his mother lodge', *The
Freemason*, 24 April, 241.
'Early Chester Masonry', *The Freemason*, 12 June,
350-1.
'The first Grand Stewards and their lodges', *The
Freemason*, 24 July, 438-9; 31 July, 454-6; 7 August
468-9; 14 August, 484-5; 21 August, 494-5.

1893 'The Grand Lodge of Ulster', *The Freemason*, 21
January, 26-7; 28 January, 40; 4 February, 53-4; 11
February, 71; 18 February, 87; 25 February, 117; 4
March, 114.
'Freemasonry Operative and Speculative', *The
Freemason*, 2 September, 114-16.

1894 'Plain questions to Brother Jacon Norton' (on the
origins of the Antients Grand Lodge), *The Masonic
Review* (Cincinnati), vol. 82, no. 5 (December 1894),
283-8.

1896 'Address to the Israel Lodge of Instruction No. 205'
(on Masonic ritual and the Old Charges), *The
Freemason*, 2 May, 250-1.

1897 'Tylers and Tyling', *The Freemason*, Christmas
Number, 9 December, 51-6.

1898 'An address to the Robert Burns Lodge No. 25' (on
the history of the lodge), *The Freemason*, 19
February, 86-8.

1901 'The Tracing Boards of Lodge No. 262 in the 7th
Light Dragoons', *The Masonic Illustrated*, vol. 1
(1901), 172-3.

1905 'An unrecorded Grand Lodge', *Ars Quatuor Coronatorum*, vol. 18 (1905), 69-78 and 84-90.

1909 'Lodges of Instruction and their probable origins', *The Freemasons' Chronicle*, 31 July, 57-8.

1910 Inaugural address to Quatuor Coronati Lodge No. 2076 (Spurious Masonry), *Ars Quatuor Coronatorum*, vol. 23 (1910), 324-9.

Subscribers' Names.

Abbott, G. Blizard, No. 1385.
Abbott, W. K., P.P.G.D. Bristol.
Addington, James, P.M. No. 217.
Akers, W. J., P.M. No. 13.
Alaway, Robert, Steward No. 1507.
Aldridge, Robert (late No. 1201).
Allcroft, John D., Past G. Treasurer.
Ames, G. A., P.M. No. 2, Past G. Steward.
Amherst, The Earl, Prov. G.M. Kent.
Amherst, W. A. T., M.P., Past J.G. Warden.
Andrews, Geo., P.M. & D.C. No. 871.
Antill, William (late No. 720).
Appleby, Thomas, No. 13.
Ashcroft, L., W.M. Elect, No. 1296.
Aspland, Lt.-Col. J. L., P.P.G. Reg. E. Lanc.
Atherton, J. L., P.M. 439, P.P.G.D.C. W. Yorks.
Atkins, H. J., P.P.S.G.W. Norths. & Hunts.

Bacon, E., Nos. 807, 1607.
Baker, Brackstone, Past G. Deacon, &c.
Barfield, Asher, P.M., P.P.G.J.D. Hants & I. W.
Barnard, G. W. G., P.P.G. Reg. Norfolk, &c.
Barratt, Thos. J., P.M. No. 3.   (3 copies.)
Barrett, Alfred E., J.D. No. 1768.
Barrett, G. R., P.M. No. 189 P.P.S.G.D. Devon.
Barron, E. J., P.M. No. 2 Past G. Deacon.
Bartlett, E. E., P.M. No. 586.
Baskett, S. R., P.P.G. Reg. Dorset.
Bassett, F., Organist No. 1382.
Batchelor, James C., G. Sec. G.L. Louisiana.
Baume, Arthur, S.W. No. 63.
Beach, Fletcher, M.D., J.W. No. 231.
Bear, Daniel, P.M. No. 1155.
Bear, T. Drew, P.M. No. 1584.
Beaumont, W. C., Past A.G.D.C.
Begemann, Dr. W., Mecklenburg.

BELTON, CHAS., F.R.G.S., Provl. S.G.W. Surrey.   (4 copies.)

BENNETT, F. T., W.M. No. 211.   (12 copies.)

BERRY, A. J., P.M. No. 1695.

BERRY, JOHN J., P.M. & Treasurer No. 554.

BERRY, HENRY, No. 217.

BERTHER, J. A., No. 1563.

BETTS, ARTHUR, W.M. No. 1351.

BILBY, R. W., N.C.A., P.M. No. 615.

BINCKES, F., Past Gd. Swd. Br., &c.   (2 copies.)

BING, HENRY F., P.M. No. 1597.

BISHOP, GEO., P.M. No. 231.

BLACK, J. J. W.M. No. 1564.

BLACKBURN, GEORGE, P.M. No. 264.

BLAXLAND, C. WILFRID, J.D. No. 709.

BLOCK, JOHN W., W.M. No. 3.

BODENHAM, JOHN, Past A.G.D.C.

BOLTON, GEO., P.M. Nos. 147 & 169.

BOND, JAMES, P.M., P.P.G.P. Norfolk, &c.

BOOTH, C. I., No. 1507.

BORTON, CHARLES, No. 2148.

BOULTON, JAMES, P.M. Nos. 28, 1056, &c.

BOWYER, EDGAR, Past G. Std. Br.

BRAMBLE, Lt.-Col. JAMES R., Past A.G.D.C., &c.

BRETTE, Rev. P. H. ERNEST, Past G. Deacon.

BRISTOW, Col. WM., Past G. Swd. Br.

BROADLEY, A. M., Past D.D.G.M. Malta, &c.

BROCK, H., P.M. No. 145.

BROCKBANK, G. P., Past G. Std. Br.   (6 copies.)

BROOKS, S., P.M. No, 1608.

BROOKS, W. E.

BROOK-SMITH, JOHN, M.A., Past G. Deacon.

BROWN, FREDERICK, P.M. No. 174.

BROWN, J. H., No. 1441.

BROWN, WM. P., P.M. No. 90.

BROWN, NICHOLSON, P.M. & Sec. No. 13.

BROWNE, LENNOX, M.R.C.S., W.M. No. 2108.

BROWNING, A. G., P.M. No. 33. S.W. No. 2140.

BUE, HENRI, Past G. Std. Br.   (2 copies.)

BULL, THOMAS, P.M. & Treasurer No. 145.

BULLEN, THOS. G., P.M. No. 197. Past G. Steward.

BULLING, CHAS. E., No. 1287,

BURDETT, Col. Sir FRANCIS, Bart., Provl. G.M. Middlesex.

BURMEISTER, CHAS., P.M. Nos. 435 & 538.

BURNE, THOMAS, P.M. & Sec. No. 162.

BURNEY, GEORGE, P.M. No. 1155.

BURT, W. H., P.M. No. 663.

BUSS, H. G., Past A.G. Sec. (2 copies.)

BUTTER, H. J., P.M. No. 913. P.P.G. Reg. Kent.

BYWATER, W. M., Grand Swd. Bearer.

CAMA, D. P., Past G. Treasurer.

CAMPBELL, GEORGE H., No. 913.

CARLETON, J. SHAW, Prov. G.D.C. Gloucestershire.

CARMAN, H., W.M. No. 548.

CARPMAEL, DEANSTON, J.W. No. 1924.

CARR, FREDERICK, P.M. No. 1607.

CARSON, E. T., P.M. Kilwinning Lodge No. 356, Cincinnati, U.S.A.

CARTER, ARTHUR ROGER, W.M. No. 1728.

CASE, ROBERT, Prov. G. Sec. Dorset.

CASSAL, C. E., Nos. 1415 & 1974.

CASTELLO, JAMES, J.D. No. 227.

CATTERSON, S. P., P.M. Nos. 548, 1891. P.P.G. Std. Br. Surrey.

CHADWICK, JOHN, Past G. Swd. Bearer.

CHANDLER, JOHN, P.P.S.G.W. Wilts, &c.

CHAPIN, JOHN J., Sec. Acanthus Lodge No. 719, New York.

CHAPMAN, ALFRED F., P.M. Massachusetts Lodge, Boston, U.S.A.

CHAPMAN, JAMES, P.M. No. 194.

CHAPMAN, JOHN, P.P.G.D. Devon.

CHAPMAN, J. WENTWORTH T., P.M. Nos. 1622 & 1922.

CHURCHILL, R., No. 586.

CLARK, CHAS. L., No. 228.

CLARKE, GEORGE, S.W. No. 1950.

CLARKE, HYDE, F.S.S., &c. Past G. Master U.S. Colombia, &c.

CLARIDGE, J. R. FITZJAMES, Sec. No. 6. Past G. Steward.

CLERKE, Col. SHADWELL H., Grand Secretary.

CLIPPERTON, J. R., P.M. No. 66.

CLOWSER, RICHARD, S.W. No. 23. Grand Steward.

COCHRANE, SAMUEL, J.W. No. 3.

COHU, THOMAS, P.M. No. 192.

COLLENS, W. J., P.M. No. 766.

COMBES, ARTHUR, S.D. No. 820.

COMBE MASONIC LIBRARY, Hayle.

COOK, GEORGE, J.D. No. 820.

COOP, GEORGE, W.M. No. 141 & Sec. 2021.

COOPER, CORNELIUS H., P.M. & Sec. No. 105. P.P.S.G.D. Devon.

COOPER, EDWARD E., P.M. No. 73.

COOPER, GEORGE, S.G. Deacon. (3 copies.)

COOPER, JAMES, W.M. No. 1950. P.M. No. 1693.

CORDWELL, GEORGE, P.M. No. 3.

CORP, JAMES, No. 2148.

CORRY, ROBERT, No. 1681.

COTTER, HUGH, P.M. No. 554.

COUPLAND, CHARLES, P.M. No. 913. P.P.J.G.W. Kent.

COX, HENRY, P.M. No. 742. P.P.G. Sup. Wks. Herts.

CRAVEN, ALFRED E., S.W. No. 263. Past G. Steward.

CRAWLEY, W. J. CHETWODE, LL.D., &c. G. Steward G.L. Ireland.

CREMORNE, LORD, Past S.G. Warden.

CRIPPS, W. C., W.M. No. 2200. P.M. No. 874.

CUBITT, ALFRED J., W.M. No. 100.

CUBITT, THOMAS, Past G. Purst.

CULL, THOMAS, P.M. & Treasurer No. 1446.

CUMBERLAND, JOHN S., P.P.J.G.W. N. & E. Yorks. (2 copies.)

CUMMINGS, Rev. HAYMAN, Prov. S.G.W. Kent. (2 copies.)

CUNLIFFE, W. J., P.P.S.G.D. E. Lanc.

CRAIG, ROBERT, P.P.G.D. W. Yorks.

CROSSLEY, HERBERT, J. W. No. 61.

CUNDY, GEORGE A., P.M. No. 901.

CURTIS, HERMAN, P.M. No. 1150. (2 copies.)

DAIRY, CHARLES, P.M. No. 141.

DANDRIDGE, A. C., No. 871.

DARCH, AUGUST, P.M. & Sec. No. 72.

DAVIS, Lt.-Col. JOHN, P.M. No. 33.

DAVIS, J. H., W.M. No. 33.

DAVISON, FREDERIC, Past S.G. Deacon.

DAWES, WILLIAM, Past P.S.G.W. &c. Sussex.

DAWKINS, EDWIN, No. 1287.

DAWSON, JOHN E., Past G. Swd. Br., D.P.G.M. Herts.

DAWSON, Hon. RICHARD, W.M. No. 2189. Prov. S.G.W. Devon.

DAWSON, W. ALFRED, P.M. No. 1768.

DEALER, ALFRED T., No. 871.

DEAR, R., W.M., No. 586.

DEAR, J. H., S.W. No. 586.

DEEVES, Captn. D., P.M. No. 1536. P.D.G.D.C. Natal.

DEHANE, H. E., P.M. No. 1543. P.P.S.G.D. Essex.

DELACOSTE, EUGENE, P.M. No. 1627.

DES GENEYS, COUNT, P.M. Nos. 1705 & 1990.

DEVONSHIRE, THOMAS H., Past G. Deacon.

DICKESON, WALTER, W.M. & P.M. No. 179.

DICKEY, HENRY, W.M. No. 1744.

DINGLE, ALFRED S., No. 871.

DIPROSE, JOHN, P.M. & Treasurer No. 957.

DIPROSE, HENRY LANDON, S.W. No. 1853.

DIVER, WALTER, W.M. No. 305. Sec. No. 100. Prov. G. Steward Norfolk.

DIXIE, A. J., W.M. No. 453.
DOCKER, J.B., P.M. No. 1687.
DODD, E. J., P.P.G.O. Kent.
DODD, WILLIAM, P.M. No. 1194, P.P.G.D. Middlesex.
DODDRELL, W. L., W.M. No. 615.
DOVE, F. W., No. 1260.
DOWDING, HENRY, No. 145.
DRUMMOND, CHARLES, J.W. No. 1629.
DUBOIS, ERNEST, Nos. 14 & 2060.
DURET, A. W., P.M. Nos. 1223 & 1768. Prov. S.G.D. Kent.

EASTES, JAMES S., Past G. Deacon, D.P.G.M. Kent. (2 copies.)
EBORACUM LODGE No. 1611.
EDMONDS, T. C., W.M. No. 1507.
EDWARDS, JOHN W., P.M. No. 317.
ELLARD, GEORGE, P.M. No. 360. Prov. S.G.W. Norths. & Hunts.
ENGLEFIELD, WILLIAM, W.M. No. 1321.
ESCOTT, ALBERT, P.M. No. 1593. (3 copies.)
EVANS, MORRIS, P.M. No. 8. Past G. Steward.
EYLES, GEORGE L., S.W. No 197. G. Steward.

FARNFIELD, JOHN A., Past A.D.C.
FARQUHAR, ALFRED, W.M. No. 1629.
FARRINGTON, G. J., P.M. No. 1271.
FENN, THOMAS, P.G.D. Pres. B.G. Purposes. (20 copies.)
FERRY, C. E., P.M. No. 65.
FESTA, G. P., P.M. & Treasurer No. 1900.
FIDLER, A. G., P.P.S.G.D. Middlesex.
FITZGERALD, J. P., P.M. No. 1364, J.W. No. 2168.
FLOWER, W., No. 586.
FORD, GERARD, Past G. Deacon, D.P.G.M. Sussex.
FORGE, R. P., P.M. Nos. 619, 1693, 1950.
FOSTER, JOHN R., No. 749.
FOWLER, Sir ROBERT N., Bart., Past G. Warden.
FRACIS, N. D., P.M. No. 255.
FRANCIS, CHARLES K., P.M. No. 265. Penna., U.S.A.
FRANCIS, THOMAS, P.M., P.P.G.D. Sussex.
FREEMAN, JOHN W., P.M. No. 147.
FREEMAN, VINCENT P., J.G. Deacon, Prov. G. Sec. Sussex.
FREEMAN, Captain GEO. WILLIAMS, W.M. No. 1068.
FRENCH, JOHN W., P.M. No. 100. P.P.G. Reg. Norfolk, &c.
FRIENDSHIP LODGE No. 44.
FROMMHOLZ, C. W., P.M. No. 141.
FRYER, H. T., P.M. No. 1155.

FULLFORD, G., J.D. No. 586.
FUTCHER, THOMAS S., P.M. No. 586. P.P.G.H. Wilts.

GARD, JOHN, P.P.J.G.W. Bristol, &c.
GARDINER, THOS. H., P.M. No. 657.
GARGINI, LOUIGI, No. 3.
GARROD, JAMES, P.M. No. 754
GARROD, HENRY, P.M. No. 749.   Past G. Purst.
GATHERCOLE, W. H., No. 1220.
GIBBINGS, ASHLEY, P.M. No. 63.
GIFFORD, JAMES, P.M. No. 105.
GILBERT, JOHN, Prov. G. Tyler. Middlesex.
GILCHRIST, JAMES, late No. 126. S.C.
GIRTON, GEO. J., No. 1572.
GLOVER, R.G., Past D.G.D. Ceremonies.
GOBLE, EDGAR, Past G. Swd. Bearer.
GOLDNEY, F. H., Past G. Deacon.
GOODACRE, WILLIAM, Past G.S. Bearer.
GOODING, RALPH, M.D., Past G. Deacon.
GORE, ROBERT L., P.M. No. 1692.
GOSLING, A. L., No. 2148.
GOSSET, M. CALLAWAY, P.M. & Sec. No. 66.
GOTTLIEB, FELIX (J.P.), Past G. Swd. Bearer. &c.   (5 copies).
GOULD, ROBERT, F., Past G. Deacon.
GRAHAM, W. J. B., P.M. No. 2041.
GRAND LODGE LIBRARY (England).
GRAND LODGE, Mark M.M. Library (England).
GRAND LODGE LIBRARY (Penna., U.S.A.)
GRANTHAM, R. F., W.M., No. 197. Past G. Steward.
GREEN, FRANK, Past G. Deacon.
GREEN, HERBERT G. E., Prov. G. Sec. W. Yorks.
GREEN, JOHN, P.M., No. 27.   (2 copies.)
GREEN, NEVILLE, P.M., No. 1962.
GREEN, WILLIAM, No. 1604.
GREENHAM, ALFRED, P.M. & W.M. No. 1884,   Prov. J.G.D.
     Hants & I. W.
GREENE, HENRY, Past G. Std. Bearer.
GREGORY, WALTER, J., J.W. No. 73.
GREY, ROBERT Past G. Deacon, Prest. B. of B.   (3 copies.)
GRIFFIN, F., P.M. No. 586.
GRIMES, MARION, W.M., Acanthus Lodge No. 719. G.L. New York.
GRUNWELL, N., J.D. No. 2200.
GUPPY, THOMAS R., No. 169.

HADDON, JAMES S., J.W. No. 1966.
HADEN, S. J., P.M. No. 1478.
HAIGH, JOHN, P.M. Phœnician Lo. Mass. U.S.A.
HAINES, A. V., P.M. No. 142.
HALES, F. R., P.M. & Sec. No. 34.
HALLOWES, RICHD. C., P.M. No. 33.
HANCOCK, THOS. W., No. 395.
HANHART, NICHOLAS, No. 222.
HARDING, Col. CHARLES. Past A.G.D.C.
HARDING, JAMES W., S.D. No. 1585.
HARLECH, LORD, Prov. G.M. North Wales.
HARRIS, G., Steward, No. 586.
HARRIS, PIERREPONT, Prov. G. Sec. Bristol.
HARRIS, WALTER, S., I.G. No. 1260.
HARRIS, WILLIAM, P.M. No. 177 & W.M. No. 1987.
HARRISON, GEORGE, No. 1607.
HARROWER, P. N., S.W. No. 181.
HASLETT, DAVID, P.M. & Sec. No. 145.
HAYWARD, STEPHEN, No. 781.
HEDGES, F. R. W., Past G. Swd. Bearer.
HEMING G. BOOTH, P.M. No. 256.
HERTFORD, THE MARQUESS of, Past S.G. Warden.
HICKLIN, WILLIAM, P.M. No. 1261.
HILL-DRURY, M.D., C. D., P.M. No. 85. P.P.G. Reg. Norfolk.
HINKS, THOMAS, Treasurer, No. 217.
HINKS, T. R. BEAUFORT, W.M. No. 217. Sec. No. 2148.
HITCHINS, H. J., J.W. No. 1319.
HOBBS, HUGH M., P.M. Prov. J.G.D. Surrey.
HOELEN, C. L., Treasurer No. 2148.
HOGARD, C. F., Past G. Std. Bearer.
HOIT, J. H., P.M. No. 856. P.P.G.S.B. Cornwall.
HOLLAND, THOS., P.M. No. 172. P.P.G.D.C. Suffolk.
HOOPER, PELLY, P.M. P.P.G. Reg. Dorset, &c.
HOOPER, STEPHEN W., P.M. No. 1924. J.W. No. 63.
HOPEKIRK, WILLIAM, A.G. Purst.
HOUGHTON, JOHN P., W.M. No. 2032.
HOWARD, Sir RICHARD N., P.P.S.G.W. Dorset, &c.
HUGHAN, W.J., Past G.Deacon. P.P.S.G.W. Cornwall. (3 copies.)
HUGHES, W. B., W.M. No. 1678.
HUKE, ALFRED N., I.G. No. 100.
HUMPHREYS, B. A. VICTOR.
HUMPHRIES, T. MOUNT, P.P.G. Sup. Wks. Staffordshire.

HUNT, JOHN E., P.M. No. 1768.
HUNT, CHARLES, P.M. No. 23.
HUSSEY, W. H., Dist. G. Sec. Bombay.
HUTCHINSON, THOMAS, No. 1900.

IMLAY, DAVID G., I.G. No. 2148.
ISAAC, H. P., P.M. No. 1693.
ITTER, C. A., Nos. 1897 & 2191.
ITTER, C. J., No. 217.

JACKSON, GEORGE, J.D. No. 2148.
JACKSON, JOHN, No. 1287.
JACKSON, ROBERT, J.W. No. 169.
JAQUES, WILLIAM, S.W. No. 1744.
JEFFS, HENRY, Past P.J.G.W. Gloucestershire, &c.
JEFFERIS, A. H., Prov. A.G.D.C. E. Lanc.
JENNER, F.S.A., HENRY (late 1964.)
JEPHSON, Surgeon-Major, W.M. No. 2094.
JERMAN, JAMES, P.M. No. 39, P.P.G. Sup. Wks. Devon.
JEW, SAMUEL, P.M. No. 105. P.P.G. Treasurer. Devon.
JEWELL, J. H., P.M. No. 1223. P.P.G.O. Kent
JOHNSTON, W. H., P.M. No. 1965, &c.
JONES, JOHN F., Steward No. 217.
JOLLY, CHARLES, P.M. No. 1472.

KEEBLE, W. D., S.W. No. 913.
KELLAND, F., W.M. No. 632.
KELL, C. F., No. 2148.
KELLY, WILLIAM, F.S.A., P.P.G.M. Leicester & Rutland.
      (2 copies.)
KEMPSTER, W. H., M.D., P.M. Nos. 890 & 1420.
KENNABY, G. L., J.W. No. 1420. (2 copies.)
KENNING, GEORGE, Past P.G.D. Middlesex.
KENTISH, W. G., P.M. No. 1293. S.W. No. 1768. (3 copies.)
KER, GEORGE, P.P.J.G.D. Kent.
KERR, ELLIS, (late of No. 241, New York.)
KING, H. L., Acanthus Lodge No. 719, G.L. New York.
KINGSWORTH, A. E., No. 874.
KIPPS, WILLIAM, P.M. P.P.G.O. Kent, &c. (3 copies.)

KNIGHT, G. W., P.M. No. 1507.
KNIGHT, J. FRANK, P.M. No. 276. Penna., U.S.A.
KNIGHTS, WILLIAM R., No. 100.
KNYVETT, FELIX S., J.G. Deacon.
KUPFERSCHMIDT, C., P.M. & Sec. No. 238.

LADD, FREDERICK, No. 169.
LAKE, WILLIAM, P.P.G. Reg. Cornwall.
LAMBERT, F.S.A., Major GEORGE, Past G.S. Bearer. (5 copies.)
LAMBERT, RICHARD, Assist. G. Sec. Louisiana, U.S.A.
LAMB-SMITH, THOS., P.P.J.G.D. Worcestershire.
LANCASTER, G. F., P.P.G. Reg. Hants and I. W.
LANE, C. S., P.P.J.G.D. Durham. (4 copies.)
LANE, JOHN, F.C.A., P.M. No. 1402. (2 copies.)
LANE, J. H., W.M. No. 1269.
LARCOME, ALFRED H., P.M. No. 3.
LARKIN, JOHN, S.D. No. 3.
LATREILLE, O. L. M., P.M. No. 1260.
LAWRENCE, SAMUEL C., Past G.M. G.L. Massachusetts.
LAWSON, CHARLES H., W.M. No. 913.
LEA-SMITH, J., P.M. No. 1159.
LECHMERE, SIR EDMUND A. H., Bart., Prov. G.M. Worcestershire.
LEE, W. H., P.P.G.D. & A.G. Sec. Middlesex.
LEFEBER, ALEX., Treasurer No. 1950.
LE FEUVRE, FRANCIS, P.P.G.S.B. Jersey.
LE FEUVRE, J. E., Past G. Deacon.
LEMON, Rev. THOS. W., M.A., P.P.G.C. Devon, &c.
LE FUEL, A. C., No. 1382.
LETCHWORTH, EDWARD, Past G. Deacon.
LEWIS, CHARLES T., P.M. No. 1472. W.M. 2184.
LEWIS, HAROLD, B.A., Sec. No. 686.
LIGHTBODY, C. RUSSELL, P.M. No. 90.
LININGER, The Hon. G. W., Past G.M. Nebraska, U.S.A.
LISTER, JAMES, W.M. No. 1745.
LITTLE, JOHN, No. 1437.
LLOYD, W. B., P.M. No. 913.
LODGE OF THE QUATUOR CORONATI No. 2076.
LOGAN, WILLIAM, Prov. G. Reg. Durham.
LONE, B. J. W., W.M. No. 1695.
LONG, PETER DE LANDE, Past G. Deacon. (2 copies.)
LOVEGROVE, HENRY, Prov. G. Treasurer Middlesex, &c.
LOW, GEORGE, P.M. & Treasurer No. 3.

* A

LUCKING, ALBERT, Past G. Purst., Prov. G.D.C. Essex.
LUNNISS, FRED., No. 1426.
LYON, D. MURRAY, G. Sec. Scotland.

MACAULAY, FRED. J., P.M. No. 142.
MADELL, ALFRED, No. 1201.
MALLETT, E., P.M., No. 141.
MANTEL, L., No. 1897.
MARSH, J. J., P.M. No. 1326. P.P.G. Std. Br. Middlesex.
MARTINS, RICHARD, P.M. P.P.G. Reg. Norfolk.
MARTYN, Rev. C. J., Past G. Chaplain. (3 copies.)
MARVIN, ALBERT, P.M. No. 1768.
MARWOOD, J. B., P.M. No. 291. P.P.G.W. Somerset.
MASON, C. L., P.P.G. Treas. W. Yorks.
MASON, JOHN, P.P.S.G.D. Middlesex.
MASON, J. J., Grand Sec. G.L. Canada.
MASON, HENRY, P.M. No. 913.
MASSIE, C. F., W.M. No. 1330. Prov. G. Purst. Leicestershire.
MASTERS, WILLIAM, P.M. No. 428. S.W. No. 2128.
MASTERS, W. F., W.M. No. 145.
MATHER, JOHN L., A.G.D.C. (3 copies.)
MATIER, C. FITZGERALD, Past G. Std. Bearer.
MATTHEWS, J. H., Past G. Std. Bearer.
MAUDSLAY, HENRY, Past G. Deacon.
MEAD, F. A., Past G. Swd. Bearer.
MERCER, D. D., P.M. No. 1641. S.D. No. 1329.
MEREDITH, T. H., P.M. No. 87. Sec. No. 1853, &c.
MERRILL, EDWIN J., No. 2148.
MEYER, C. E., Rep. G.L. Wisconsin, nr. G.L. Penna, U.S.A.
MEYER, HERMANN, No. 2148.
MICKLEY, GEO., M.B., P.P.S.G.W. Herts.
MIDDLEMIST, R. P., P.M. & Sec. No. 5. Past G. Steward.
MILLER, JAMES M., S.W. No. 700.
MILLINGTON, H., No. 632.
MITCHELL, G. W., P.M. No. 615.
MOFFREY, R. W., S.W. No. 957.
MOLLET, L. C., No. 765.
MONCK, A. J., No. 228.
MONCKTON, F.S.A., SIR JOHN B., Past G. Warden.
MONEY, E. M., P.M. No. 28.
MONTAGU, J. M. P., Past G. Deacon.
MOON, JOHN, Steward No. 2148.
MOORE, G. L., P.M. No. 169.

Morgan, Frederick, P.M. No. 1155.
Morgan, Walter V., P.M. No. 96.
Morgan, William W., P.M. No. 211. (4 Copies.)
Morgan, W. W. (J.P.), P.P.G. Sec. Mon., &c.
Morley, R. J., Organist, No. 1326.
Morley, William, Nos. 1769 & 1924.
Morris, Edwin, S.D. 1789.
Morse, Rev. Herbert G., Past G. Chaplain.
Munt, George W., No. 3.
Murton, Charles A., Past G. Deacon.

Nash, Henry F., No. 2032.
Neeld, J. G., P.M. & Sec. No. 169, &c.
Nelson, Richard, P.M. & P.Z., &c.
Newman, Gerard R., No. 1950.
Newton, James, P.P.S.G.D. E. Lanc
Newton, John, F.R.A.S., P.M. No. 174.
Nicols, D., P.M. Nos. 12 & 60. Past G. Steward.
Noakes, F. M., No. 2148. (3 Copies.)
Norris, Edwd. S., W.M. No. 32.
Norris, W. R., P.M. No. 181.
North, Chas. J. (late No. 473.)
Norton, Jacob, Boston, U.S.A.
Nott, William, P.P.S.G.W. Wilts.
Nuding, Henry, P.M. No. 140. S.W. No. 1924.
Nunn, G. G., No. 586.
Nutting, W. J., I.G. No. 231.

Ockenden, T. W., P.M. 1768, P.P.G.D. Middlesex, &c.
Oldham, Saml. B., Dep. G. Sec. Ireland.
Ohren, Magnus, Past A.G.D.C.
Ohren, Charles M., P.M. No. 452.

Packman, E. G., No. 1260.
Page, John A., P P.S.G.W. Bristol.
Pakes, John J., P.M. & Sec. No 871.
Palmer, Edward, P.M. No. 913,
Palmer, Rev. J. N., Past G. Chaplain.
Palmer, John S., P.P.G.W. Oxon.
Parker, H. J., P.M. G. Tyler G.L. Massachusetts, U.S.A.
Parkhouse, S. H., P.M. No. 511. P.M. & Treas. 1642.
Parry, W. E., W.M. No. 686.
Parvin, T. S., G. Sec. G.L. Iowa, U.S.A. (2 copies)

* A 2

PASCOE, W. H., Organist No. 1223.
PATCHITT, E. C., P.P.G. Swd. Br. Notts.
PAUL, JOHN, W.M. No. 1472.
PEACHEY, G. S., Steward No. 1194.
PEARCE, GILBERT B., P.J.G.W. Cornwall
PEARSE, M.D., W. E. GRINDLEY, P.M. No. 63.
PECK, ANDREW, Acanthus Lodge No, 719. G.L. New York.
PEMBROKE, E. LINDSAY, No. 211.
PENDLEBURY, A. A., Assist. G. Sec.
PENFOLD, ABEL, P.M. No. 913. P.P.S.G.D. Kent.
PERRY, R. J., S.D. No. 1382.
PERRYMAN, W. H., P.M. No. 3, G. Purst.
PHIPOS, T. J., J.D. No. 1950.
PICKERING, G. A., I.G. No. 890.
PICKERSGILL, HENRY T., No. 217.
PINCKARD, G. J., Rep. G.L. Eng. near the G.L. Louisiana.
PLATT, WILLIAM, W.M. No. 1313.
POLEY, T. WELLER, Past G. Deacon.
PORTAL, REV. CANON G. R., Past G. Chaplain.
POTTER, JOHN, No. 100.
POTTER, R. F., P.M. No. 749.
POWDRELL, J, No. 1744.
POWELL, GEORGE, P.M. & Sec. No. 142.
POWELL, J. A., No. 186.
POWELL, W. A. F., Past G. Deacon, D.P.G.M. Bristol.
PRATT, T. C., P.M. No. 957.
PRATT, W.T., J.W. Acanthus Lodge 719. G.L. New York.
PPITCHARD, HENRY, P.M. No. 1415.
PROV. GRAND LODGE. W. Yorks.
PULLEY, ALFRED, P.M. No. 169, &c.
PURNELL, WILLIAM, P.M. No. 103.

RADCLIFFE, WILLIAM, P.M. No. 211.
RADWAY, C. W., P.M. & Sec. No. 41. P.P.S.G.W. Somerset.
    (2 copies.)
RAWLES, JAMES (late No. 507).
READ, GEORGE, P.M. No. 511.
READ, WILLIAM (late No. 172).
READE, F. T., J.W. No. 1584.
RECKNELL, G. S., P.M. & Sec. No. 1728.
REDDALL, DAVID G., J.W. No. 2148.
REDDALL, WILLIAM, No. 49.
REYNOLDS, GEORGE, J.W. No. 1614. Sec. No. 2191.
RICHARDSON, FRANK, Past S.G. Deacon. (3 copies.)

RIDDLE, T. P., No. 3.
RIDLEY, SIR MATTHEW W., Bart., P G.M. Northumbrld. (2 copies.)
RILEY, J. RAMSDEN, P.P.G.D.C. W. Yorks, &c.
ROBERTSON, J. ROSS, D.G.M. G.L. Canada.
ROBINSON, J.C., P.P.S.G.D. Cheshire.
ROBINSON, R. W., No. 879.
ROBINSON, REV. THOMAS, M.A., Past G. Chaplain.
ROOM, H. H., P.M. No. 2090.
ROPER, GEORGE, P.M., No. 69.
ROSENSTOCK, JULIUS, P.M. No. 169, &c.
ROSS, R., No. 1744.
ROWLEY, WILLIAM, S.W., No. 2148. J.W. No. 1924.
RUCKER, JOHN A., Past G. Deacon. (5 copies.)
RUSSELL, WILLIAM, P.M. No. 77. P.P.S.G.D. Kent.
RYLANDS, W. H., F.S.A., J.W. No. 2. G. Steward. (2 copies.)

SAMPSON, W. E., No. 14. (3 copies.)
SANDEMAN, HUGH D., Past District G.M. Bengal.
SAUNDERS, AUBREY. Past District G.M. Madras.
SAUNDERS, W. J. H., W.M. No. 139. Michigan, U.S.A.
SCHUMANN, Prof. GIUSEPPE, Lodge Universo, G.O. Italy.
SCURRAH, W. A., W.M. No. 2206., P.P.G. Sup. Wks. Middlesex.
SCOTT, WILLIAM G., G. Sec. G.L. Manitoba, Canada.
SEAGER, SAMUEL, No. 179.
SETON, Sir BRUCE M., Bart., Past G. Deacon.
SHELDRAKE, SPARHAM, W.M. No. 313. G.L. Canada.
SHEPPERD, CHARLES (late No. 1158.)
SHRYOCK, Genl., Grand Master. G.L. of Maryland, U.S.A. (2 copies.)
SILLITOE, J. H., Past G. Std. Bearer, &c.
SIMPSON, JOHN D., W.M. No. 1952.
SIMPSON, Rev. R. J., Past G. Chaplain.
SINGLETON, W. R., G. Sec. G.L. Dist. Columbia, U.S.A.
SMEATON, JOHN, No. 1507. (4 copies.)
SMITH, ALBERT, No. 100.
SMITH, HENRY, Past G. Deacon. D.P.G.M. W. Yorks.
SMITH Rev. J. HENRY, P.M., No. 279. W.M. No. 2157, P.P.G.C.
　　　Leicestershire & Rutland.
SMITH, J., W.M. No. 1478.
SMITH, WILLIAM M., S.W. Acanthus Lodge No. 719 New York.
SMITHETT, WILLIAM, P.M. No. 58. Past G. Steward.
SMYTH, Rev. T. C., Grand Chaplain. (3 copies.)
SNOOK, G. F., S.W. No. 1693.
SOUTHEY, JAMES F., No. 100.

SPARKS, JAMES, P.M. No. 1271.

SPARROWHAWK, W., S.W. No. 1223.

SPAULL, W. H., Prov. G. Sec., Shropshire

SPENCER, ALFRED, Past G.S.B. Prov. G. Sec. Kent.

SPETH, G. W., P.M. No. 183. Sec. No. 2076.

SPICE, ROBERT P., P.M. No. 21. Past G. Steward.

SPICER, RICHARD W., P.M. No. 1629.

SPILLING, HENRY G., No. 2148.

SPILLING, WALTER F., I.G. No. 435.

SPRATLING, W. J., B.Sc. P.M. No. 1924. Sec. No. 2033.

SPRY, DANIEL, Past G. Master G.L. Canada.

SQUIRE, JAMES, P.M. & Sec. No. 3.

STATON, JAMES W., P.M. No. 154 Kentucky, U.S.A.

STAITE, EDWIN M. H., No. 2200.

STEELE, RICHARD S., No. 100.

STEVENSON, GEORGE D., S.D. No. 2148.

STEWART, RAYNHAM W., Past G. Deacon.

STILES, WILLIAM M., P.M. No. 1507, &c.

STILLWELL, EDWARD W., P.M. No. 1, &c. (2 copies.)

STORR, EDWIN, P.M. No. 167.

STRANGE, EDWIN S., P.M. No. 1223.

STRANGE, H. S., No. 1223.

STRANGE, NICHOLAS, I.G. No. 2200.

STRATTON, JAMES, No. 913.

STUART, WILLIAM, P.M. No. 141, &c.

SUDLOW, ROBERT CLAY, P.M. No. 263. P.P.S.G.D. Kent, &c.

SUTHERLAND, HENRY, M.D., W.M. No. 99. Past G. Steward.

SUTTON, EDWARD B., Past G. Deacon. (3 copies.)

SWAN, GEORGE F., P.M. No. 1321, &c. (3 copies.)

TACON, J. W., P.M. No. 1196.

TAYLER, CHARLES. P.M., No. 1624.

TAYLOR, GEORGE, Prov. G. Sec. Worcestershire.

TAYLOR, R. J., P.M. Nos. 144, 1922, &c.

TERRY, JAMES, P.M. Past G. Swd. Bearer, &c.

TEW, THOMAS W., Prov. G.M.W. Yorks.

THOMAS, JAMES LEWIS, Past A.G.D.C.

THOMAS, CHARLES, late No. 77.

THOMAS J. G., W.M. No. 871.

THORPE, B. KELLY, Past G. Std. Br, Prov. G. Treasurer. Kent.

THRUPP, RAYMOND H., Past A.G.D.C. D.P.G.M. Middlesex.

THURKLE, E., P.M. & Treasurer No. 87.

TIBBITTS, F. H., P.M. No. 1950.

Todd, Joseph, P.P.G. Reg. N. & E. Yorks.

Tomkins, Alfred Savill, Prov. S.G.D. Surrey.

Tracy, Nathaniel, P.P.J.G.W. & Prov. G. Sec. Suffolk.

Trevanion, Hugh C. B., P.P.G.W. Essex.

Trewinnard, A. H., P.M. Nos. 228 & 1693.

Trollope, M.D., Thomas, Past G. Deacon.

Trott, E. C., No. 103.

Troup, James, No. 3.

Truscott, Charles, P.P.J.G.W. Cornwall.

Tufnell, Henry, No. 700.

Tunbridge, R. H., No. 100.

Turberville, H. Smith, late No. 1608.

Tweddell, Geo. Markham, Author of *A Hundred Masonic Sonnets, &c.*

Vail, William, W.M. No. 1155.

Venable, Rowland Geo., Past A.G.D.C. D.P.G.M. Shropshire.

Very, James, No. 754.

Vincent, William, P.P.G.S.B. Middlesex. (2 copies.)

Waghorn, F. R., No. 871.

Wakeman, Sir Offley, Bart., Prov. G.M. Shropshire.

Walford, E. L., W.M. No. 2148. S.W. No. 905. (3 copies.)

Walker, L. V., W.M. No. 22.

Walkley, Arthur, P.P.S.G.D. Somerset.

Ward, Horatio, P.P.G.W. Kent, &c. (3 copies.)

Wardlaw, John, P.P.G.W. Norths. & Hunts.

Warne, Thomas S., P.P.S.G.W. Kent.

Warren, Frank L., No. 871.

Warren, James Syer, No. 979.

Warrington, Richard S., P.M. No. 197. Past G. Steward.

Waters, E., I.G. No. 586.

Waters, John, No. 87.

Waterlow, James R., No. 537. New York.

Waterlow, Philip H., P.M. No. 1491, &c.

Watkins, William, P.P.S.G.W. Mon., &c.

Watson, William, P.M. No. 289, &c.

Webb, C. H., P.M. No. 174.

Webber, Walter, J.W. No. 700.

Weddell, J. C., M.D., W.M. No. 1837.

Weeden, Charles, P.M. No. 813.

Weller, William, P.M. No. 1564

WELSFORD, W. OAKLEY, No 1321.
WENDT, E. E., D.C.L., G. Sec. G.C. Eng.
WESTCOTT, W. F., W.M. No. 70.
WESTCOTT, Dr. WYNN. P.M. No. 814, P.P.G.D.C. Somerset.
WETZLAR, CARL G., No. 141.
WHEELER, W.N.C., W.M. No. 1271.
WHILE, JOHN, P.M. No. 228.
WHITMARSH, THOMAS W., P.M., &c., Sec. No. 1150, &c.
WHYMPER, H. J., Past D.D.G.M. Punjab. (4 copies.)
WHYTEHEAD, T. B., P.M. No. 1611, P.P.S.G.W., N. & E. Yorks.
WICKS, H. J., J.W. No 1269.
WILKINS, BUTLER, Past G. Std. Br. D.P.G.M. Norths. & Hunts.
WILLIAMS, F. H., S.W. No. 18.
WILLIAMS, S. E., No. 749.
WILLIAMSON, W. B., P.P.J.G.W. Worcestershire.
WILLING, JAMES, Jun., P.M. Nos. 177, 1319, &c.
WILLMOT, JOSIAH, Steward No. 2200.
WILLIS, T. L., No. 11.
WILSON, G. M., Steward, No. 586.
WILSON, JAMES, P.M., No. 317.
WILSON, J., P.M. No. 1155.
WINSON, C. T., J.W. No. 586.
WOOD, H. TRUEMAN, Past A.G.D.C.
WOODS, SIR ALBERT W. (Garter), Past G. Warden & G.D.C.
WOODFORD, Rev. A. F. A. Past G. Chaplain.
WOODMAN, W. R., M.D., Past G.S. Bearer.
WOODWARD, A. C., P.M. & Sec. No. 1538.
WOODWARD, J. F. H., Past G.S.B. Prov. G. Sec. Middlesex.
WRIGHT, WILLIAM W., No. 871.

YARKER, JOHN, P.M. Past S.G.W. Greece, &c.
YARKER, JOHN L., No. 163.
YOUNG, BENJAMIN, No. 27.
YOUNG, J. L., P.M. &c. Penna., U.S.A.

ZETLAND, The EARL OF, Prov. G.M. N. & E. Yorks.

AUTHOR'S PREFACE

"MASONS don't read" is a complaint often heard, but in my opinion scarcely justified. If true, there has been, during the last hundred and fifty years, a most lamentable waste of printing materials; for, without entering the region of statistics, I have no hesitation in saying that of no kindred institution has so much been written and printed during the period named as of the Society of Free and Accepted Masons. The Order, including in its ranks every class, profession and calling, cannot reasonably be expected to be all scholars and students, but my experience leads to the conclusion that a rapidly growing desire has been evinced by a large number of brethren in different parts of the world to make themselves acquainted with the antecedents of the various bodies to which they owe allegiance. To this desire I have endeavoured to minister by offering to the English-speaking fraternity what I venture to hope will prove to be a readable book, at a price which places it within the reach of the humblest member, and while making no claim to being considered a general History of Masonry, it will throw considerable light on the character and early proceedings of the two branches of the Order which eventually formed the *United Grand Lodge of England*. The accompanying List of Subscribers will show how nobly I have been supported, and the fact that the book has been advertised and sold in about three months only of the dullest portion of the Masonic year should be a sufficient answer to the cry that "Masons don't read." The title of the work will not, I sincerely hope, mislead anyone. Masonic literature, especially that of the last century and the first half of the present, contains many fictions, and to deal with them all effectually would require a much larger amount of knowledge and patience than I can fairly claim to possess, as well as a volume far exceeding the limits of the one before the reader. I have therefore confined myself to noticing a very few of the more important ones, without materially deviating from my original undertaking: that of disposing to the best of my ability of what I consider to be *the greatest fiction in the history of English Masonry.*

"Masonic Facts and Fictions" was chosen as being a title easily remembered, and because I could not think of a name better suited to the character of the book.

A most agreeable duty now devolves upon me, namely, to record permanently my warmest gratitude to those brethren who have so generously assisted in my labours.

To Col. Shadwell H. Clerke, Grand Secretary of England, I am deeply indebted for permission to use the records and documents in the archives of the Grand Lodge; for several hints which have been of especial value in the, to me, somewhat difficult task of compilation; and for his ready and brotherly assistance whenever I have had occasion to seek it.

Thomas Fenn, President of the Board of General Purposes, also merits my sincere acknowledgments, not alone for the honour he has done me in accepting the dedication of this my first book, but for the aid and encouragement extended to me from the commencement of my literary labours.

One particular act of kindness on the part of these two brethren seems to me to deserve special recognition ; they having not only read the proof sheets while the work was in the press, but with a beneficence worthy of the grand principles of our Order, performed the very tedious and somewhat difficult operation of perusing the whole of the original manuscript; and had it not been for their sympathy and encouragement, it is more than probable that "Masonic Facts and Fictions" would never have arrived at maturity.

To my much esteemed friend and brother, W. J. Hughan (whose readiness to assist in every good work is proverbial), I owe many thanks for his kindly aid in correcting the proofs, and for generously placing at my disposal his most extensive and varied experience in the paths of Masonic literature.

For the excellent Page of Seals (the exact size of the originals), I am much indebted to W. H. Rylands, F.S.A., whose artistic skill and accuracy of delineation cannot fail of being appreciated. The *facsimiles* of autographs are from the pencil of my good friend G. D. Stevenson, A.R.I.B.A., they are carefully executed and offer facilities for the study of character by handwriting. If, however, serving no other purpose, they will at all events furnish conclusive evidence that some of our "Ancient" brethren were well able to write their own names.

Everyone interested in Masonic Archæology will doubtless agree that we cannot be too grateful to Henry Jenner, F.S.A., for the great care and patience exercised by him in revising and correcting my previously imperfect transcript of the Ancient Charges. His great experience and willing aid has without a doubt considerably enhanced the value of the book.

I beg to acknowledge with heartfelt gratitude the generous and active support of numerous brethren who have taken considerable trouble in bringing the Work under the notice of their friends, thereby largely contributing to a most satisfactory result.

I am also under many obligations to the firm of Diprose, Bateman & Co., not only to the principals themselves for practical and valuable advice, but to the employés for their courtesy and careful attention during the progress of the undertaking.

In conclusion, I sincerely hope that the reader will be as well satisfied with my labours as I am with those of the printers and publishers, we shall then have no reason to regret our connection with "Masonic Facts and Fictions."

London, 1887.

CONTENTS.

CHAPTER I.

CHAPTER II.

CHAPTER III.

Lau: Dermott: del.

Plan.

A Scale of ten Cubits.

A Scale of ten Cubits or 240 Inches according to Jofephus.

FROM A DRAWING BY LAU. DERMOTT IN THE
"H.R.A. GRAND CHAPTER REGISTER" ("ANCIENTS")

MASONIC FACTS

AND

FICTIONS.

CHAPTER I.

MAY BE CONSIDERED INTRODUCTORY, BUT OUGHT TO BE READ.

" No pleasure is comparable to standing on the vantage ground of truth."
Francis Bacon.

IN no portion of society has the enquiring spirit of the age been more strongly manifested than amongst the fraternity of Free and Accepted Masons. The feeling which prompted us to believe and accept, without hesitation, nearly every assertion that appeared in print, is a thing of the past. In many instances our confidence in our most cherished traditions has been severely shaken, leaving doubt and indecision where before was simple child-like faith ; but whether we as a body are benefited or otherwise by this alteration is a question I shall not at present attempt to discuss. For my own part I yield to none in a regard for well-founded traditions and old-established customs ; but where a wrong could be righted and justice be ensured to the memory of an individual, or a stigma removed from a community, were it not that tradition or a questionable assertion stops the way, I say, down with the obstacle, and let the truth prevail, even though the error may have been handed down " from generation to generation " as indisputable fact. It is on this principle that I venture to appear in the somewhat unusual character of a " bookmaker," and should I fail to convince, I feel sure that my efforts in the cause of truth and justice will be generally appreciated.

B

That there were four Grand Lodges existing in England at the same period is a subject of wonderment to many who are not intimately acquainted with the history of our Institution; it will, therefore, perhaps not be deemed a waste of time if I briefly mention them all in chronological order before entering upon the more immediate object of my undertaking.

The senior of these organizations, the mother of all Grand Lodges was established in London in 1717, and has had an unbroken although chequered existence from the time of its formation down to the present day.

In 1725 an old lodge which had been held in the City of York, from a period so remote, that it may fairly be designated "time immemorial," formed itself into a Grand Lodge, and either then or subsequently assumed the high-sounding title " Grand Lodge of *all* England," an assumption scarcely justified by its ultimate position and influence, for its importance was chiefly vested in its name, and its dissolution, about the year 1792, may be justly ascribed to inanition.   Nevertheless, the records of its proceedings are so highly entertaining as well as instructive, that I would refer those desirous of fuller information to the pages of Hughan's " *Sketches and Reprints*," or Gould's " *History of Freemasonry.*"   The lodges chartered by this body are also given in " *Masonic Records*" recently compiled by John Lane, of Torquay.

Next in rotation is the Grand Lodge of the " Ancients," established in London in 1753, and it is to the character and proceedings of this Society that the following pages are mainly devoted.   London was also the birthplace of the fourth Grand Lodge, which was prematurely brought into existence by a few of the members of the Lodge of Antiquity, in the year 1779, under the somewhat egotistical title of " *The Grand Lodge of England, South of the River Trent,*" although to my thinking, it scarcely merits the distinctive

appellation of a Grand Lodge, for it came to an inglorious
end after an insignificant reign of ten years. If one were
disposed to moralize on the futility and emptiness of grand-
iloquent titles, an opportunity presents itself in the histories
of these Masonic bodies, for the functions of the "Grand
Lodge of ALL England" never extended beyond the counties
of York, Cheshire and Lancashire, unless we include a
charter granted to the FOURTH Grand Lodge, whose jurisdiction was still more limited, being confined to the Metropolis only; whereas the two that originated in a very humble
and unpretending manner, and at first had no ambition
beyond "the Cities of London and Westminster," ultimately
spread their branches over every habitable part of the
globe, contributing more than anything else to the realiza-
tion of the prophetic words of a gifted member of our Order,
who says :—

> " It's comin' yet for a' that,
> That man to man, the warld o'er,
> Shall brothers be for a' that."

Without entering at length into the causes which led to
the collapse of the two organizations mentioned, I may
here express an opinion that their failure is to be attributed
to the agencies which are chiefly instrumental in bringing
about the downfall of other structures and enterprises, *i.e.*,
insecurity of foundations, and a want of proper material,
and, I might safely add, that in this case there was neither
room nor demand for them.

At no previous period has so much trouble been taken
to elucidate the early history of Masonry as within the last
twenty years. I allude more particularly to the labours of
Gould, Hughan, Woodford, Lane, Findel, Kloss, and other
less known, but equally careful writers, whose works are
easily accessible and might be studied with " profit and
pleasure" by all who aspire to become familiar with the
antecedents of the Order to which they belong. While

confessing the utmost regard for these indefatigable labourers in the field of Masonic research, whose arduous toil, patience and assiduity cannot be too highly recognized (and I think I may say without an atom of egotism that very few understand their difficulties and appreciate their labours better than I do) I beg to state, if not quite "with fear and trembling," yet with considerable diffidence, that there is one important point on which I totally disagree with them all. I allude to the circumstances which led to the formation and establishing of the "Ancient" Grand Lodge in 1753, undoubtedly the most remarkable Masonic event of the last century. To the diligent searcher after truth this subject presents many difficulties which former writers overcame with little trouble to themselves by the simple and expeditious process of copying their predecessors. Hitherto, there has been abundance of speculation, but very few facts have been brought to bear upon it. It is not my intention to repeat the opinions of the various authors, for although some of them differ in matters of detail, yet all seem to agree, with an unanimity "worthy of a better cause," that the founders of this body were originally seceders from the Mother Grand Lodge of 1717, and they are invariably referred to as "the schismatics." Several reasons have been given for their withdrawal from parental authority, none of which in my opinion are satisfactory or sufficiently conclusive. Although fully sensible of the boldness of the attempt, I shall now endeavour to prove that those who have applied the term "*seceders*" to this section of our Order, have done so under a wrong impression; for after having most carefully considered the subject I am of opinion that there is no evidence yet brought to light which would justify me in believing that any considerable number of them ever owned allegiance to the regular Grand Lodge of England; and I venture to express a hope that future historians will, after having read these pages, find a name more in accordance with the principles of justice and equity, for a portion of our community to which we of the present day are deeply indebted. As I shall frequently have occasion to refer to the two rival bodies, I shall for the sake of brevity follow the course usually adopted in the present day, *i.e.*, to designate the older or regular Grand Lodge by the term " Moderns," and the other body by that of " Ancients." It is a well-known fact that up to a comparatively .recent period the rulers of our Order held the strongest objections to anything appearing in print concerning the affairs of the Craft, hence the difficulties we now labour under as to many interesting epochs in our past history, and this applies with equal truth to both sides. The only information vouchsafed by the " Moderns " was through the medium of the Book of Constitutions, which was supposed to contain a history of Masonry from the earliest period down to the date of issue, compiled under the careful supervision of the Grand Lodge officials, and containing, of course, just as much as it suited their purpose to make public. The quarterly reports of both bodies even when issued in a printed form contained scarcely anything besides figures showing the amount of money received from the different lodges.

Information with regard to the doings of the "Ancients" was still more difficult to obtain, their *Ahiman Rezon,* or Book of Constitutions, being compiled by the Grand Secretary himself, and from the first edition to the last it contains nothing in the form of a record of their proceedings. I presume this omission is to be accounted for by the fact that when the book first appeared in 1756 they had no particular history to tell, the author therefore exercised considerable wit and ingenuity in endeavouring to bring into ridicule the opposition book.

These two works, with the exception of the engraved lists of lodges issued by the " Moderns " annually, were the only sources of information on which the great body of the

Craft in England had to depend. The "Ancients" published no regular lists of their lodges, although two are mentioned in their printed reports for 1795 and 1803, and two others are given in the later editions of the *Ahiman Rezon*, viz., 1807 and 1813, both of these latter are reprinted by R. F. Gould in his "*Atholl Lodges*," and the earliest lists taken from their MS. register are to be found in Jno. Lane's "*Masonic Records*."

What amount of reliance ought to be placed on publications of this kind, will be shown by the following which appears in the form of a note or addition to page 239 of the Constitutions of 1784. It refers to a complaint against irregular makings, adjudicated upon in Grand Lodge on the 12th December, 1739 :—" The Grand Lodge justly considered such proceedings as an infringement on the original laws, an encroachment on the privileges, and an imposition on the charitable fund of the Society. It was therefore resolved to discountenance those assemblies and to enforce the laws against all brethren who were aiding or assisting in the clandestine reception of any person into Masonry, at any of these illegal conventions. This irritated the brethren who had incurred the censure of the Grand Lodge ; who, instead of returning to their duty, and renouncing their error, persisted in their contumacy, and openly refused to pay allegiance to the Grand Master, or obedience to the mandates of the Grand Lodge.

" In contempt of the ancient and established laws of the Order they set up a power independent, and taking advantage of the inexperience of their associates, insisted that they had an equal authority with the Grand Lodge to *make, pass, and raise Masons*. At this time no private lodge had the power of passing or raising Masons ; nor could any brother be advanced to either of these degrees but in the Grand Lodge, with the unanimous consent and approbation of all the brethren communication assembled.

" Under a fictitious sanction of the antient York constitution which was dropped at the revival of the Grand Lodge
in 1717, they presumed to claim the right of constituting
lodges. Some brethren at York continued indeed to act
under their original ccnstitution, notwithstanding the revival
of the Grand Lodge of England ; but the irregular Masons
in London never received any patronage from them. The
ancient York Masons were confined to one lodge which is
still extant, but consists of very few members, and will probably be soon altogether annihilated. This illegal and
unconstitutional claim obliged the regular Masons to adopt
new measures to detect these impostors, and debar them and
their abettors from the countenance and protection of the
regular lodges. To accomplish this purpose more effectually,
some variations were made in the established forms which
afforded a subterfuge, at which the refractory brethren
readily grasped. They now assumed the appellation of
Antient Masons, proclaimed themselves enemies to all
innovation, insisted that they preserved the antient usages of
the order, and that the regular lodges on whom they conferred the title of *Modern Masons* had adopted new measures,
illegal and unconstitutional. Thus by a new species of
deceit and imposition they endeavoured to support an existence, using the necessary precautions taken by the Grand
Lodge to detect them, as grounds for a novel and ridiculous
distinction of *Antient and Modern Masons.* This artifice
strengthened their party in some degree, the uninformed
were caught by the deception ; and in order to procure farther support to their assumed authority, they also determined
to interrupt the regular mode of succession to the office of
Grand Master, by electing a chief ruler under that designation, and other officers under the title of grand officers
appointed from their own body, convinced that the most
probable means for establishing their opposition would be by
liberally conferring honours on their votaries to secure their

allegiance and to induce others to join them. They framed a code of laws for their government, issued patents for new lodges, and exacted certain fees of constitution, from which they hoped to raise a fund sufficient to support their power. They so far succeeded in their new plan as to be acknowledged by many ; some gentlemen of family and fortune entered among them ; and even many regular Masons were so unacquainted with their origin, or the laws of the society, as to attend their lodges, and give a tacit sanction to their proceedings. Of late years, however, they have not been so successful. The laws being more generally known, the impropriety of countenancing their measures has been more clearly discovered, and their meetings have not only been less encouraged, but many of their best members have deserted them."

This *ex-parte manifesto*, concocted for an obvious purpose, without a particle of evidence to support its pretensions, seems to have been received as gospel truth by the generality of Masonic writers, although it evidently failed to have the effect intended by its promulgators ; indeed, it invariably happened that whenever the " Moderns" adopted any particular measures with the view of discrediting or damaging the prestige of their rivals, those astute individuals contrived to utilise these measures very much to their own advantage, as is admitted in one particular instance in the foregoing extract ; and many years afterwards this identical manifesto was turned against them with crushing effect by the body against which it had been aimed. I shall probably have occasion to recur to this subject at a future stage, my present purpose is to point out an erroneous assertion made by the writer of the document in question, whether accidental or otherwise, I will leave to the judgment of the reader ; certainly there is no excuse for it. I refer to the passage on passing and raising brethren in Grand Lodge only, wherein it is deliberately stated that private lodges had no power to confer those degrees at that time, viz., in 1739. There can be no doubt that the records of Grand Lodge were as accessible to the compiler of the Book of Constitutions in 1784 as they would be in the present day if wanted for a similar purpose, yet this is what the minute book tells us :—

"27th November, 1725.

"A motion being made that such part of the 13th Article of the General Regulations relating to the making of masters only at a Quarterly Communication, may be repealed, and that the master of each lodge, with the consent of his wardens, and the majority of the brethren, being masters, may make masters at their discretion. Agreed, *Nem. Con.*"

This palpable mis-statement is in my opinion quite sufficient to impair the value of the whole of the remaining assertions. However, in strict justice to our brethren of the last century, I must admit that they have had plenty of imitators, some of whom in regard to reckless assertions far outshine them; even the worthy and enthusiastic Dr. Oliver was not quite faultless in this respect, and was evidently not unaccustomed to draw liberally on his imaginative powers, in the production of some of his numerous works on Masonic History. For example, wishing to refresh my memory as to the reverend author's opinions of the "Ancients," I turned to his "*Revelations of a Square,*" and found in company with the old time-honoured story about excluded brethren, seceders, etc., etc., the startling intelligence that Dr. Manningham, when Deputy Grand Master consulted with Dr. Anderson on the subject of a new prayer for the first degree, "and together they drew up a prayer for that particular ceremony, which was submitted to Grand Lodge for its sanction." Now as Dr. Anderson died, and I presume was decently buried in

1739,* and whereas Manningham did not appear on the Masonic stage until 1747, and was not appointed Deputy Grand Master till 1752, how these two worthy doctors could have held a consultation passes my comprehension. However, using the words of the reverend brother in the preface to another of his works (*The Discrepancies of Free-masonry*). "Discrepancies in masonic work are of common occurrence in many of our lodges," he might safely have added, and out of them also. Now Oliver could easily have ascertained the date of Anderson's death in the same way as I did, by referring to the register in one of the magazines of the period; he is therefore equally as culpable as the other writer quoted. It is not my intention however to point out the inaccuracies to be found in Masonic publications generally; no doubt these two examples will sufficiently show how very easy it is for an ordinary reader to be led astray, especially on matters of historical import. In dealing with this subject I shall take what I may be permitted to designate, a common-sense view of the question (and I must ask my readers to look at it from a similar point of view), in so doing I shall endeavour to keep my mind perfectly free from bias or partiality for either one side or the other, a task which earlier writers found somewhat difficult, but which will be comparatively easy now that the two former rival bodies are amalgamated into one harmonious whole, and invidious distinctions are unknown. I shall doubtless have occasion to support my arguments by means of extracts and references, but for these I shall in nearly every case go to the fountain head, viz., the written records of the two Grand Lodges.

Various dates have been adduced for the beginning of

---

* *Gentleman's Magazine*, 28th May, 1739. (Register of Deaths). "Dr. James Anderson, an eminent Dissenting Minister, author of the Constitutions of the Freemasons, and Royal Genealogies."

what is generally described as " The Great Masonic Schism," the majority of writers taking their cue from the foregoing manifesto, are content with the date of 1739. Others go back to the year 1735, when certain privileges were asked for and acquired by the past Grand Stewards, which it is alleged caused such discontent amongst the rank and file of the Order, that many of them seceded and formed irregular lodges, ultimately setting up an independent governing body in opposition to the established Grand Lodge.

I shall deal with this view of the question in its turn, but at present will ask the reader to bear me company to a period somewhat anterior, in order to take a brief glance at the condition of speculative Masonry in its earliest stages.

It is pretty generally known that in the year 1717 certain old lodges held a meeting in London and agreed to establish what was at first intended by its promoters, merely to be a Grand Lodge for the cities of London and Westminster, and which grew so rapidly that it became not only the Grand Lodge of England, but in a comparatively short space of time had extended its branches and influence to many distant parts of the globe.

Previous to this period there was no recognized head of symbolical Masonry (notwithstanding that our learned historian Dr. Anderson gives a long list of Grand Masters, in which he includes nearly every person of importance mentioned in both ancient and modern history in connexion with operative Masonry or the science of Architecture), the lodges therefore acted quite independently of each other, and acknowledged no higher Masonic authority than the master for the time being ; no doubt when a lodge grew too large for the comfort of its members, or a difference of opinion arose between them, providing the requisite number could be got together, they would remove to another house and set up a lodge on their own account, without troubling themselves about warrants of constitution, consecrating officer, or indeed any of the grand ceremonials considered so essential at the opening of a new lodge in the present day. There was no regular subscription, each member contributing a small sum towards the expenses of the evening, with something in addition for the benefit of the sick and distressed; this with the entrance fee (generally about a guinea), and the fines inflicted on brethren for omitting to bring their aprons, or for using profane language, constituted the only source of income. That the social status of the general body of the fraternity was much lower than it is now, is plainly evinced by the fact that their first Grand Master and several of the earliest Grand Wardens were subsequently relieved from the fund of charity. Masonic clothing was of the simplest and most inexpensive description, consisting of a plain white lamb-skin for an apron, with gloves to correspond. I am inclined to think that in the earliest period the Grand Master himself wore no other ornament. Collars were unknown, and when jewels came into use they were at first suspended from the neck by a plain white ribband.* The portrait of "Anthony Sayer, Grand Master of the Freemasons," painted by Highmore, and engraved by Faber, both Masons, shews the apron only. Jewels are not mentioned in the Constitutions of 1723, neither are they depicted in the beautifully engraved frontispiece to that work. †

---

* Jewels are first mentioned in the Grand Lodge minutes of the 24th June, 1727, when it was " Resolved *Nem. Con.*, that in all private Lodges and Quarterly Communications and Generall Meetings the Mar. and Wardens do wear the Jewells of Masonry hanging to a White Ribbon (vizt.) That the Mar. wear the Square, the Senr. Warden the Levell, and the Junr. Warden the Plumb rule."

† I have heard several versions as to the identity of the two most prominent and evidently noble personages in this picture. My own opinion is that they are intended for the Dukes of Montague and Wharton; the former attended by his deputy, Dr. Beal, and his two Grand Wardens,

Unfortunately we have no record of what actually occurred in connexion with the newly formed Grand Lodge during the first six years of its existence, other than the very meagre account given by Anderson in the Constitutions of 1738. Minutes of the proceedings may have been taken, but I think it more than probable that they were not. Certainly there was no secretary before 1723, and it is worthy of notice that from the very day William Cowper was appointed to that office, the 24th of June, in the last named year, we have an unbroken record down to the present time. There is therefore a wide field for speculation as to the details by which the grand idea of consolidating the whole of the fraternity in London under one acknowledged head was carried out, and it is much to be regretted that we know not to whom the praise is due for its conception. It would appear from Anderson's account that there was no difficulty at all in the matter, but bearing in mind the absence of unity amongst the various lodges and the tenacity with which our early brethren invariably clung to their established customs and peculiarities we can well imagine it was not all smooth sailing. Anderson, in the Constitutions, 1738, p. 109, says, " the few lodges at London finding themselves neglected by Sir Christopher Wren, thought fit to cement under a Grand Master as the centre of union and harmony, viz., the lodges that met :—

" 1. At the Goose and Gridiron Alehouse, in St. Paul's Churchyard ;

" 2. At the Crown Alehouse, in Parker's Lane, near Drury Lane ;

Josias Villeneau, and Thomas Morris, one of whom is holding the aprons and gloves in readiness for the investiture of their successors in office, while the Duke of Montague is represented in the act of handing over the new Constitutions, and compasses, the Grand Master's emblem, to *his* successor, the Duke of Wharton, in the rear of whom stands Dr. Desagulier, his deputy, and his Grand Wardens, Joshua Timson and William Hawkins.

" 3. At the Apple Tree Tavern, in Charles Street, Covent Garden ;

" 4. At the Rummer and Grapes Tavern, in Channel Row, Westminster."

It is rather curious that in a very scarce book entitled " *The Complete Free Mason, or Multa Paucis for Lovers of Secrets* " (by an anonymous author), having no date, but which was evidently published about 1764, the writer puts the number of lodges at six, but he does not tell us where they were held. We must not lose sight of the fact that Anderson's account was written about twenty years after the event, for he does not enumerate the particular lodges in the first edition of the Constitutions. It is somewhat difficult therefore to reconcile his statement, that these four were the only lodges in London at that time, with the fact that the engraved list for 1723 as well as the written register for that year, give four lodges as taking precedence of the one which he describes as No. 4, but which is fifth on both the last mentioned lists. Now this lodge, I mean the No. 5 of 1723 was, without a doubt, the strongest and by far the most influential lodge in London at that period ; the Duke of Richmond was its Master, George Payne, a Past Grand Master, its Deputy Master, and in a list of seventy-two members are to be found the names of many other noblemen and officers of distinction, as well as those of Anderson himself and William Cowper, the first Grand Secretary, in fact the lodge was composed of the very *elite* of the Order. It is most unlikely that a lodge of this character would have permitted another, and apparently a very insignificant lodge, there being only twelve members returned in 1723, to occupy the senior position on the roll, had it been constituted since the formation of the Grand Lodge. It is true this old lodge disappears from the list in 1725, when the former No. 5 becomes No. 4, but that does not alter the fact of its existence prior to 1723, and there is no doubt whatever in my mind that it was also in existence in 1717. Here again is conclusively shewn that we must not consider official historians infallible, even when we find the distinctive prefix Reverend, in company with their names.

For my part I decline to look at these interesting events through the glasses of our learned genealogist. Whether there were four or six lodges that took part in establishing the Grand Lodge, is not, in my opinion a matter of vital importance, but considering all the circumstances, something more reliable than Anderson's bare statement is required to convince me that these were the only lodges in London at the time. The engraved list for 1723 gives the signs of 51 houses at which lodges were supposed to be meeting at the date of publication, all of them being in the metropolis with the exception of two, one at the " Duke of Chandois' Arms," Edgworth,* the other at the " Crown," at Acton, and thirty-six of this number returned a list of their members to Grand Lodge in that year. It is scarcely feasible that all these could have been entirely new lodges, doubtless some were ; but in my opinion many of them were in existence prior to the formation of the Grand Lodge, and on finding that Institution patronized by persons of wealth and distinction (or as Anderson grandly gives it in 1723 :—" Several Noblemen and Gentlemen of the best Rank, with Clergymen and learned Scholars of most Professions and Denominations") they agreed to accept of a Constitution, for which in those days no payment was required in order to be placed on the official list of regular lodges. †

---

* It is rather curious that there should be at the present time in the village of Edgware (which I presume is identical with the Edgworth of 1723), a small roadside public-house having the old sign of the Masons' Arms.

† A fee of £2. 2s. was first paid for a " Constitution" in 1730 by the Lodge which is now No. 5 on the register, in conformity with a resolution passed in Grand Lodge in the previous year.

CHAPTER II.

THE WRITTEN RECORDS OF THE FIRST GRAND LODGE.

" History is Philosophy teaching by examples."
Bolingbroke.

 THINK the written records if carefully studied, will in some measure support the views previously expressed, for instance, the last item in the Grand Lodge minutes for the 25th November, 1723, is as follows : " Mr. Henry Prichard's case was recommended by the Grand Master to the Grand Lodge that he should not be a sufferer."

What particular service Prichard had rendered does not appear, but he must have been held in very high esteem, for at the next meeting of Grand Lodge, on the 19th February, 1724, a collection was made, headed by the Earl of Dalkeith, Grand Master, with £2. 2s., resulting in the handsome sum of £28. 17s. 6d. being handed over to the poor brother, his acknowledgment for which is written in the minute book.

At this time the lodges paid no regular contributions to the Grand Lodge, and whatever expenses were incurred at the Quarterly Communications were paid by the Grand Master for the time being. The Earl of Dalkeith who seems to have been a very benevolent person, was the first to suggest the formation of a permanent fund for relieving the distressed. This he did on the 21st November, 1724, by a series of four propositions which were agreed to without opposition, but were not acted upon until the 25th of November, 1729, when the five following Lodges contributed between them the sum of £9. 8s. 6d., viz. :—

	£	s.	d.
The King's Arms, St. Paul's Churchyard (now the Lodge of Antiquity, No. 2)	4	10	0
The Rose and Rummer in Holborn (defunct)	1	1	0

	£	s.	d.
The One Tun, in Noble Street (now the Royal Alpha, No. 16)	0	5	6
The Queen's Head, in Knave's Acre (now the Fortitude and Old Cumberland, No. 12)...	1	10	0
Paul's Head, in Ludgate Street (defunct) ...	2	2	0

But to return to poor old Prichard, who seems to have been rather a hard bargain, another petition from him was read on the 27th of December, 1729, in which he is described as a joiner, but the Master and Wardens of the lodge at the Queen's Head, in Knave's Acre, on being asked their opinion concerning the petition, " said they had relieved Prichard in their own lodge, and had advised him not to present it this night. The petition was then handed back to the Master and Wardens to be kept by them till the General Charity was established upon a proper ffooting, and they shall think fit to recommend his case again." On the 28th August, 1730, ten petitions for relief were read and referred to the Committee of Charity, one of them being from Prichard; he sent in another in the December following, but a brother having stated that he had recently been relieved by several lodges, also by the Committee of Charity, and that he had received an offer to be provided for in St. James's Workhouse, but had refused, the petition was dismissed.

This case has been selected as an illustration of the social condition of some of the Masons of the old school, and I will now direct attention to the following additional extracts from the Grand Lodge minutes:—

" 24th June, 1731.

" The Petition of Henry Pritchard (a regular Mason upwards of FFORTY YEARS) was also read, setting forth his Poverty, Age, Blindness, and other Misfortunes, and notwithstanding his having formerly received £3. 0s. 0d. out of the General Charity, yet that by reason of his Blindness and other Infirmities, he was incapable of helping himself. Br. Sharp and several other worthy Brethren giving him a Good Character,

"The Grand Lodge considering Br. Pritchard's Condition, in consideration thereof were pleased to order

"That the Treasurer of the General Charity do pay to Br. Henry Pritchard the sum of five Pounds towards his further releife, and desired that Dr. Desagulier would be pleased to see the same applyed in the best manner for that purpose."

The only lodge in which I find the name of Henry Pritchard in 1723 is No. 15 on the register, "The Half Moon, in the Strand," consisting of 17 members.

In the 1725 register the lodge is No. 12, and the members reduced to ten, but Pritchard's name is not amongst them. I cannot trace this lodge later than 1725, probably it died out shortly after that year, as in 1730 Pritchard is said to have been a member of the "Queen's Head, in Knave's Acre," although his name does not appear in any list of members of that lodge, but it is hardly likely that, poor as he was, he would have belonged to two lodges at one time, and moreover, a law had only recently been passed prohibiting brethren from belonging "to more than one lodge at one time within the Bills of Mortality."

From the fact of Pritchard's lodge being No. 15, and he a Mason of over forty years' standing, we may fairly presume that it was one of the old lodges which, as I have suggested, joined the confederation of 1717, after the Grand Lodge was established. This was not an isolated case, as the following extract from the minutes of March 2nd, 1732, will prove: "The petition of Brother Edward Hall, a Member of the Lodge at the Swan, in Chichester, being there made a Mason by the late Duke of Richmond, Six and thirty years agoe, and now recommended by the present Duke of Richmond, as a proper object of the Charity of Free and

Accepted Masons, his Petition was read, and Br. Hall was called in, and after some questions asked him, he withdrew and the question being put,

"Resolved: That Six Guineas be given to Br. Edward Hall for his present subsistance."

The lodge at the "Swan in Chichester," first appears in the register of 1725, with a list of fifteen members, two of whom were evidently added after the list of thirteen had been entered. In the engraved list for 1729, the earliest I have seen in which the dates of Constitution are given, the space for the date of that lodge is blank, but in the subsequent lists it is given "July 17, 1724."

The Duke of Richmond was present in Grand Lodge at the time Hall's petition was read, indeed the record implies that he brought it forward himself, at all events he must have had some good reason for believing in the truth of the story; the applicant must also have satisfied the other brethren or, notwithstanding the recommendation of the noble Duke, I am fully convinced that they would not have unanimously voted him six guineas.

The early records contain many other instances of old Masons appealing to the newly-formed Grand Lodge for pecuniary aid, but as the Masonic age of the petitioners is not stated, it is unnecessary to enumerate them, especially as they will have no direct bearing on my argument as to the existence of pre-1717 lodges, although this fact will be of some little value when the question of a social distinction between the old and the new school is considered. The reader will please to bear in mind that in order to avoid unnecessary repetition the initials G. L. M. signify "Grand Lodge Minutes." I have before remarked that the only reliable records of Grand Lodge commence with the written minutes of the 24th June, 1723. At this early period there were evidently two distinct parties, and the following extracts will show a want of unanimity on what were considered matters of vital importance.

c 2

The first item of the minutes on the above date relates to the appointment of a Secretary, to which there seems to have been no opposition, but whether the brother was elected by the members, or personally appointed by the Grand Master is not quite clear ; however, Anderson himself on Page 161 of the Constitution of 1738, says, " On 24th June, 1723, the *G. Lodge* chose *William Cowper*, Esqre., to be their *Secretary*. But ever since then, the *New G.M.* upon his commencement appoints the *Secretary*, or continues him by returning him the Books. His *Badge* is of *two Golden Pens* across on his *Left* Breast." As Anderson was present as Jr. Grand Warden on the day he mentions, I have no doubt he is correct as to the mode of selection.

The next business was the confirmation of the General Regulations, or what is now known as the Constitutions of 1723. On this subject there appears to have been some difference of opinion. " Then, ' the question was moved that the said General Regulations be confirmed so far as they are consistent with the Ancient Rules of Masonry.' The previous question was moved and put, whether the words [so far as they are consistent with the Ancient Rules of Masonry] be part of the question.

" Resolved in the affirmative.

" But the main Question was not put.

" And the Question was moved.

" That it is not in the Power of any person, or Body of men to make any Alteration or Innovation in the Body of Masonry, without the Consent first obtained of the Annual Grand Lodge.

" Resolved in the affirmative.

" Then the Grand Master being desired to Nominate his successor, and declining to do so, but referring the Nomination to the Lodge.

" The Right Honble. the Earl of Dalkeith was proposed to be put in Nomination as Grand Master for the year ensuing.

" And two Brethren of his Lordship's Lodge (he being absent in Scotland) acquainted the Lodge that his Lordship had declared he would accept the Office if chosen.

" The Earl of Dalkeith was agreed to be put in Nomination as Grand Master for the ensuing year.

" The lodge was also informed, that (in case of his election) he had nominated Dr. Desaguliers for his Deputy.

" And the 35th General Regulation, purporting that the Grand Master being Installed shall next nominate and appoint his Deputy Grand Master, &c., was read.

" Then, the question was proposed and put by the Grand Master,

" That the Deputy nominated by the Earl of Dalkeith be approved.

" There was a Division of the Lodge, and two Brethren appointed Tellers.

"Ayes 43
"Noes 42

" Then the Grand Master in the name of the new Grand Master, proposed Brother Francis Sorrell, and Brother John Senex for Grand Wardens the ensuing year.

" Agreed, ' That they should be Ballotted for after dinner.'

" Adjourned to Dinner.

" After Dinner, and some of the regular Healths drank, ' The Earl of Dalkeith was Declared Grand Master according to the above-mentioned Resolution of the Grand Lodge.'

" The late Grand Master declaring he had some doubt upon the above-mentioned Division in the Grand Lodge before Dinner, whether the Majority was for approving Dr. Desaguliers, or whether the Tellers had truly reported the Numbers, proposed the said Question be now put again in the General Lodge.

" And accordingly insisting on the said Question being now put, and putting the same, his Worship and several

Brethren withdrew out of the Hall, as dividing against
approving Dr. Desaguliers.

" And being so withdrawn,

"Brother Robinson producing a written authority from the
Earl of Dalkeith for that purpose, did declare in his name,
that his Worship had agreeably to the regulation in that
behalf appointed, and did appoint Dr. Desaguliers his Deputy,
and Brothers Sorrell and Senex Grand Wardens; and also
Brother Robinson did in his said Worship's Name and
behalf of the whole Fraternity protest against the above proceedings of the late Grand Master in first putting the
Question of Approbation, and what followed thereon as un-
precedented, unwarrantable, and Irregular, and tending to
introduce into the Society a Breach of Harmony, with the
utmost disorder and confusion.

" Then the said late Grand Master and those who withdrew with him being returned into the Hall and acquainted
with the aforesaid declaration of Brother Robinson,

"The late Grand Master went away from the Hall
without any ceremony."

The preceding extracts include nearly the whole of the
minutes taken at this meeting; nothing is omitted that
could possibly be of the least value from an historical point
of view. The earliest authentic records of the proceedings of
the Mother Grand Lodge of the World cannot fail to interest the brotherhood generally, while those who derive
more than ordinary pleasure from a study of its history will
I doubt not concur with me in opinion that every line is
worthy of careful consideration, and that there is evidently
more in these transactions than appears upon the surface. I
think it a great pity that the new Grand Secretary did not
record the names and lodges of the movers of the different
resolutions, especially as by so doing he would have enabled
me to make more clear that which some of my readers may
be inclined to look upon as somewhat hypothetical. Having

examined the incidents in all their bearings, and carefully considered the attendant circumstances, I can come to no other conclusion than that this meeting was in reality a contest for supremacy between the old or operative class, represented on this occasion by the ambitious but harebrained Duke of Wharton, with his Grand Wardens, the blacksmith and stonemason, and their followers on the one side, and the more aristocratic brethren of the new or modern school of Dalkeith, Desaguliers, Payne and Anderson, whose cause appears to have been very ably supported by Captain Robinson, one of the Wardens of the noble Earl's lodge. It is but fair that I should mention my reasons for arriving at this conclusion, and in order to render myself explicit it will be necessary to go back to the year 1722, but as we have no written records of that year I must again call to my aid our only historian of that eventful period. Anderson, on page 114 of the Constitutions of 1738, says : " Grand Master Montague's good government inclin'd the better Sort to continue him in the Chair another Year, and therefore they delay'd to prepare the Feast.

" But Philip, Duke of Wharton, lately made a Brother, though not the *Master* of a *Lodge*, being ambitious of the Chair, got a Number of Others to meet him at *Stationers' Hall*, 24 June, 1722, and having no *Grand* Officers, they put into the Chair the *oldest Master Mason* (who was not the *present* Master of a Lodge, also irregular), and without the usual decent Ceremonials, the said *old Mason* proclaimed aloud, Philip Wharton, Duke of Wharton, Grand Master of *Masons*, and *Mr. Joshua Timson*, Blacksmith, } *Grand*
Mr. William Hawkins, Mason, } *Wardens.*
but his Grace appointed no *Deputy*, nor was the *Lodge* opened and closed in due Form.

" Therefore the *noble* Brothers and all those that would not countenance Irregularities, disown'd *Wharton's* Authority, till worthy Brother Montague heal'd the Breach of Harmony, by summoning the Grand Lodge to meet 17th January, 1723, at the *King's Arms* foresaid, where the Duke of Wharton promising to be *True* and *Faithful, Deputy Grand Master Beal* proclaimed aloud the most noble Prince and our Brother,

" Philip Wharton, Duke of Wharton, Grand Master of Masons, who appointed Dr. Desaguliers the *Deputy Grand Master.* Joshua Timson, foresaid, } Grand James Anderson, A.M., } Wardens. for Hawkins demitted as always out of town."

This is the account given by Anderson of what was undoubtedly a serious split in the Masonic camp, which was only healed by the Duke of Montague and his friends giving way to Wharton & Co., for the meeting called by the former at the " King's Arms " (at which house Wharton's lodge was held), was clearly little else than an unconditional surrender on the part of " the noble Brothers and those of the better sort," who had previously " disown'd Wharton's Authority." We must not forget that this incident is described by Anderson about sixteen years after it occurred, and that he not being a member of Wharton's lodge, was scarcely likely to have been present at any of the proceedings he describes. Unfortunately, we have no record of the members of that lodge in the 1723 register, or I am very much mistaken if we should not find Timson and Hawkins, his two Grand Wardens, amongst them. I cannot find either of them in any other lodge of that period.

Anderson's statement reads as though Hawkins had demitted previous to the meeting for reconciliation, and that he (Anderson) was there and then appointed in his stead ; but on examining the written register of the old Grand Officers, I find William Hawkins entered as J.G. Warden for 1722, and in another handwriting undoubtedly added subsequently, these words, " who demitted and then James Anderson, A.M., was *chosen* in his place." It is but natural to conclude that between 1722 and 1725 Wharton's lodge had undergone some little alteration with regard to the social status of its members. His *Grace* figures as Master in the latter year, and has for his Wardens Sir Thomas Mackworth, Bart., and the Honorable John Trevor, Esq. In a list of twenty-nine members there are seven designated " Esqre.," one Captain, and one Baronet, the rest have the ordinary prefix " Mr." only, and amongst them are several whose names I find in the previous register, who were, without question, old Masons, including a brother Cordwell, who was J.G. Warden in 1718.

In April, 1730, Br. Timson, Wharton's S.G. Warden, was a petitioner for relief from the newly established Charity Fund (the sum total of which was then about £80), and in consideration of his having been Grand Warden he was granted £14, at the same time Anthony Sayer, first Grand Master, was voted £15. In December the same year Timson's widow was an applicant for relief, but her petition was unanimously rejected on the ground that " her husband had received £14 in May last."

I think I have said enough to show that Wharton had thrown in his lot with the lower class of Masons, although I do not wish to imply that he was in any way responsible for his Wardens; from the fact of his insisting upon those officers being balloted for in 1723. I feel confident that personal appointments were looked upon as an innovation by the old brethren, also that Anderson himself was *elected* and not *appointed*, or the word "chosen " would not have been used in connexion with his name as J.G. Warden. It was evidently no " hole and corner meeting " at which Wharton was proclaimed Grand Master, even our one-sided historian admits that he "got a *number* of others to meet him at Stationers' Hall, 24th June, 1722." It is worthy of notice that it was at Stationers' Hall just twelve months before that his predecessor Montague had been installed. Anderson says, "but his Grace appointed no Deputy," as though this omission was an irregularity on his part, whereas that office was not known in Masonry till Montague appointed Dr. Beal in 1721, and from the very close division in Grand Lodge on the question of Desaguliers' appointment, and Wharton's palpable opposition to that brother, there is no doubt the office was looked upon as another innovation.

Between the 24th of June, and the 25th of November, 1723, no meeting of Grand Lodge appears to have been held, and judging from the records of the last named date the business then transacted consisted chiefly in confirming what had been done at the preceding Communication.

At this meeting the Earl of Dalkeith presided as Grand Master, supported by his Deputy, Desaguliers, and his two Grand Wardens, Sorrell and Senex.

"The following Questions were put :—

"1st. Whether the Masters and Wardens of the several Lodges have not power to regulate all things relative to Masonry at their Quarterly Meetings, one of which must be on St. John Baptist's Day ?   'Agreed, *Nem. Con.*'

"2nd. Whether the Grand Master has not power to appoint his Deputy ?   'Agreed, *Nem. Con.*'

"Agreed, that Dr. Desaguliers be Deputy Grand Master from the last Annual Meeting.

"Ordered, that Br. Huddleston, of the King's Head, in Ivy Lane, be expelled that Lodge for laying severall aspersions against the Deputy Grand Master which he could not make good, and the Grand Master appointed Mr. Davis Senr. Warden, Master of the said Lodge in Ivy Lane.

"Agreed, that no new Lodge in or near London, without it be Regularly Constituted, be countenanced by the Grand Lodge, nor the Master or Wardens admitted at the Grand Lodge.

"3rd. Whether the two Grand Wardens, Brother Sorrell and Brother Senex are confirmed in their office ?

"Agreed, *Nem. Con.*"

Then follows the before mentioned recommendation of the Grand Master on behalf of Henry Pritchard, and the record ends. We are left entirely in the dark as to what led to the passing of the foregoing resolutions, also as to the discussions which doubtless arose before they were agreed to.

We must therefore take these early minutes for what they were undoubtedly intended to be, simply a register of results, and in order to be able to arrive at anything like an accurate knowledge of the real proceedings we must read between the lines. It is not at all likely that these questions were brought forward for prospective purposes only ; something must have occurred, and that recently, to have rendered them necessary. In my opinion a solution for most of them can be found in the rather stormy transactions of the 24th of June, although it is not at all improbable that difficulties may have arisen at this same meeting which called for immediate action.

I will now briefly examine the different questions in the order in which they appear in the book.

It would seem from the tone of the first paragraph that the powers of the Masters and Wardens had been disputed, nothing however of the kind appears in the minutes ; although it does not necessarily follow that no such dispute occurred. Here again, by taking a retrospective glance at Anderson's account of the Installation, or as he puts it, the proclamation of the Duke of Wharton, I think we may find light. It will be observed that he makes it a ground of complaint that Wharton was proclaimed by the oldest Master Mason " (who was not the *present* Master of a Lodge, also irregular)" the italics are his own, and I understand his meaning to be that the brother in question was a Past Master. Hence, I infer that amongst the older members of the Fraternity, Past Masters were considered *eligible to attend Grand Lodge,* a privilege which the new regulations denied them, unless by dispensation from the Grand Master.

There can be no doubt that this restriction would have the effect of rapidly increasing the number of lodges, an object which it is more than probable that the new or gentlemanly portion of the Order had in view. Whether or no, this was certainly the result, and in proportion as new lodges accumulated the old ones decayed and dropped out, as will be seen from an examination of the different lists.

A reference to the proceedings of the 24th June, will sufficiently explain the second and third questions relating to the Deputy Grand Master and the two Grand Wardens.

The order for the expulsion of Bro. Huddleston appearing immediately after the confirmation of Desaguliers' appointment as D.G.M. seems to me to indicate that the offence in question had been committed during a discussion on the subject of that appointment. Unfortunately, we have no means of ascertaining the nature of these aspersions, but in my opinion they were not of a very serious character, although the punishment, at first sight, appears rather severe; it was, however, not an expulsion from the Craft, nor even from his own lodge, but from the Grand Lodge for that meeting, as his name appears in the list of members returned in 1725 for the "King's Head, in Ivy Lane," and there is no record of his having been reinstated.

From the fact of the lodge being an old one, I am inclined to think that Bro. Huddleston's grievance had something to do with the new regulations supposed to have been concocted by Anderson and Desaguliers. Up to 1767, the members of this lodge were for the most part of the artizan class, but in that year it was joined by the Duke of Beaufort and some of his friends, consisting of the leading members of the Order, and was then removed from Holborn to the "Thatched House Tavern," St. James's Street. It is now the Lodge of Friendship, No. 6, one of the most select, as well as one of the best conducted lodges in London.

The paragraph referring to new lodges merits careful

attention, it seems to point to some trouble about lodges having been formed without official sanction, and from the word " *new* " being used, might imply that the regulation was not intended to interfere with old lodges then working. It might also signify that all the lodges in London were to be found under the banner of the Grand Lodge ; but of the latter interpretation, I am somewhat doubtful, for supposing it to be correct, the word " *new* " would not have been wanted.

At the next meeting of Grand Lodge, the 19th February, 1724, the whole of the business appears to have consisted of passing resolutions of a repressive character; being exceedingly brief, I will give them in full, viz. :—

" The following Questions were put and Agreed to.

" 1st. That no Brother belong to more than one Lodge at one time within the Bills of Mortality.

" It is the Grand Master's Order that every Master or Warden bring with them the List of every Member belonging to his Lodge at the next Quarterly Meeting.

" 2nd. That no Brother belonging to any Lodge within the Bills of Mortality be admitted to any Lodge as a Visitor unless personally known to some Brother of that Lodge where he visits, and that no strange Brother however skilled in Masonry be admitted without taking the Obligacon over againe, unless he be Introduced or vouched for by some Brother known to, and approved by the majority of the Lodge. And whereas some Masons have mett and formed a Lodge without the Grand Master's leave.

" Agreed, That no such person be admitted into Regular Lodges."

It seems to me most improbable that the Grand Lodge should have spent a whole sitting in discussing and adopting these measures for the express purpose of putting down one irregular lodge ; it would be like bringing out a whole regiment as well as a battery of artillery to shoot a single deserter. To my thinking the first part of the last resolution applies to surreptitious or spurious Masons rather than to irregular ones, or in plainer language, to people who might have obtained a knowledge of the secrets without going through the recognized and usual ceremonies, or why the order to re-obligate strangers ?

The following is the next reference to Irregular Makings, 21st November, 1724 :— "That if any Brethren shall meet Irregularly and make Masons at any Place within ten miles of London, the persons present at the making (The new Brethren excepted), shall not be admitted even as Visitors into any Regular Lodge whatsoever, unless they come and make such Submission to the Grand Master and Grand Lodge as they shall think fit to impose on them.

"Agreed, *Nem. Con.*"

On the 27th December, 1727, it was " Agreed, That it shall be referred to the succeeding Grand Master, Deputy Grand Master, and Grand Wardens, to enquire into the Precedency of the several Lodges, and to make Report thereof at the next Quarterly Communication, in order that the same may be finally settled, and entred accordingly."

Hence, it is quite clear that up to this time no record had been kept of the dates of Constitution of the various lodges, and it is equally conclusive that the authorities themselves knew very little on the subject. At the same meeting " A Letter from the Master, Wardens and Brethren of the Lodge held at the King's Head, in Salford, near Manchester (praying that the List of their Members may be entred in the Grand Lodge Book, and that they may be under the Care and Patronage of the Grand Lodge) was read.

"Agreed, *Nemine Con*. That they be entred accordingly."

We have no means of ascertaining how long this lodge had been working before the application for recognition was made, but from the fact of the List referred to containing twenty-four names, it had probably been several years in existence. In the engraved List for 1729 it appears amongst the lodges constituted in the latter part of 1727, but no date is assigned to it until 1740, and then the year only (1727) is given, the actual date of Constitution being omitted, and so it continues until its erasure in 1754.

It will be observed that this lodge does not ask to be constituted into a regular lodge. They merely wish to have their names entered in the Grand Lodge book, and to be under the care and patronage of the Grand Lodge ; being probably under the impression that they never had been irregular, and therefore required no Constitution. I have no doubt this was the case with many other old lodges in different parts of the country as well as in London ; for instance at the meeting on the 10th May, 1727, a letter was read from the Provincial Grand Lodge of Chester (in which city three prosperous lodges were established numbering between them eighty members,* and on the 24th June in the same year a similar communication was read from the Provincial Grand Lodge of South Wales.

G. L. M. 17th April, 1728.

"Then most of the Lodges present delivered the Dates of the time of their being Constituted into Lodges in order to have Precedency in the printed Book."

The following rather curious letter appears in the minutes of this meeting which I consider of sufficient importance for reproduction, as it affords a striking example of the loose method of establishing lodges in the old time, and of the readiness of the Grand Lodge to receive into its fold all comers whether lawfully constituted or not.

" The Deputy Grand Master acquainted the Brethren, that he had received a Letter from several Masons at a Lodge at Madrid, in Spain, which he read to them, and the Grand

---

* See " Early Chester Masonry," in " Freemason," 12th June, 1886.

Lodge unanimously agreed to what was prayed for in their Letter, which is as followeth :—

" Right Worshipful Master,

" We here undersigned Masons, free and accepted, residing at present in Madrid, and other places of the Kingdom of Spain, take the Liberty of this Letter, as our Duty oblige us, to acquaint our Most Right and Worshipful Grand Master, his worthy Deputy, the Grand Wardens, and all the Lodges of Masons now constituted in England, that having been always very desirous to see our Ancient Society propogated, its true and virtious Designs encouraged, and the Craft flourish in every place where our affairs have called us ; Resolved accordingly to propagate it in this Kingdom whenever it could be done in a lawful manner. And as we had sometime agoe the Opportunity of the Presence of his Grace the Duke of Wharton, we petitioned him to Constitute a Lodge in this Town, the which he readily granted and executed, and after our Lodge was formed we accepted and made Masons, three persons hereunder mentioned, and just after it was Resolved unanimously to acquaint with our Proceedings our Grand Master and the General Officers in England to all which his Grace submitts himself intirely, having acted in this occasion as second Deputy.

" Be pleased therefore to acquaint our Grand Master, and all the Lodges in general at the next Quarterly Communication with the contents of this Letter, and we expect the favour to be inserted in the Book under the Name of the Madrid Lodge, and Meetings being fixed at Present on the first Sunday in every Month, we hope to send at the next Quarterly Communication that shall be held about St. John Baptist's day of this present year, a longer List of Members of our Lodge, and a copy of such By Laws, as we Resolve upon, as they are thought proper for the Country wherein we are at present for the Union amongst us, and the Charity to the Poor, so much recommended and exercised in our Ancient Society, upon which in general, We pray God Almighty to shed his most precious ffavours and Blessings. We are,

"Sr. And Right Worshipful Master,
"Your most dutiful Brethren
and humble Servants,

"Dated in our Lodge at Madrid,
this 15th ffebruary, 1728. N.S.

"By his Grace's orders,

"Philip Duke of Wharton, &c., Deputy G. Master.
"Sic Subscribitur.

"Charles De Labelye, Master.   ⎫
"Richards,   Senr. Warden. ⎬ Pro tempore.
"Thomas Hatton,   Junr. Warden. ⎭
"Eldridge Dinsdale.
"Andrew Gallwey.

"Then the Grand Lodge drank prosperity to the Brethren of the Lodge at Madrid, and desired the Grand Master to write them word of their being acknowledged and received as Brethren, or in what manner he shall think proper."

This Lodge was continued in the Engraved Lists up to 1767, when it was erased, but no further list of Members is registered, and only the foregoing names appear in the Grand Lodge Book. The self-appointed "second Deputy Grand Master" who had formerly opposed the Duke of Montague and Desaguliers, seems to have had nothing whatever to do with the Grand Lodge from the time he "went away from the Hall without ceremony" on the 24th June, 1723; indeed, he left the country shortly afterwards, and probably never returned, he could therefore have had no more real authority for constituting a lodge (according to the new regulations) than he had to call himself Deputy Grand Master, and yet this lodge was deemed to have been

D

lawfully constituted, and was received, as it were, with open arms by the regular Grand Lodge. I can only account for this by the supposition that Wharton had simply followed the old method of forming and establishing a lodge, and that at this period there was still a numerous body of his former associates attending the Quarterly Communications. It is quite evident that Wharton, though comparatively a young man, had considerable influence over the Fraternity. Our present mode of constituting a lodge is unquestionably merely an elaboration of the primitive ceremony described by Anderson in the Constitutions of 1723, and judging from the heading here given I should say it was added at the instigation of the noble Duke himself.

"Postscript. Here follows the Manner of constituting a New Lodge, as practis'd by his Grace the Duke of Wharton, the present Right Worshipful Grand Master, according to the ancient Usages of Masons."

The following item in the minutes of this meeting is worthy of notice, as it goes far to confirm my previously expressed opinion that all the offices in Grand Lodge were elective under the old system.

" The Grand Master having appointed Brother William Reid to be Secretary to the Grand Lodge, the Deputy Grand Master signified his Lordship's pleasure of the same to the Brethren, and further acquainted them that his Lordship, notwithstanding such appointment would not insist upon Brother Reid's being Secretary without their unanimous consent.

"To which they all agreed. *Nemine Con.*

" And he was declared as such accordingly."

I may also mention that the previous meeting was the Installation Festival, and at the end of the names of the officers then appointed, and evidently written subsequent to the rest of the minutes, being in a different hand and interlined, are the words, " Br. William Reid *chosen* Secretary."

G. L. M. 25th June, 1728.

" The minutes of the last Q.C. having been read :—

" Pursuant to an Article in the aforesaid Minutes (requiring all the regular Lodges to give in the exact time when they were severally Constituted) some of the Members delivered the account as required, and such as had not complyed with the aforesaid Order were directed to do it before the next Quarterly Communication."

Under the circumstances it is not surprising that some of the lodges, especially the older ones, should have experienced a difficulty in determining the exact date of their being constituted.

The frequent use of the term " regular lodges " in the Grand Lodge minutes leaves no doubt in my mind that there must have been other lodges in existence at this time that were considered irregular by the *regime* of 1717 ; although probably the members themselves were of a different opinion, unquestionable evidence of which will be found in the following extracts from the minutes of Grand Lodge:—

26th November, 1728.

" A petition was presented to the Deputy Grand Master by Wm. Benn, Master, and Job Beardsly, Senr. Warden of the Lodge held at the Mag Pye, against Bishopgate Street Church, signed by Gerard Hatley, Joseph Burr, and Obadiah Wynne, the Master & Wardens of a Lodge held for some time past at Bishopgate Coffee house, declaring their Intention and earnest desire to be constituted as soon as it will suit the Conveniency of the Deputy Grand Master to confer that Honour upon them, and humbly praying to be admitted among the regular Lodges at this Quarterly Communication.

" The Deputy Grand Master did (upon the recommendation of the Gentlemen who appeared for them, and also upon their application to him some time agoe for the said purpose) dispence with their being at present irregular, and admitted them into the Grand Lodge.

" Copy of the Deputation for Constituting a Lodge in Gibraltar (*L.S.*) Kingston.

" Whereas application was made to our Rt. Worshipfull Brother His Grace the Most Noble Charles Lenox Duke of Richmond, late Grand Master by our Brother John Bailie, Master, and Thomas Wilson, and Benjamin Radenhurst, Wardens of a Lodge of St. John's, at Gibralter, for and on the behalfe of several of our Brethren Commissioned and non-commissioned Officers and others; representing : That as they have nothing more at heart than their duty to God, our King and Country, and to his Grace as Grand Master, They desire that they may be constituted a regular Lodge in due fform.

" These are therefore to Impower and authorize our well-beloved Brother John Bailie, Thomas Wilson, and Benja min Radenhurst to convene our Brethren at Gibralter aforesaid, and that they do in our place and stead, consti-tute a regular Lodge in due fform, at Gibralter aforesaid (taking especial care that they and every of them have been regularly made Masons) with like Priviledges as all other regular Lodges do enjoy, and that they be required to con-form themselves to all and every the Regulations contained in the Printed Constitutions, and observe such other Rules and Instructions as shall from time to time be transmitted to them by us, or Nathaniel Blackerby, Esqr., our Deputy Grand Master, or the Grand Master, or his Deputy Grand Master for the time being, and that they do with the first opportunity send to us, or our Deputy a List of the Members of their Lodge, together with the Rules agreed on to be by them observed, to the end they may be entred in the Grand Lodge Book. Given under our hand and Seal of Office at London this 9th day of March, 172$\frac{8}{9}$, and in the year of Masonry 5728.

　　" By the Grand Master's command,
　　　　" Nat. Blackerby, Deputy Gd. Master.
　　　　" J. Thornhill,　⎫
　　　　" Mn. O'Connor,　⎬ Grand Wardens."

This Deputation is particularly interesting, for although in point of date it has only second place in the records, the petition upon which it was issued seems to have been the first received for a Constitution abroad, as the Duke of Richmond, to whom the application was made was Grand Master in 1724, and there is no reason to doubt that it was received during his term of office. The first Deputation was for a lodge at Fort William, in Bengall, and is dated " the 6th day of ffebruary, $172\frac{8}{9}$," followed by the above mentioned for Gibraltar, dated a month later; and the third was for the lodge at Madrid, which although acknowledged by Grand Lodge in 1728, and the Grand Master was desired to write the brethren to that effect, nothing appears to have been done in the matter until the 27th of March, 1729, when " The Master of the Lodge at Madrid stood up and represented that his Lodge had never been regularly constituted by the Authority of the Grand Master, Deputy Grand Master and Grand Wardens in England, and therefore humbly prayed a Deputation for that purpose.

" Ordered, that the Secretary do likewise prepare a Deputation to Impower Charles Labelle, Master of the said Lodge, to constitute them with such other Instructions as is likewise necessary for that purpose."

It will be observed that this petition from Gibraltar is similar in one respect to those already mentioned; it is not for permission to form a new lodge, but for constituting or legalizing one already established. There is, however, one peculiarity about it to which I wish to call attention, viz., the title " Lodge of St. John's."

Hitherto the records contain no mention of St. John, except with reference to the Annual Festivals of the Order, and it is well known that lodges had no distinctive names at this period, being only known by their numbers on the list, and the signs of the houses at which they were held. That the lodge was so described by the applicants and the designation

acknowledged by the authorities is evident from the following
letter read in Grand Lodge on the 27th December, 1729 :—

"A Letter from the Lodge of St. John of Jerusalem
lately Constituted at Gibralter by authority from the present
Grand Master was read, and ordered to be entred, viz :—

"Most Noble and Right Honourable Grand Master.

"My Lord,

"We the Master and Wardens of the Lodge of St.
John of Jerusalem, established by your Lordship's Letters of Consecration, dated the seventh day of March,
172$\frac{8}{9}$, in this His Majesty's Garrison of Gibralter, do for
ourselves and Fellow Masons, beg Leave to return our most
humble Thanks for the Honour your Lordship hath been
pleased to do us, in impowering us to hold a Lodge in as
due and ample manner as hath been hitherto practised by
our Brethren; In pursuance of which we did on the fifth
Instant, hold our first Lodge, and as our Number was then
but small: We admitted six Brothers, whose names are
distinguished in the List of the Members of the Lodge,
which together with the Orders thereof, We now transmitt to
you.   And we further beg Leave to assure your Lordship
that we shall in every respect conform to what you have
prescribed to us, and shall keep an exact account of our
Proceedings in order to lay them before your Lordship or
our Grand Master for the time being when it shall be
necessary or by you required.   And so We humbly Salute
your Lordship, the Right Worshipful the Deputy Grand
Master and Wardens, and the rest of our Brethren, and in
the name of our Lodge We remain with great Respect,

"My Lord,

"Your Lordship's most humble and most
"Obedient Servants and Brethren,

"John Baylie,   Master.
"Josias Wilson,   } Wardens.
"Benjn. Rodenhurst, }

"From our Lodge at Gibralter,
the 19th day of October, 1729."

" A List of the Members of the said Lodge being 21 in Number was also transmitted with the above Letter."

I have given this letter in the order in which it appears in the records, but I shall have something more to say at a future stage on the subject of Lodges of St. John.

G. L. M., 28th August, 1730.

" Dr. Desaguliers stood up and (taking Notice of a printed Paper lately published and dispersed about the Town, and since inserted in the Newspapers, pretending to discover and reveal the Misteries of the Craft of Masonry) recommended several things to the consideration of the Grand Lodge, Particularly the Resolution of the last Quarterly Communication for preventing any false Brethren being admitted into Regular Lodges, and such as call themselves Honorary Masons.

" The Deputy Grand Master seconded the Doctor, and proposed several Rules to the Grand Lodge to be observed in their respective Lodges, for their security against all open and secret enemies of the Craft."

Ibid, 15th December, 1730.

" The Deputy Grand Master took notice of a Pamphlet lately published by one Pritchard who pretends to have been made a regular Mason : In violation of the Obligation of a Mason which he swears he has broke in order to do hurt to Masonry, and expressing himself with the utmost Indignation against both him (stiling him an Impostor) and of his Book as a foolish thing not be regarded. But in order to prevent the Lodges being imposed upon by false Brethren or Impostors, Proposed, till otherwise ordered by the Grand Lodge, that no person whatsoever should be admitted into Lodges unless some Member of the Lodge then present would vouch for such visiting Brother's being a regular Mason, and the Member's Name to be entred against the Visitor's Name in the Lodge Book, which Proposal was unanimously agreed to."

The foregoing paragraphs appear to refer to one publication. Notwithstanding that the Deputy Grand Master in his righteous indignation, describes it as a "foolish thing, and not to be regarded," it seems to have occasioned nearly as much excitement as would a bombshell dropping into the midst of a pic-nic party. It would be very interesting and most valuable could we but find out the "several things recommended to the consideration of the Grand Lodge." The fact of their not having been written induces me to think that some portion of them, at any rate, were of an esoteric character.

Assuming that both these extracts refer to one pamphlet, it appears as though something unusual had occurred between the 28th of August and the 15th of December, or the second and more emphatic notice would not have been either judicious or necessary. What that something was, is of course, impossible to decide with certainty, but it is worthy of remark, that Prichard is said to have made an affidavit before an Alderman on the 13th of October to the effect, that his publication was a "true Copy of Freemasonry." It seems to me most unlikely that he should have taken this extraordinary step unless under the fear that his book was in danger of being discredited in consequence of some important alteration having taken place in the recognized ceremonies. I have every reason to believe that something of the kind suggested was done either during this year or as is stated in the mendacious manifesto previously referred to, some time subsequent to the year 1739; my own opinion inclines to the former period as will be seen more clearly hereafter. While on this subject I may as well mention that having carefully searched the Register, I can find no person bearing the name of Samuel Prichard in either of the lists of members returned to Grand Lodge; these lists are not entirely reliable, as the first or 1723 register gives the members of 36 lodges only, out of 52 mentioned in the book. The next is in 1725, and is much more complete; it includes 77 lodges, only four of which are without the names of the members. It is in this register I should have expected to find Prichard, had he been as he asserts on his title page, " Late member of a Constituted Lodge." It is just possible he may have been related to the before mentioned poor old brother Henry Prichard and so obtained a surreptitious knowledge of the ceremonies. The Deputy Grand Master says, " *who pretends to have been made a regular Mason,*" thereby insinuating that Prichard had no real claim to that title; it is therefore a question of whom to believe, and as it is not a matter of very great import I shall leave it to the reader's own option.

Another incident is mentioned in the minutes of this period, which is worthy of attention, although I do not attach so much importance to it as some of our brethren of the pen. I allude to a complaint against Anthony Sayer the first Grand Master of the Order. The description of this transaction, is, in my opinion, not sufficiently explicit to render it of real historical value. Yet I am reluctant to pass it by unnoticed, it being the only occasion on which a Past Grand Master has been called upon to defend himself in Grand Lodge against accusations made by the Master and Wardens of a private Lodge. The recorded facts are as follows :—

G. L. M., 28th August, 1730.

" A Paper signed by the Master and Wardens of the Lodge at the Queen's Head, in Knaves Acre, was presented and read, complaining of great Irregularities having been committed by Brother Anthony Sayer, notwithstanding the great ffavours he hath lately received by order of the Grand Lodge. *

---

* He had recently been relieved with £15 from the Charity Fund.

" Ordered, that Br. Sayer be summoned to attend at the next Quarterly Communication to answer the said Complaint, and that the persons who signed the same do also attend at the same time."

Ibid, 15th December, 1730.

" Brother Sayer likewise attended to answer the Complaint made against him, and after hearing both parties, and some of the Brethren being of opinion that what he had done was clandestine, others that it was irregular : The Question was put whether what was done was clandestine or irregular only, and the Lodge was of opinion that it was irregular only. Whereupon the Deputy Grand Master told Br. Sayer that he was acquitted of the charge against him, and recommended him to do nothing so irregular for the future."

This reads very much like a verdict of " not guilty, but don't do it again." It is, however, another proof that there were two parties in Grand Lodge who were accustomed to take very different views of the same question. If Anderson's account is correct, it seems to me that the Duke of Wharton's action in 1722 was a far greater irregularity than anything that poor old Sayer could have been guilty of.

It is nevertheless to be regretted that the precise nature of our old Grand Master's offence is not stated ; the general opinion is that he had taken part in irregular makings, or something of that kind, and it may have been so, although I at one time was inclined to think that there was no justification for this view of the case, and that the irregularities complained of were in some way connected with his own lodge, as it was from the Master and Wardens of that lodge the charge emanated. A more careful investigation has, I must confess, led to a modification of my views ; yet I am fully convinced that it was not considered a very serious matter, or he would not have been treated so leniently, and whatever his failings may have been, his poverty should prompt us to "temper justice with mercy;" he at least was not ashamed of them or afraid to face his accusers. It is useless to conjecture with such vague materials, I will therefore leave the solution of the problem to some future Dr. Oliver.

G. L. M., 29th January, 1731.

"Dr. Douglas observed that several Brethren that are not of any regular Lodge, and yet are good and faithful Brethren, can have no Notice (of the Grand Festival) without publick advertisement.

"Ordered, That this affair be left to the Direction of the Stewards."

This is somewhat paradoxical; it may mean either, that there were "good and faithful brethren" who were not members of any lodge; or that the persons indicated belonged to irregular or unconstituted lodges. If the first rendering be the true one, I cannot understand why the word *regular* should have been used; and if the second is correct, it is strange that they should have been described as "good and faithful;" in either case the adjectives seem a little out of place. We must not however judge the Masonry of this early period by our present standard of almost perfect discipline and organization.

Having, from official sources alone, furnished fairly conclusive evidence of the fallacy of some of Anderson's statements as to the formation and early career of the Grand Lodge, I will here venture to express an opinion that not only did he take no part in the events he describes, but, that he was not even a member of the Order prior to 1721, or he would in all probability have been made, at least, a Grand Warden before 1723, and his name would have been mentioned in connexion with the first General Regulations which he states were compiled by Bro. George Payne in 1720, and approved by Grand Lodge on St. John Baptist's Day 1721, and which he, Anderson, within a few months, was ordered by the Grand Master, "to peruse, correct and digest into a new and better method," the result being the Constitutions of 1723, wherein his name appears as Master of a lodge, although this fact does not in my opinion weaken the probability of his having but recently joined the Order ; indeed, considering the work he had undertaken it would have been strange had he not been either a Master or Warden at the time his labours were being discussed in Grand Lodge.

As doubtless many of the brotherhood have not an opportunity of referring to this most interesting and important book, I will here give the concluding paragraph of the "*Approbation*" which is supposed to have been written by the Duke of Wharton, and was signed by him as Grand Master, by his Deputy, the two Grand Wardens, and the Masters and Wardens of twenty private lodges.

" And we ordain That these be receiv'd in every particular *Lodge* under our Cognizance, as the Only Constitutions of *Free* and *Accepted Masons* amongst us, to be read at the making of *new Brethren*, or when the *Master* shall think fit ; and which the *new Brethren* should peruse before they are made."

The words " every particular Lodge under our Cognizance" read very much like an admission that at this period there were lodges outside the jurisdiction of the Grand Lodge.

G. L. M., 24th June, 1731.

" Then the Petition of Br. William Kemble was read, but he not appearing, nor satisfaction given to the Grand Lodge, how long he had been made *a regular* Mason, the same was dismissed.

" A Petition was presented and signed by several Brethren praying that they may be admitted into the Grand Lodge and Constituted into a regular Lodge at the Three Kings in Crispian Street, Spittle Fields. After some debate, several

Brethren present vouching that they were regular Masons, they were admitted, and the Grand Master declared, that he or his Deputy would Constitute them accordingly, and signed their Petition for that purpose."

It is impossible to ascertain whether this lodge was regularly Constituted in conformity with the Grand Master's promise. I cannot find that the usual fee for a Constitution was ever paid; 10s. 6d. is recorded to its credit on the day the Petition was read, and the same amount on the 3rd of December following, after which I can find no trace of it in any of the lists of lodges extant; it had either removed to some other house or was never further acknowledged.

Nothing applicable to the subject on hand is to be found in the records between the date last mentioned and the 24th February, 1735, when the following Resolution was agreed to :—

"That if any Lodge for the future within the Bills of Mortality shall not regularly meet for the space of one year, such Lodge shall be erased out of the Book of Lodges, and in case they shall afterwards be desirous of meeting again as a Lodge they shall lose their former Rank and submitt themselves to a new Constitution."

On the 24th of June following this regulation was extended to country lodges.

I mention this circumstance because some writers have referred to the number of lodges struck of the roll a few years later as having some influence on the formation of the "Ancient" body; whereas a comparison of the previous lists of lodges will show that such erasures had taken place from the earliest period, although no formal resolution to that effect had been passed in Grand Lodge, a single example will suffice. The latest list for 1725 is the one reproduced by Jno. Lane as a frontispiece to his excellent volume, "*Masonic Records*," and it comprises exactly 70 lodges, while the next available which is known as the 1729 list, has only 54 lodges, ten of which are stated to have been Constituted after 1725, thus clearly shewing that at least twenty-six lodges were erased between the publication of these two lists.

Another reference to making Masons irregularly appears in the Minutes of the 31st March, 1735.

" The Grand Master took notice (in a very handsome speech) of the Grievance of making extranious Masons in a private and clandestine manner upon small and unworthy considerations, and Proposed that in order to prevent that Practice for the future; No person thus admitted into the Craft, nor any that can be proved to have assisted at such Makings shall be capable either of acting as a Grand Officer on occasion, or even as an Officer in a Private Lodge, nor ought they to have any part in the General Charity which is much impaired by this clandestine Practice."

It will doubtless be remembered that in 1724 a resolution on this subject had been carried in Grand Lodge, indeed it seems to have cropped up periodically from the earliest period of which we have any reliable data, and although only mentioned occasionally in the minutes, yet bearing in mind, the totally different condition of Masonry to what it now is, I have not the least doubt that the offence complained of was continuous, and not spasmodic as would appear at first sight. Grand Lodge certificates were not known in those days, nor were certificates of any kind used except when a brother resigned his lodge or "declared off;" and as there was no register of members at head quarters from about 1730 to 1770, it would seem to me rather a difficult matter to distinguish *regular* from *irregular* brethren, except of course by their lodges.

I have already directed attention to the great social difference between the old and the new order of Masons, and by way of emphasising my remarks on that subject, I

will here give a list of brethren of distinction present at the
Installation of Lord Weymouth, April 17th, 1735.

"The Rt. Honble. The Earl of Crawfurd, G.M.

" Sir Cecil Wray, Bart., D.G.M.

"John Ward, Esq. ⎫
"Sir Edward Mansell, Bart. ⎬ Grand Wardens.

"The Rt. Honble. The Lord Viscount Weymouth, G.M.
elect.

" Duke of Richmond.

"Duke of Athol.

"Earl of Winchelsea.

" Earl of Balcarrass.

" Earl of Wymes.

" Earl of Loudoun.

" Marquess of Bowman.

" Lord Cathcart.

" Lord Vere Bartee.

"Together with a vast appearance of late Grand Officers
and Gentlemen (being Masons) all clothed in white Aprons
and Gloves."

I will now deal with the question of the before mentioned privileges of the Grand Stewards, to which some of
my predecessors appear to have given, what I consider undue
importance as affecting the Origin of the " Ancients."

I will first briefly state the nature of those particular
privileges, but it must not be forgotten that the Stewards
had obtained most important concessions from Grand Lodge
without opposition only a few years before the period now
under examination. I allude to the privileges of nominating
their successors, wearing their jewels pendent to red
ribbons, and having their aprons lined with red silk, the
particulars of which are to be found in my articles on the
Grand Stewards and their lodges, published in the *Freemason*
of the 24th and 31st July ; 7th, 14th, and 21st August,
1886. The next concession is recorded in the transactions
of Grand Lodge, 31st March, 1735.

"Then a motion was made that Dr. James Anderson should be desired to print the Names (in his new Book of Constitutions) of all the Grand Masters that could be collected from the beginning of time, together with a List of the Names of all Deputy Grand Masters, Grand Wardens, and the Brethren that have served the Craft in Quality of Stewards, which was thought necessary, Because it is Resolved, That for the future all Grand Officers (except the Grand Master) shall be selected out of that Body."

I have given the whole of the paragraph in order that my readers may see the ambiguity of that portion of it which relates to the Grand Stewards. We can well imagine the fate of such a motion had it been brought forward in Grand Lodge at a more recent period, but at the risk of being thought tedious I will again repeat, that we must entirely lose sight of our latter-day Masonry in order to properly understand and appreciate the doings of our earlier brethren. The only Grand Officers acknowledged at this time were the Grand Master, Deputy Grand Master, and the Grand Wardens ; it was not till 1741 that the Treasurer, Secretary, and Sword Bearer were considered as Grand Officers, or even members of the Grand Lodge, which I presume is the reason they are not mentioned in the foregoing extract.

Unfortunately, the record does not state that this motion was seconded or put to the vote, we are therefore left in doubt as to whether the Grand Master, who, as I have previously shewn, had the power of appointing the Grand Officers, had himself resolved to select those brethren from amongst the Past Grand Stewards, or whether a Resolution to that effect was then proposed to Grand Lodge ; however, nothing in the shape of opposition or even dissatisfaction is recorded in the minutes, and after all the business was over Grand Lodge is said to have been "closed with an uncommon appearance of Harmony." A statement which I see no reason to doubt.

G. L. M., 24th June, 1735.

" An Address from the Body of the Gentlemen who had served the Society in the Quality of Stewards directed to the Grand Lodge was then read, Praying certain Priviledges in consideration of such their services, &c.

" 1. That they might meet monthly or otherwise as a Lodge of Master Masons (under the Denomination of the Stewards Lodge) and be enrolled among the Number of the Lodges as usual with the times of their meeting.

" 2. That they might be so far distinguished (since all the Grand Officers are for the future appointed to be chosen out of their Number ; and in order to qualify themselves to the right discharge of those Offices when called to the same) send a Deputation of twelve from the whole Body of Stewards to each Quarterly Communication, all the twelve to have voices, and all that come to pay half a Crown a peice towards the Expence of that occasion.

" 3. That no person who had not served the Society as a Steward might be permitted at a Quarterly Communication or elsewhere to wear their coloured Ribbonds or Aprons," But

" That such as had been Stewards might be indulged with wearing a particular Jewel by way of distinction suspended in their proper Ribbond whenever they appeared as Masons, the Pattern of which they then offered. These were granted them upon a Division, 45 of the Assembly being on the Affirmative side, and 42 on the Negative.

" It was also Declared, That,

" The twelve Stewards for any current year might attend in their proper Colour, &c., paying as usual for four Lodges, but they are not allowed votes, nor are to be heard in any debate unless something relating to the ensuing Feast be under Consideration."

I cannot see sufficient grounds for the belief that the granting of the preceding privileges would be likely to materially contribute to the establishing of an opposition Grand

E

Lodge ; no doubt these innovations and repeated concessions to rank and social distinction were not without their influence on the old-fashioned and more humble members of the community, but I am of opinion that the observations made with reference to former close divisions in Grand Lodge, will apply with equal truth to the proceedings just mentioned, as well as to what occurred at the next meeting, viz., a struggle between the two classes.

G. L. M., 11th December, 1735.

" A Petition and Appeal was presented and read, signed by several Masters of Lodges against the Privileges granted to the Stewards Lodge at the last Quarterly Communication. The Appellants were heard at large, and the Question being put whether the determination of the last Quarterly Communication relating to this matter should be confirmed or not. In the course of the collecting the votes on this occasion there appeared so much confusion that it was not possible for the Grand Officers to determine with any certainty what the Numbers on either side of the Question were, they were therefore obliged to dismiss the Debate and close the Lodge."

The Grand Officers evidently had rather a lively time on this occasion. It seems to me that the most reasonable explanation of this strong opposition is to be found in the second paragraph, with reference to allowing twelve Past Grand Stewards the right of membership of Grand Lodge, with the same powers as were possessed by the Masters and Wardens of the private lodges, hitherto the only acknowledged representatives of the general body of the Craft.

It is but natural to conclude that if any particular persons felt aggrieved at these concessions it would have been those members who attended and so strongly opposed their confirmation, and that they would have been the seceders, if there *was* a secession. A comparison of the numbers attending Grand Lodge immediately before, and for some years after the events just described will shew a decided increase in the attendances as well as in the amount of money received :—

							Cash received.		
							£	s.	d.
1735,	31 March,	41	Lodges represented.	123	members attended		24	13	6
,,	24 June,	31	,,	,,	90	,,	,,	5	15	6
,,	11 Dec.,	57	,,	,,	171	,,	,,	46	4	0
1736,	6 April,	61	,,	,,	176	,,	,,	33	1	6
,,	17 June,	38	,,	,,	99	,,	,,	12	1	6
,,	27 Dec.,	53	,,	,,	152	,,	,,	38	17	0
1737,	13 April,	76	,,	,,	211	,,	,,	43	11	6
1738,	25 Jan.,	68	,,	,,	190	,,	,,	40	8	6
,,	6 April,	61	,,	,,	161	,,	,,	43	11	6
1739,	31 Jan.,	93	,,	,,	268	,,	,,	57	4	6

This is exclusive of the Grand Officers present, about the same number of whom attended on each of the occasions mentioned, and were too few to have any material effect on the question as viewed from my stand-point.

To a regular attendant at Grand Lodge, comment on the foregoing figures will be quite superfluous, but to others less familiar with our legislature a few words of explanation may not be out of place. Then as now, the summer meetings were but thinly attended, and as *agenda* papers were not then in use the members were evidently " caught napping " on the 24th of June, when the subject of the Stewards' privileges was first brought forward, this will account for the limited number present ; meanwhile, the interval between June and December during which no meeting was held, had doubtless been utilised by both parties to the best advantage. We have had several instances in recent years of what can be done by means of a " whip up," hence the strong muster and violent opposition ; but as there were at this time about 80 London lodges on the roll the matter does not appear to have excited the amount of enthusiasm one might have expected, considering its importance. We cannot decide with certainty how many of these 80 lodges were actually

E 2

in working order, but I have good reason for believing that at least ten of them were dormant, and on a re-examination of the attendance list I find that with one exception the whole of the lodges represented were situated in the metropolitan district, the only outsider being a member of a lodge in Bengal, who had brought the handsome donation of ten guineas to the Charity Fund; this with a like amount paid for five new Constitutions, three guineas from the newly-formed Stewards Lodge, and five from another lodge recently established, will sufficiently explain the comparatively large sum received at the meeting in question. It will thus be seen that the celebrated battle of the Stewards' privileges was really fought by the London Masons, but from what transpired at the ensuing meeting I am disposed to believe, that other than the legal representatives of the lodges gained admission on the occasion referred to, and probably contributed in no small degree to the confusion which prevailed.

G. L. M., 6th April, 1736.

"Then the acting G. Master acquainted the Assembly that himself with others of the Grand Officers then present had thought of some proper Laws which he had then in his hands to propose to the Society for their approbation or amendment, if they were disposed to have them read. This being generally acceptable, His Worship proceeded to read the first, viz. :—

"That none be admitted to any future Quarterly Communications except such Masons as appear in the Character of and are the known and declared members of the Grand Lodge on any pretence whatsoever, unless they shall be called in as Witnesses or as Petitioners, or that shall be admitted on a Motion publickly made by Permission of the Society sitting, for which the cause is always to be assigned.

"On reading this Article a long Debate arose relating to the words, who ought to be understood by the ' Known and Declared Members of the Grand Lodge,' and after a long

Debate it was agreed and Declared that the following persons were the members and had a right to be present at all Quarterly Communications of Masons :—

" 1. The four Present and all Past Grand Officers.

" 2. The Masters and Wardens of all Constituted Lodges.

" 3. The Master and Wardens and nine Representatives of the Stewards Lodge.

" With this explanation the Law above said was *unanimously* agreed to."

This was followed by several new regulations for the better preservation of order in Grand Lodge; on the mode of taking divisions, receiving appeals, and the conduct of the members generally during debates, which seem to have been framed with the view of preventing a repetition of the late disturbance, and were agreed to without a division. According to the figures taken from the Grand Lodge Book this appears to have been even a larger meeting than that of the 11th December ; and in addition to the 171 Officers of Private Lodges there were no less than 15 Grand Officers and Past Grand Officers present, whereas only four attended the former Communication. Yet the very question which appears to have then caused such dissension, is stated to have been " *unanimously* agreed to " at the latter meeting ; this apparent inconsistency is easily explained by the adoption of my suggestion as to outsiders having gained admission, possibly in support of the Masters who presented the " Petition and Appeal," as up to this point the proceedings seem to have been of the most harmonious character.

Were further evidence wanted in order to show the improbability of the privileges of the Grand Stewards having any relation to the supposed secession, I might mention that the records from 1735 to 1739 contain no indications whatever of a rupture or even of aught but the most perfect harmony in the governing body of the Craft, nor is there any reference during that period to irregular makings until

the 30th June in the last-named year, when a complaint of
this nature was made against several persons, only one of
whom is mentioned by name, a Brother Stephenson, who
attended and " excused himself to the satisfaction of the
Lodge," but as the others did not put in an appearance it
was "Ordered that the farther consideration thereof be de-
ferred till some other opportunity."

The subject cropped up again at the next meeting of
Grand Lodge, 12th December, 1739.

"Whereupon the G.M. took notice that altho' some
Brethren might have been guilty of an offence tending so
much to destroy the Cement of the Lodge, and so utterly inconsistent with the Rules of the Society, yet he could not
bring himself to believe that it had been done otherwise
than through inadvertency, and therefore proposed that if
any such Brethren there were, they might be forgiven for
this time, which was ordered accordingly.

" Ordered, that the Laws be strictly put in execution
against all such Brethren as shall for the future countenance,
connive, or assist at any such irregular Makings."

The minutes of the 23rd July, 1740, contain a most interesting paragraph on this subject.

"Br. Berington moved that the 8th Regulation might
be read, which being done he informed the Lodge that
several Irregularities in the making of Masons having been
lately committed and other Indecencies offered in the Craft
by several Brethren, he cautioned the Masters and Wardens
against admitting such persons into their Lodges, and thereupon several Brethren insisting that such Persons should be
named. The same was, after a long debate and several
Questions put, Ordered accordingly, when Br. Berington
informed the Lodge that Br. George Monkman had a List of
several such persons. He, on being required to do so, named
Esquire Cary, Mansell Bransby and James Bernard late
Stewards who assisted at an irregular making.

" When it being very late the Lodge was closed."

It is rather curious that all the persons mentioned in this transaction had been Grand Stewards.

Berington served in 1734, Monkman in 1738, and the three last named had served the office at the Festival immediately preceding the meeting at which the charge was made.

This incident certainly does not favour the theory of irregularities being confined to brethren who had seceded from the main body on account of certain privileges granted to the Grand Stewards in 1735, but it may serve as an additional link in the chain of evidence in support of the proposition already advanced, that from the earliest period lodges were in existence that were considered irregular by the confederation of 1717, never having accepted a Constitution from that body, but which lodges considered themselves perfectly independent.

Some curiosity may be felt by those who have not at hand a copy of the old Constitutions, as to the nature of the " 8th Regulation," but as it is too long to be reproduced here, I may mention that, as may be supposed, it refers to irregular lodges, and includes the whole of the old law contained in the 1723 Constitutions, as well as the different measures relating to that subject passed in Grand Lodge subsequently, all of which will be found in the preceding pages.

Another remarkable feature in this business is that the complaint seems to have been dropped as suddenly as it had been taken up, it is not mentioned in the records again, nor is there any other reference to irregular makings until the 26th of May, 1749, when, " The complaint against Bro. Mercado for making Masons irregularly was heard, when he acknowledged the same, and expressed his Concern that he had given occasion for the Complaint and promised to behave as a Mason for the future, and it appearing that persons so made had at his request agreed to be regularly made the next Lodge night at the *George*, in Ironmonger Lane, he was at the Intercession of the Master and Wardens of the said Lodge fforgiven."

The next mention of this subject is in the G. L. M. of the 18th June, 1752.

"A Complaint was then made in general of the Frequency of irregular Makings, when the D.G.M. recommended it to the Brethren to send to him or the G.S. the names of such as shall be so irregularly made and of those who make them."

There is nothing in the records showing that the Deputy Grand Master's recommendation was ever acted upon, although at this time the "Ancient" Grand Lodge may be considered as being fairly established, having ten working lodges on its roll.

On the 30th November following, "The Petition of the Master, Wardens, and seven of the Brethren of the Lodge held at the 'George,' in Piccadilly, complaining against the Landlord of that House for setting up a *Spurious* * *Lodge* under their Constitution, and for refusing the Petitioners their Jewels, and for making Masons clandestinely," was read in Grand Lodge.

"Ordered, that the consideration of the said Petition be referred to the next C.C., and that the Petitioners do then attend, and that notice be given to the said Landlord to attend likewise."

It is a continual source of regret to Masonic students that no trace has been found during the present generation of the minutes of the Committee of Charity prior to the year 1761. Were these records available, I feel sure that much light would be thrown upon those portions of the history of our Order which are now veiled in obscurity.

---

* The first time the term "*Spurious*" is used in the Grand Lodge Minutes.

The subject of the petition with reference to the Lodge at the "George," is not again mentioned in the Grand Lodge minutes; how therefore the matter was settled it is impossible to determine. The engraved list for 1752 shows that No. 50 at the *Moon & Seven Stars*, Park Street, Grosvenor Square, removed in that year to the "George," Piccadilly, and in 1753 to the Masons' Arms, Old Palace Yard, thence to various other places mentioned in Lane's "*Masonic Records*," until the year of its erasure (1775). This lodge is said to have been Constituted in 1728, but the actual date of Constitution is not given in any list, hence, I presume it to have been one of the old lodges previously referred to which came in voluntarily, and that like many other similar lodges there was a difficulty in determining the precise time of its being deemed "regular."

The "Ancients" had two lodges at this period meeting at the "George," Piccadilly, viz., (Nos. 23 and 29). According to Lane the former was Constituted at the White Lyon, Hemming's Row, 10th October, 1753, and met for a very short time at the "George." It is under a new warrant of that number that No. 30 now meets. The latter (No. 29), was Constituted 15th November, 1753, and lapsed in 1755, but was revived in 1812 at Deal. It seems to me that we have pretty clear evidence of *a split* in regard to one of these "Ancient" lodges and the "Modern" No. 50; one party keeping to the original warrant and removing to fresh quarters, the other setting up a new lodge under the recently formed Grand Lodge of the "Ancients." In support of this view I tender the following extracts from their minutes of the 6th March, 1754 :—

"Heard a Complaint against Wm. Holford, Junr., Warden of No. 29, for an Irregularity in the Lodge, &c.

"Ordered that Br. Holford shall ask pardon in the Gd. Lodge and on refusal he shall be excluded."

I presume Bro. Holford *did* "ask pardon in the Grand

Lodge," for although the record is silent on that point it tells us further on that he was installed as Deputy Grand Master for the year 1755.

The first Master and Wardens of this lodge (No. 29 of the Ancients) were Wm. Turner, Walter Smith, and Wm. Holford. Turner, I find from the "Ancient" register was a member of original No. 11, but the names of the two Wardens do not appear in the register prior to the Constitution of No. 29, hence I presume they were either unattached Masons or former members of the "Modern" lodge previously held at the same house. In some few cases the word "modern" is written against names of members in the column headed "*from whence*" of the old register, but it is not so in this instance. Where these two Wardens came from must therefore be left an open question. I ought also to state that notwithstanding its very brief existence this lodge registered 32 members before it fell into abeyance.

Originally I had only intended to have carried my examination of the minutes of the "Modern" Grand Lodge up to the period of the formation of its rival; but I am reluctant to omit the episode of the Ben Jonson's Head Lodge, on which however, I do not place much historical value, beyond the fact of its being the first occasion on which the "Ancients" are distinctly mentioned in the records.

I shall nevertheless continue the practice hitherto followed, and give the particulars *verbatim*, it being not improbable that some of my readers may see more in the affair than I do.

G. L. M., 24th March, 1754.

"The G.S. informèd the Lodge that Br. John Merigeot from the Ben Johnson's Hd., Spital Fields, from a true sense of his misconduct and misbehaviour at the last Q.C. desired their forgiveness and to be admitted to ask pardon.*

---

* Br. Merigeot's name is not mentioned in the minutes of the preceding Quarterly Communication.

" Whereon the G.M. expressed his readiness to forgive, and tho' in justice to the Society (as the Bro.'s offence affected them) he would not do it without their Consent, yet his Worship in the most affectionate manner recommending it to the Brethren to forgive him Br. Merigeot was called in and making a proper Submission, thereon obtained Grace and was restored to his place in the Lodge."

Ibid, 29th November, 1754.

" The three following Articles recommended by the last C.C. for Laws of the Grand Lodge were taken into Consideration.

" 1st. That no Lodge shall for the future be deemed regularly removed until the removal thereof shall be approved and allowed by the G.M. or his Deputy for the time being.

" 2nd. That if any Mason shall without the especial Licence of the Grand Master or his Deputy for the time being attend as a Mason cloathed in any of the Jewels or Cloathing of the Craft at any Funeral or Funeral Procession, he shall not only be for ever incapable of being an officer of a Lodge but even of tyling or attending on a Lodge or partaking of the General Charity if he shall come to want it.

" 3rd. That if any Mason shall attend, tyle or assist as Tyler at any Meetings or pretended Lodges of Persons calling themselves Masons, not being a regular constituted Lodge, acknowledging the Authority of our Rt. Worshipful Grand Master, and conforming to the Laws of the Grand Lodge, he shall be forever incapable of being a Tyler or Attendant on a Lodge or partaking of the General Charity.

" Ordered, that the said three proposed Laws be & be entred as Laws of the Grand Lodge."

This seems very much like beginning at the wrong end, or trying to kill a snake by treading on its tail.

Ibid, 20th March, 1755.

" The D.G.M. made a Complaint to the Grand Lodge of the Master and Wardens of the Lodge No. 94, held at the

Ben Johnson's Head, in Pelham Street, Spital Fields, for forming and assembling with other members of that Lodge under the Denomination of a Lodge of Ancient Masons who as such consider themselves as independant of this Society and not subject to our Laws or the authority of our Grand Master, when he took notice of the great necessity there was to discourage all such Meetings, not only as the same were contrary to our Laws, &c., particularly that made at the last Q.C., and were also a great Insult on the Grand Master and the whole Body of Free and Accepted Masons. But as they likewise tended to introduce into the Craft the Novelties and Conceits of opinionative Persons and to create a Belief that there have been other Societies of Masons more ancient than that of this Ancient and Honourable Society.

"When Part of the 8th Old Regulation and the new Regulation made the 19th day of February, 1724, touching the forming Lodges without leave of the G.M. being read, the D.G.M. desired the said Master and Wardens to give their Reasons for such their Behaviour.

"The said Brethren thereon insinuated that as at those Meetings they in nowise interfered with this Society, either by making Masons or otherwise, and met together only as Private Persons, that they apprehended they had a right so to do, but on being asked they acknowledged the Charge against them with respect to their Forming and assembling as a Lodge of Masons independant of this Society and under no subjection to our laws or the Authority of our Grand Master, and that they were generally tyled and that their Tyler was one Micajah Cross, who not long ago was releived at a Committee of Charity.

"A Question was then put, that the meeting of any Brethren of this Society as or under any Denomination of Masons other than as Brethren of this our Ancient and Honourable Society of Free and Accepted Masons, is inconsistent with the Honour and Interest of the Craft, and a high Insult on our Grand Master and the whole Body of Masons, which was carried in the affirmative, one of the Brethren complained of, only Dissenting.

" Another Question was also put that the said Micajah Cross be for ever incapable of being a Tyler or attendant on a Lodge or of partaking of the General Charity, which was in like manner carried in the Affirmative.

" The D.G.M. moved that the Consideration of the irregular Proceedings of the said Lodge at the Ben Johnson's Head might be postponed till next Q.C., hoping that a thorough sense of their Misconduct and a Determination not to be guilty of the like for the future will then appear and reconcile them to the Grand Lodge, which was Ordered accordingly."

Ibid, 24th July, 1755.

" The Complaint against the Lodge held at the Ben Johnson's Head, in Spital Fields, postponed at the last Q.C. was taken into consideration, and the Master and Wardens of the said Lodge being present and the minutes of the said last Q.C. touching the said Complaint read to them, The D.G.M. informed them that the Grand Lodge was ready to hear what they had to say.

" The said Master and Wardens thereupon spoke what they thought proper for their Defence, which they were many times (and more particularly Bro. John Merigeot one of the said Wardens) indulged the liberty of doing, and they sometimes insinuated (contrary to the admission of their Master and Wardens at the last Q.C.) that the Charge against them was unsupported by any Proof and attempted to induce a Belief that their Meetings complained of were regular and in consequence of their Constitution from this Society, and that those Meetings and the Transactions therein were no novelties but agreeable to those of this Society and free and open to every Brother. But the contrary was made appear by Bros. Jackson and

Pollard who had been refused Admittance at those Meetings until they had submitted to be made in their own novel and particular manner, under the Denomination of 'Ancient Masons, for which they paid the expence of the Meeting.'

"The said Master and Wardens then insinuated (as was done at the last Q.C.) that they apprehended they had a Right to meet as Private Persons under any Denomination, and thereupon after some Debate about the Question to be proposed, the following Question (in Compliance with what they themselves desired) was put, viz. :—

"That the Members of the Lodge at the Ben Johnson's Head be permitted to meet independant of their Constitution from this Society under the Denomination of a Lodge of Ancient Masons.

"Which was carried in the negative almost unanimously, the said Master and Wardens and those of the Lodge held at the Fish and Bell, Soho, only holding up their hands for it.

"The said Master and Wardens were then exhorted to refrain from their said irregular meetings, and to reconcile themselves to the Grand Lodge, but without effect.

"A Question was then put, That the Lodge No. 94, held at the Ben Johnson's Head, in Pelham Street, Spital Fields, be erased from the Book of Lodges, and that such of the Brethren thereof as shall continue those irregular meetings be not admitted as visitors in any Lodge.

"Which was carried in the Affirmative almost unanimously, the same Brethren as above only Dissenting."

No. 94 was constituted, in 1732, at the Nag's Head Audley Street, but owing to the lamentable gap in the register of "Moderns" (from 1730 to about 1768) there is not a list of its members accessible. Judging from the amount of its contributions to the Charity Fund, I should say it could not have been a very high class lodge. The records show a fairly regular attendance on the part of its representatives at the Grand Lodge, and there is nothing to indicate that up to 1754 the conduct of its members had been other than strictly orthodox ; yet it is possible that the irregularities complained of had been in practice for some years prior to a definite charge being brought against them. Hitherto lodges had only been erased for non-attendance at Grand Lodge or for not contributing to the " General Charity."

In 1755 the " Ancients " had about forty lodges on their roll, and it may be that the knowledge of this fact, prompted the " Moderns" to take some decided steps for the purpose of consolidating their forces with a view to counteract the rapidly increasing power of the opposite party, which was not deemed necessary during their former disorganised condition.

There is one fact in this transaction about which there can be no mistake, viz., that the defendants had the strongest sympathy and support throughout the whole business, of the representatives of a very old, if not the oldest, lodge, in the Craft—a lodge to which the honour belongs of having not only assisted in establishing the Grand Lodge, but of having furnished the Order with its first Grand Master.*

It is evident, therefore, that the Master and Wardens of this venerable lodge either saw no great amount of harm in the irregularities complained of, or that these practices, or some portion of them, were really such as they had been accustomed to consider quite correct in the old time, and we have it on very good authority that—

> " A fellow-feeling makes one wondrous kind."

I may also mention another curious fact in connexion with this incident, which caused me some little surprise, and that is my inability to identify the offending lodge with any

---

* Now the Fortitude and Old Cumberland Lodge, No. 12.

one on the list of the "Ancients" for the period indicated. It is true the materials available are exceedingly scanty, being only the sign of the house at which the lodge was held and the names of two of the persons implicated, viz., John Merigeot, and Cross the poor old Tyler, for whose annihilation those terrible laws seem to have been specially concocted; but I can safely say that neither of *their* names are to be found in the register of the "Ancients."

The Grand Lodge minutes of the 14th January, 1757, furnish the following scrap of intelligence, which ought not to be passed over :—

"The Grand Lodge received Information that the following 14 Persons (amongst others) who are not Masons, meet the 1st and 3rd Tuesday in every month, at the Marlbro's head in Pelham St. Spital Fields and hold what they call a Lodge, viz. :—

"Jacob Peirce, Brewer, — Malawson Dyer,
    Wm. Dupree, Weaver, Thos. Swain, Weaver,
    Jas. Dupree, do., Michael Bandy, do.,
    Peter Landy, Dyer, — Reeds, Dyer,
    Wm. Caster, Weaver, Daniel Marchant, Weaver,
    John Gill, do., Rowland Taylor, Cooper,
    Thos. Warrington, Cooper, Mathew Nicole, Weaver.

"Ordered that a List of their names be printed and sent to every Lodge that they may be on their Guard in their respective Lodges least any of those Impostors should gain Admittance amongst them."

The observation made with reference to the Lodge at the "Ben Jonson's Head" will apply with equal justice to this one, viz., that the lodge cannot be identified on the "Ancients'" list, neither are any of the foregoing names to be found in their register, which I may state is as near complete as possible, from the period of their starting as an organised body, forming in this respect a striking contrast to that of their more aristocratic rivals.

Having now brought my examination of the minutes of the "Modern" Grand Lodge up to a period when the rival Institution may be considered to be in a fairly prosperous condition, it is unnecessary to continue my researches in this direction. I may, however, mention that every item of intelligence to be found in those records that could possibly be construed as having the least bearing on the question of the origin of the "Ancients" has been placed before my readers, and I hope it will not be thought very presumptuous on my part if I venture to express an opinion that a most powerful imagination would be required to detect any trustworthy evidence or even indication of a secession from the regular body having occurred previous to the year 1752.

With regard to the various references to irregularities and clandestine makings, the records of both Societies will show that offences of this character were not confined to either party, and that they came to the front occasionally even up to within a few years of the Union, but as a general rule these complaints were made by the two Grand Lodges against their own adherents, and not by one Society against the members of the other ; unless as it sometimes happened, the delinquents had two strings to their bow, as was the case with the last Deputy Grand Master of the "Ancients" (Thos. Harper) who was initiated in No. 24 of that body in 1761, and took an active part in its affairs for upwards of half a century ; he also joined the Globe Lodge of the "Moderns" in 1787, of which he was Master in 1793, and served as Grand Steward for that lodge in 1796. The truth of the proverb, "A man cannot serve two masters" was forcibly exemplified in the case of our distinguished old brother, who seems to have been highly respected by both sides and to have devoted much of his time and attention to the service of the Craft generally, irrespective of party, but who, nevertheless, met with expulsion from the "Modern" Grand Lodge in 1803 on account of his refusal to sever his con-

F

nection with the opposition body with which he had been so long associated and of which he was then Deputy Grand Master, in which office he took a prominent part in the arrangement for the Union of the former antagonistic bodies: notwithstanding his great age and increasing infirmities his zeal for Masonry never slackened. He scarcely ever missed a meeting of the United Grand Lodge or the Lodge of Benevolence until within about a year of his death, which occurred on the very day of the Grand Festival, 25th April, 1832.

There are many similar instances on record of brethren being mixed up with the affairs of both Bodies at the same time, and no doubt it is to this state of things that the Union at last came to be almost inevitable, and was only retarded by the inability of the parties to reconcile themselves to certain details and conditions.

If an apology be needed for this little digression, I must plead a reluctance to miss an opportunity for paying my humble tribute of respect to departed merit, which, in this instance, will serve as a sort of introduction to the next portion of my task.

CHAPTER III.

AN EXAMINATION OF THE RECORDS OF THE "ANCIENTS."

"Of a truth he was a wise man who said 'Thou shouldst not decide till thou hast heard what both sides have to say.'"—*Aristophanes.*

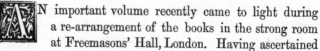AN important volume recently came to light during a re-arrangement of the books in the strong room at Freemasons' Hall, London. Having ascertained by a glance at the opening pages that it contained an alphabetical list of the members of the "Ancient" lodges, I placed it on the shelf with the rest of the Registers of that body, where it remained until I handed it to Br. John Lane, for examination little thinking at the time, that it was the

book described by Dermott in a footnote added to the transactions of February 5th, 1752, and which in common with everyone familiar with the otherwise complete set of records of the "Ancients" I had long deplored as lost. Br. Lane soon found that the book was something more than a mere register of names of members; that it contained what was of the greatest interest to Masonic students generally, but especially valuable to himself, viz., the first lists of the "Ancient" lodges, of the existence of which certainly no one of the present generation had any previous knowledge. He also made another important discovery, viz., that the "Ancients" had erased two of their original lodges for disobedience so early as 1752. On calling my attention to these facts we readily came to the conclusion that this was the "missing link," the long lost "Vol. 1. A." of the "Ancients."

A full description of this book has been given in the columns of the *Freemason*, first, briefly by Br. Lane on October 24th and November 28th, 1885, and at greater length by G. B. Abbott in a series of articles commencing April 3rd, 1886, on "The Early Organization of the ' Ancient' Masons "; it is, therefore, unnecessary for me to do more than direct attention to such of its contents as are likely to assist the enquiry on hand. The last-named writer has aptly described the book as " a large folio with very little in it," but what it does contain is undoubtedly of great historic value, notwithstanding that it leaves much to be desired, especially so with regard to the place and date of initiation of the original members. It is much to be regretted that the first portion of the register throws no light on this important subject; the columns headed "From Whence" and "When Made" being a perfect blank down to the sixty-ninth name in the register, when the date of making is given as May 20th, 1751.

According to Br. Abbott's computation there were but

six lodges with a total membership of about seventy or eighty on the roll of the " Ancients " in July, 1751, when it was decided to start a Grand Lodge on their own account. Whether this was their first General Assembly, and how long these lodges had been working, we have no means of ascertaining. The members for the most part seem to have consisted of mechanics and shop-keepers; many of them were evidently from the Sister Isle, as will be seen by the names of those who comprised the Committee for framing the regulations, whom I presume we may fairly consider as the leading spirits of the movement.

All that I can learn of these old brethren is from the register, and meagre though it be, it is worth recording.

Philip McLoughlin, belonged to No. 6 (present No. 11). Occupation, not stated; Time of Discharge, July 29, 1751. "Gone to Ireland."

Saml. Quay, belonged to No. 2 (present No. 3); first name in the General Register; described as a "Habit Maker at the P. W. D., Tavistock St." (1st Senior Grand Warden).

James Shee, belonged to No. 4 (present No. 7). Attorney, Fetter Lane. "Gone to Ireland."

Joseph Kelly was also a member of No. 6. The register says he was "excluded for non-payment."

John Morgan, belonged to No. 2. Occupation not stated; resigned 4th March, 1752. "Gone on board a stationed ship."

The first name in the index is that of Abr$^{m.}$ Ardizorf; in the register he is No. 23. This name savours of the Hebrew persuasion; his address is given as "Broad Court, Bow St., Covent Gard^{n,};" occupation not stated. Strange to say he seems to have been excluded on the very day of the General Assembly, the 17th July, 1751, being "Deem'^{d} unworthy of ye Society," but must have been re-admitted, as his name appears in the Minutes of Grand Lodge, 6th

December, 1752. With the name of Jno. Hamilton, No. 80 on the register, we have a distinct clue to the Masonic antecedents of some our "Ancient" brethren. Under the heading "From Whence" is written "St. John," followed by the words "New Constitu^n by Pet$^{n.}$" This new Constitution, the date of which in the list is given as 29th July, 1751, was for No. 7, at the Fountain. Hamilton was first Master of this lodge, which was erased in December, 1752, "for disobedience of the 21st Rule of the Grand." It is not quite clear what this Rule was, for in July, 1752, only eighteen regulations are recorded. Up to August 28, 1752, the register shows, as having joined the different lodges, twenty-two brethren, who, under the heading "From Whence," have "St. John" written against their names."

The first mention of the "Moderns" is on June 6th, 1752, on which day Thos. Floyd is registered as having joined No. 9 from the "Moderns," and is said to have been "made antient" on that day; altogether seven brethren are so described, but none after August, 1753.

I think we ought not to take it for granted that the number mentioned comprised the whole of those who claimed to be considered "Ancients" at the time of the formation of their Grand Lodge, doubtless there were others who did not belong to any lodge, but readily joined the concern when they found it established on what appeared to be a firm basis—as had been the case in the early days of the older Grand Lodge. At the end of the year 1755 the register of the "Ancients" contains the names of considerably over a thousand members.

Immediately after the index of names is the following code of eighteen rules, and as in no instance do they refer to any former regulations, we may fairly assume them to be the first written laws of the Ancient Grand Lodge. There are in existence about 127 lodges constituted by that body, whose members will probably deem these early regulations

worthy of reproduction, especially when I state that I have
never met with them in print until they were embodied in
the before mentioned Articles by Abbott; for, strange to say,
they do not appear to have been incorporated by Dermott
in the first edition of the *Ahiman Rezon*, or Constitutions
of the " Ancients."

RULES & ORDERS
to be Observe'd
By the Most ANCIENT and HON^BLE. Society of
FREE and ACCEPTED MASONS.

As agreed and Settled by a Committee appointed by a
General Assembly held at the Turk's head in Greek Street,
Soho, on Wednesday, the 17th of July, 1751, And in the
Year of MASONRY 5751.

By { Phil^p. McLoughlin | James Shee }
{ Saml. Quay | Jos^ph. Kelly }

& Jno. MORGAN, G^d. Secret^y.

Viz^t.

For the GRAND.

1st.

THAT the Masters and Wardens do meet on the First
Wednesday of every Month at the Turk's head, in Greek
Street, Soho, or such other place as shall be agreed on, there
to hold a Monthly Committee for the better Regulation &
Government of the Lodges, AND to hear and determine all
Matters and Disputes that may or shall arise in any of the
Regular Lodges. AND that the Chair shall be taken the
First Night by the Master of the Senr. Lodge, and every
other Night by the other Masters each in his turn according
to Seniority, until such time as there shall be a Grand
Master & Grand Wardens appointed, and then every Grand
Lodge Night the Grand Master to take the Chair, and in
his Absence by the Deputy Grand, and in the Absence of
both by the Senr. Grand Warden, and in their Absence by
the Junr. Grand Warden, and if all the Grand Officers

shou'd be Absent, then the Master of the Eldest Lodge, & so on by all the Masters in their turn according to Seniority.

2nd.

THAT such meeting do consist only of the Masters and Wardens of all Regular Lodges, and in the Absence of a Mast^r or Warden, a Past Mast^r may attend and bear the Office in their absence for the time being, and to have a Voice in the Grand equal to the present Members.

3rd.

AND if any Members do not appear before the Roll is call'd the s^d Members shall be Fine'd in the Sum of Two-pence, and in case of Absence the whole Night, Sixpence, Except Sick, Lying in Confinement, or three Miles from the place of Meeting, that none be admitted but Mast^{rs} Ward^{ns} & Past Mast^{rs} of Regular Lodges, & such as have been Regularly Install'd, and at the time of their Comeing to be members of a Regular Lodge of ANCIENT MASONS.

4th.

THAT No Brother be made either a Master or Warden of any Lodge except he hath been made a Mason One half Year, and Member of a Regular Lodge for that time.

5th.

NO Person shall be made a Mason in any Lodge until first his Name, Occupation and Place of Abode shall be reported to the Secretary with the time he is intended to be made in Order that the Secretary may apprize all Lodges of the same.

6th.

THAT no Old Mason be admitted a Member of any Lodge except he hath been made in a Regular Lodge and hath a proper Certificate of his good behaviour and his not owing any thing in such Lodge and in case a Member of any Regular Lodge shall be desierous to become a Member of any other with an intent to belong to two or more Lodges then such Lodge he sues to come into must be assur'd that he is not Indebted to the Lodge he then belongs to— Regist^y. 6d.

7th.

THAT all Complaints and Appeals must come before this Lodge by Petition.

8th.

NO Admission or Warrant shall be granted to any Brothers to hold a Lodge until such time they have first form'd a Lodge of Ancient Masons and sitt regularly in a Credible house and then to Apply by Petition and such Petition to be Attested by the Masters of three Regular Lodges who shall make a Proper Report of them.

9th.

THAT on St. Johns day the 24th of June & St. Johns day the 27th of Decem^r. the Master of every Lodge shall deliver into the Secretary of the Grand Lodge the Names of the Masters & Wardens that are appointed to serve for the Ensueing Half Year.

10th.

THAT on the first Grand Lodge Night after each St. Johns day the Master of every Lodge shall deliver into the Grand Secret^y. the Names of the Members of his Lodge together with their Half Year's Dues. THAT is the Members of each Regular Lodge, for the use of Indigent Brethren or otherways as the Grand Lodge shall think Proper, One Shilling each Member pr. Quarter.

11th.

THAT if a Lodge should grow to Numerous, that Lodge to appoint Masters & Wardens to form a New Body, they applying to the Grand Lodge for Warrants & Constitution in one Month after the first Sitting Night & that no Lodge shall sitt on the First Wednesday of each Month, it being Grand Lodge Night when the Mast^rs. & Wardens are re-quir'd to attend.

12th.

THAT every Person who shall be made a Mason in any

Regular Lodge shall pay for his Register in the Grand Lodge Book for the sum of One Shilling.

13th.

THAT No Person or Member of the Grand Lodge at the time of Sitting shall Interupt the Grand Master or Grand Officers or any Brother then Speaking to the Grand Master ti'l such Brother hath done, and not then to Speak without first asking liberty in a Proper manner. Nor to hold any Private Committees during the Sitting of the Lodge, nor depart the Lodge without leave from the Grand Master under Penalty of being Fine'd at the Discretion of the Grand.

14th.

THAT if any member of a Private Lodge shall be desierous of leaveing the Lodge he belongs to to join another, he must have a proper Certificate from the Mast^r of that Lodge and Notice to be given to the Secret^y of the Grand Lodge of his leaveing the same, and the Mast^r of Lodge the s^d Brother shall join shall report him to the Grand Lodge in Order to have him Register'd in the Grand Lodge Book to ye Number of the Lodge he is then removed to and to Pay for the same the sum of Sixpence.

15th.

THAT the following be the Charges & Paid for the Constitution of a New Lodge.

Viz^t.

		£	s.	d.	
FOR the Warrant	... ...	0	10	6	
Regester for each Member	...	0	1	0	Each.
Pursevant } of ye Grand Lodge		0	3	6	
Tyler }		0	2	6	

AND that all Warrants Constitutions Registers & Petitions for Constitutions be the Fees of ye Grand Secretary, and that no Petitions be receiv'd but such as are wrote by the s^d Secret^y and he paid for the same.

16th.

THAT the Grand Master have Power to Call a Committee at Pleasure or Deputy G.M. or G.W. or whoever shall be in the Chair in their Absence; and such Committee to Consist of Masters of Lodges only, & their Resolutions to be laid before the Grand Lodge, the Next insueing Night after such Committee held and that the s^{d.} Committee have Power to Adjourn from time to time not exceeding three Grand Lodge Nights.

17th.

THAT each officer, viz., Masters & Wardens of all Regular Lodges under the Constitution of this Grand Lodge, who thro : Negligence or Omission will be absent on a Grand Lodge meeting (he or they having a proper Summons sent him or them) shall be fin'd as the Grand Rules Specify, and that all such fines shall be paid by the Body such Absenttee belongs to and that if any of the Members refuse paying his or their Devidend of said fines, Such Member upon Such his Refusal shall be Excluded.

18th.

THAT upon the death of any of our Worthy Brethren whose names are or may be hereafter Recorded in the Grand Registry, &c., the Master of such Lodge as he then belonged to Shall immadiately Inform the Grand Secretary of his Death and the intended time for his funeral, and upon this notice the Grand Secretary shall summon all the Lodges to attend the funeral in proper Order, And that Each Member shall pay One Shilling towards Defraying the expences of said funeral or otherwise to his widow or nearest friend provided the Deceased or his friends Realy want and Require the same, otherwise the money so raised to be put to some other Charitable use, or as the Committee shall think proper, &c.

It is further Agree'd (To support the Dignity of this W.G. Lodge) that no Mem · hereof (on any Grand Lodge meeting) be admited to Sit herein without his proper Cloathing and jewell, &c., Except upon some great Emmergency, in which case the Trangressor shall give Sufficient Reason for so doing.

There are notes written in the margin against some of these Rules.

The 6th has—"All good men accept^{d.} upon proper Recommendation" against the upper part, and against the lower is "No Re-Registry p^{d.} to ye G. Sec. Except the B^{r.} absolutely quit his former Lodge."

The 10th—"July the 1st, 1752. Jno. Doughty in the Chair, Agreed that no half year's dues be paid into the Grand Committee until there be a Grand Master."

The 15th—"This Rule was farther confirmed July 13, 1753 Vide Transactions."

The 17th—"Apr. 6th 1752. Jno. Morris in the Chair."

The 18th—"July 1st, 1752. Jno. Doughty in the Chair."

Sixteen of these rules were evidently written by John Morgan, who, in the absence of evidence to the contrary, we must look upon as the first Grand Secretary of the "Ancients"; they are exceedingly well written and carefully framed, as will be seen. Nos. 17 and 18 were, I think, written by Dermott, who, in this instance, seems to have tried to imitate the handwriting of his predecessor. No doubt they answered the purpose for which they were intended, until the rapid extension of the Order rendered more pretentious regulations both desirable and necessary.

What always strikes me whenever I look at them is the improbability of their being the work of a journeyman shoemaker, the description given of Morgan by a Grand Secretary of the "Moderns" about twenty years later.

Next in order to the regulations is the following Agreement in Dermott's well-known hand :—

" WHEREAS it is highly expedient for the Universal Benefit of the Ancient Craft that a **Grand Master** and

Grand Lodge shou'd govern and direct the proceedings of the several Ancient Lodges held in and about the Cities of London and Westminster. And as the present low condidition of the Ancient Society of Free and Accepted Masons renders the hope of obtaining a Noble Personage to preside over us at this time very precarious.

"In Order to preserve the present remains of the true Ancient Craft, &c., We, the under Named, being the present Masters and Wardens of the Several Masonical Meetings called Lodges of true Ancient Masonry aforesaid, do agree (pursuant to the powers vested in us by our Respective Brethren of the several lodges) to form a Grand Committee (we mean such a Committee) as may supply the deficiency of a Grand Master untill an opportunity offers for the Choice of a Noble Personage to govern our Ancient Fraternity. And that We will therein (by the Authority Aforesaid) make Statutes or laws for the better government and well Ordering the said Fraternity, Receive petitions, hear Appeals, and Transact Business (that is to say such Business as ought to be peculiar to a Grand Lodge) with Equity and Impartiality.— Dated in our Grand Committee Room on Thursday, the fourteenth day of September, New stile, 1752, And in the year of Masonry 5752. In the presence of

No. 2 John Doughty Master	Rich. Coffy Sen. Warden	Petr. Britain Junr. W.
„ 4 Geo. Hebden Do.	Honble. Edwd.	
	Vaughan Do.	Chr. Pidgeon Junr. W.
„ 5 Rich. Stringer Do.	Owen Tudor Do.	Barth. Scully Do.
„ 6 Edwd. Ryan Do.	John Dally Do.	John Wilson Do.
„ 8 Thos. Blower Do.	Alexr. Fife Do.	John Smith Do.
„ 11 Andw. Francis Do.	Wm. Turner Do.	William Weir Do.
„ 12 John Cartwright Do.	James Ryan Do.	Barnaby Fox Do.

James Hagarthy and Henry Lewis, Past Masters of No. 4. and Thomas Kelly, Past Master of No. 6.   Lau. Dermott, G.S.

"And whereas several of the lodges have congregated and made Masons without any Warrant (not with a desire of Acting wrong, but thro : the Necessity above mention'd), in order to Rectify such irregular proceedings (as far as in our power) it is hereby Order'd That the Grand Secretary shall write Warrants (on Parchment) for the Unwarranted Lodges, viz., The Lodges known by the Title of No. 2, 3, 4, 5, 6, and that all the said Warrants shall bare date July the Seventeenth One thousand Seven hundred fifty and One being the day on which the said lodges met (at the Turk's head Tavern, in Greek street, Soho), to revive the Ancient Craft.

"That the Secretary shall leave proper Spaces for the Grand Mast^r, Deputy G.M., and Grand Wardens to sign all the said Warrants according to Ancient Custom.

"That as soon as we shall arrive at the Great happiness of installing proper Grand Officers, the possessors of the Unsigned Warrants shall present them to the Grand Master for His Worship's Signature or Renewal, Until which time the said Warrants, as well as those which have or may be (thro : necessity) granted in the like manner, shall be deem'd good and lawfull.

"lastly, this our Regulation shall be Recorded in our Registry, to shew posterity how much we desire to revive the Ancient Craft upon true Masonical principles.

"Signed, by Order, Lau. Dermott, G.S."

In the margin is written, "Sepr 14, 1752, N. Stile. Geo. Hebden, Mast^r No. 4, in the Chair."

Although this old Register leaves us somewhat in the dark with regard to the antecedents of the originators of the Ancient Grand Lodge there is no mystery about their ultimate proceedings, they were evidently thoroughly in earnest and above-board in all their doings, as their records from February, 1752 to 1813, will prove. We see from the heading of their first rules that the title "Ancient" was not, as some imagine, an after-thought, adopted with the view of depreciating their rivals. A careful perusal of the "Agreement" can leave no other impression than that those who signed it must have had some good reason for their assertions of antiquity.

Before finishing with the old register I may state that the first mention I have met with of Deacons as officers of a lodge in England is given in connection with the Constitution of No. 34, April, 1754; it is rather curious that the Wardens are not indicated. The entry runs thus:—

" Michael Thorpe	Mastr.
" Robt. Fisher	S.D.
" Jas. Murray	J.D.
" Abrm. Meinzies	Sec."

The D. therefore may have been inserted accidentally instead of W. There is, however, no mistake in the case of of No. 37 Constituted on the 19th August following, the Master, Wardens, Deacons, and Secretary being all mentioned in the order here given.

The first page of the earliest Minute Book of the Ancient Grand Lodge is headed " Transactions of the Grand Committee of the Most Ancient and Honorable Fraternity of Free and Accepted Masons.

" At the Griffin Tavern, in Holborn, London, Feb. the 5th, 1752.

" Mr. James Hagarty in the Chair.

" Also present the Officers of No. 2, 3, 4, 5, 6, 7, 8, 9 and 10, being the Representatives of all the Ancient Masons in and adjacent to London.

" Brother John Morgan, Grand Secretary, Informed the Committee that he being lately appointed to an office on board of one of His Majesty's Ships, he recd. Orders to prepare for his departure, and therefore advised the Grand Committee to chuse a new Secretary immediately.

" Upon which Brother John Morris, Past Master of No. 5, and Brother Laurence Dermott of No. 9 and 10, and Past Master of No. 26 in Dublin were proposed and admitted as Candidates for the Office of Grand Secretary.

" And Grand Secretary Morgan was ordered to examine

the Candidates seperately & report his opinion of their Qualifications.

"After a long & minute Examination Relative to Initiation Passing, Instalations, and General Regulations, &c., &c., &c., Brother John Morgan declared that Brother Laurence Dermott was duly qualified for the office of Grand Secretary. Whereon the Worshipful Master in the Chair, put the names of John Morris, and Laurence Dermott, seperately, when the latter was Unanimously chosen Grand Secretary; and accordingly he was installed (in the Ancient manner) by the Worshipful Mr. James Hagarty, Master of No. 4 then Presiding Officer, assisted by Mr. John Morgan, late Grand Secretary and the Masters present.

"After which Brother Morgan (at the request of the President), proclaimed the new Grand Secretary, thrice, according to ancient custom, upon which the new Secretary received the usual salutes. And then the President and late Grand Secretary, John Morgan delivered the books, &c., &c., into the hands of the new Secretary, upon certain Conditions which was agreed to by all parties, and which Conditions the said Worshipful Bro. James Hagarty can explain.*

"The Grand Committee unanimously joined in Wishing Bro. Morgan Health and a successful voyage, and then Closed with the greatest Harmony, having Adjourned to Wednesday the fourth of March next."

---

* "Be it Remembered that Mr. John Morgan, late Grand Secretary, had a certain claim on the Manuscripts here said to be delivered to Laurence Dermott, which claim was acknowledged by the Gd. Committee as good and lawful. And for that and other good Reason which cannot be committed to writing, The Worshipful Grand Committee did agree with Bro. John Morgan, late Grand Secretary, That the new Secretary, Lau. Dermott should be solemnly bound never to deliver the said manuscript (viz., a large folio bound in white vellum) to any person, but him the said John Morgan or his Order in Writing.

"Note, the above Mr. James Hagarty is a painter, and lives now (1752), in Leather Lane, London."

The foregoing minutes, as indeed, the whole of the first book ending with the Proceedings of the Grand Lodge on December 7th, 1768, appear to have been written by the new Grand Secretary, Laurence Dermott, who, as will be seen hereafter, figures prominently in the subsequent progress of the "Ancients," and although we have no direct evidence of his connection with that body prior to the 1st of February, 1752, it seems almost incredible that he should have been unanimously elected Grand Secretary only four days afterwards, over the head of a brother who was undoubtedly one of the 70 or 80 who had agreed in July, 1751, to start a Grand Lodge; either the brethren must have been well acquainted with the man, or the Hibernian element was strong enough to carry the election with flying colours. I shall reserve my comments on the Masonic career of this remarkable person until a later stage, when I purpose dealing briefly with that of the brethren who formed the first Committee of Organization, as well as those who signed the subsequent articles of agreement.

I have given the first minutes *verbatim*, but in future I shall only give an occasional extract from the Minutes of the Proceedings of the next two or three years, wherein anything of historical import is mentioned, whether it be in accord with my own views or otherwise.

"Grand Committee, April 1st, 1752.

"The Copy of the Bye-laws for private Lodges as written by the late Grand Secretary, was read and compared with Br. Dermott's Copy of the Bye-laws of his former Lodge, No. 26, in the City of Dublin, and the latter being deemed the most correct, it was

"Unanimously Resolved, that the most correct copy should be received & acknowledged as the only Bye-laws for private lodges in future, and public thanks given to Bros. Philip M'Loughlin and J. Morgan for their good intentions, and trouble in drawing up the former bye-laws.

" The new President called on John Morgan, James Hagan, and Laurence Dermott, to know what success they had in petitioning Lord George Sackvile to accept the Chair. Their report was that they had waited on Lord George Sackvile at Somerset House, in the Strand, that having read the petition, His Lordship told them politely, that he had the highest veneration for the Ancient Craft, and wish to promote it. But he was engaged to attend His Father, the Lord Lieutenant of Ireland, and was inform'd that the Grand Lodge of Ireland had lately chosen him Grand Master; and that upon his return to England he would accept the Chair, or recommend them to another Noble Man.* Unanimously Resolved, and Ordered that the thanks of the Ancient Craft be given to the Right Honorable Lord George Sackvile for His Lordship's polite and very kind answer."

A Committee had evidently been deputed to wait on Lord Sackville or some other nobleman for the purpose here indicated, but as no previous reference to this Committee appears in the minutes, and Morgan, who bade adieu to his brethren two months before, being one of the persons mentioned, it is probable that the appointment was made during the time he officiated as Grand Secretary; the fact of Dermott being also on the Committee seems to point to an earlier connection with the " Ancients " than the date given in the register.

The Sackville incident reads very much like truth, but as I cannot find his Lordship's name on any list of Grand Masters of Ireland, I presume he was misinformed on that point; he was, however, doubtless an Irish Mason, for he is not mentioned in the proceedings of the " Moderns," whose Grand Festivals were generally well attended by the nobility. There is no doubt as to one portion of the story, Lord George's father *was* Lord Lieutenant of Ireland at the

* " The report was made by Hagan & Dermott, Mr. Morgan being then out of Town."

time mentioned; assuming the remainder to be equally veracious, he, at all events, does not appear to have looked upon the " Ancients " as an irregular or schismatic body, or his answer would probably have been of a different character.

I ought to have mentioned that a Committee of three was appointed to convey the before-mentioned vote to his Lordship, but a foot note informs us that " Lord Sackvile was out of town, and went to Ireland without their seeing him."

The next meeting was held May 6th, 1752, when " A motion was made by John Hamilton, Past Master of No. 7, That this Grand Committee be removed back to the Turk's head Tavern, in Greek Street, Soho, where it had been long held under the title of the Grand Lodge of Free and Accepted Masons of the old Institution; this motion was not seconded and therefore dropt."

The Grand Committee ultimately decided to remove to the Temple Eating House, near Temple Bar.

As we have no means of either verifying or disproving the statement made by Br. Hamilton, it must be taken for what it is worth. Our acquaintance with the Ancients, it will be remembered begins at the Tavern mentioned, but how long they had been located there and under what title, is at present not quite clear.

The only business recorded on July 1st, 1752, consists of a complaint by John Robinson of No. 9, against Moses Willoughby of the same lodge, for defrauding him of the sum of nine shillings in a " bargain in the exchanging a loomb." This matter had been referred to a Committee of Weavers, who decided against the defendant, and he was ordered to refund the money on pain of expulsion, but Moses was evidently a hardened sinner; " he declared they might expell him, for he would not conform to the Rules of any Society upon Earth by which he should lose nine shillings.

" Therefore he was Unanimously Expell'd, and deem'd unworthy of this or any other good Society."

" Grand Committee, Nov. 5th, 1752.

" The names of several Noble and Honorable Gentlemen said to be Ancient Masons, were laid before this Committee, in order to petition some one of them to undertake the Grand Mastership & Government of Craft. The principal personages spoke of were the Rt. Honble. Lords Chesterfield, Ponsonby, Inchiquin, Blesinton.

" Ordered, that the Grand Secretary shall draw up a proper petition to the Rt. Honble. Philip Earl of Chesterfield, an Ancient Mason, beging his Lordship's sanction as Grand Master.

" Ordered, that the Gd. Secretary with the Masters of five lodges shall wait on the Rt. Honble. Lord Chesterfield with the said petition.

" The Secretary return'd thanks for the honor done him in appointing him of the Committee to wait on Lord Chesterfield, and beged the Grand Committee would postpone the business untill they had made choice of some proper place to receive and Install his Lordship, the Temple Eating House being very unfit for that business.

" Brother James Bradshaw and other friends of Br. Robt. Glave the Landlord objected to the Grand Secretary's request, upon which there were many altercations on both sides, not fit to be written, the consequence and conclusion was that the matter was wholly postponed and the Committee closed and adjourn'd to the first Wednesday in Dec. next."

We learn on the authority of Anderson (Constitutions 1738, pp. 112 and 129) that the first-mentioned nobleman, the celebrated Earl of Chesterfield, then Lord Stanhope, was made a Mason in a Grand Lodge held at the King's Arms Tavern, St. Paul's Church Yard, on the 24th June, 1721, and that while Lord Ambassador at the Hague he was present at the initiation of Francis Duke of Lorrain in a lodge presided over by Dr. Desaguliers for which a Deputation or Warrant had been granted. The same writer says: "Our said Royal Brother Lorrain coming to England this year (1731) Grand Master Lovel formed an Occasional Lodge at Sir Robert Walpole's house of Houghton Hall, in Norfolk, and made Brother Lorrain and Brother Thomas Pelham, Duke of Newcastle, Master Masons."

Lord Ponsonby I have failed to identify as a Mason in the records of either "Ancients" or "Moderns." Lord Inchiquin was Grand Master of the latter body in 1726. He attended Grand Lodge occasionally subsequent to his Grand Mastership, his last appearance in that assembly being on the 27th April, 1738. His Lordship died in 1777.

I confess to a little surprise at not finding the name of this nobleman on the Register of 1725. He may have been an Irish Mason, and, if he joined an English lodge, probably it was one of the lodges that did not register their members at that period.

The Earl of Blessington, who as Lord Mountjoy had been Grand Master of Ireland in 1738–9, was the first nobleman elected Grand Master of the "Ancients;" he served that office from 1756 to 1760. I cannot, with a strict regard for truth, say that he filled the Chair during the time mentioned, for, strange to say, he never attended a meeting, not even to be installed, that ceremony being performed privately by the Grand Officers in his own library in Margaret Street. The following correspondence is worth perusal :—

"Grand Lodge, 27th Decr., 1756.

"The Grand Secretary acquainted the G.L. that he had wrote to the Grand Master Elect, a Copy of which he read as follows :—

"To the Right Honorable William Earl of Blesinton in Margaret Street.

" My Lord,

" I have the Honour of conveying the Unanimous thanks of the Grand Lodge of the most Antient and honorable Fraternity of Free and Accepted Masons, for the great honour your Lordship has done the Fraternity in condescending to fill Solomon's Chair. I am also order'd to assure your Lordship that the several members which compose this Grand Lodge are firmly resolved to pursue such measures as will convince your Lordship that this great favour is not ill bestowed.

" I have the honour to be,

" My Lord, &c., &c.,

" Lau. Dermott, Gd. Secretary.

" The Grand Secretary having waited on the Grand Master Elect with the foregoing letter but could not gain admittance, he return'd and wrote another letter in which he enclosed the former and sent them by post to his Lordship.

" Upon Receipt of these letters his Lordship wrote the following Answer which he sent by William Holford, Esqr., whom his Lordship appointed Deputy Grand Master.

"To Mr. Dermott, Secretary to the Grand Lodge of Free and Accepted Masons at the Five Bells Tavern in the Strand.

" Sir,

" I am much concern'd that I happen'd not to see you when you call'd on me the other day, but my being denied was owing to a mistake, having given my orders not with regard to you but another person who has been very troublesome. As I shall be out of Town St. John's Day I must beg leave to act by Deputy. I am very sensible of the Honour done me by the Fraternity in Chusing me Grand Master, And if you shall hereafter have any business to transact with me, you have but to let me know before hand when you will call, and I shall give proper orders to receive you.

" I am, Sir,

" Your Humble Servant,

" (Sign'd)   Blesinton."

Ibid, December 6th, 1758.

" The Grand Secretary read the copy of a letter sent to the Grand Master, as follows :—

"My Lord and Rt. Worshipful Sir,—

" We the Grand Lodge of Free and Accepted Masons of the Old Institution beg leave to return your Lordship our most sincere and hearty thanks for the great Honour your Lordship has been pleased to have done the Fraternity in condescending to be our Grand Master for two years last past, and we hope your Lordship will excuse our non-attendance in a public manner which we shou'd have (gladly) done, but were given to understand that it would be more agreeable to your Lordship if sent by our Secretary in this private manner.

"The number of Warrants sign'd by your Worship is a convincing proof of the prosperity of the Craft under your Lordship's sanction. And we have the pleasure to assure your Worship That (notwithstanding the troublesome time of War, the bane of all good Society) we have not only been able to relieve a great number of Indigent Brethren, but have also bought an Hundred pounds stock in the 3 P C Annuities, 1726, and have still money enough in the Grand Lodge Chest to answer all demands that are likely to be made on us. We are sensible that it will be very pleasing to your Lordship to hear of a great number of Worthy Freemasons Ardently and Industriously engaged in Brotherly love and Charitable works. As such we most humbly entreat your Lordship may be pleased to continue to us the great honour of being our Grand Master for the year 1759, and as Masons we firmly promise that it shall be our constant care to endeavour by every laudable means to deserve the great Honour conferred on,

"My Lord,
"Your Lordship's
"Most Oblidged
"Most Humble Servants and
" For the Antient Fraternity,   " faithfull Brethren,
"Sign'd Willm. Holford, D.G.M."

" His Lordship's answer :—

" I am very sensible of the great Honour done me by the Fraternity, and very glad to hear of their prosperity, and with all my heart accept of their kind offer and shall always be willing to promote the Antient Craft.

" (Sign'd)   Blesinton."

These extracts will probably be considered a sufficient reply to an assertion made in the year 1769 by the Grand Secretary of the "Moderns" in an official letter to the purport that Lord Blessington had forbidden the " Ancients " to use his name any longer, under pain of prosecution. I shall give this document in full later on, but will now return to the Transactions of the Grand Committee of 6th December, 1752 :—

" The Grand Secretary desired to know whether there was any other books or Manuscripts more than had been delivered to him by the Worshipful Mr. James Hagarty, the presiding officer, upon the 2nd of Feb., 1752, and Mr. John Morgan, late Grand Secretary. To which several of the Brethren answer'd that they did not know of any.

" Others, viz., Brothers Samuel Quay, James Hagan, John Doughty, John Smith, Richard Price, John Bandy, and others said that they knew Mr. Morgan had a Roll of parchment of prodigious length, which contained some Historical matters relative to the Ancient Craft, which Parchment they did suppose he had taken abroad with him. It was further said that many Manuscripts were lost amongst the lodges lately Modernized, where a vestige of the Ancient Craft was not suffered to be revived or practized, and that it was for this reason so many of them withdrew from lodges (under the Modern sanction) to support the true Ancient System. That they found the freemasons from Ireland and Scotland had been initiated in the very same manner as themselves, which confirm'd their system & practice as right and Just. Without which none could be deem'd legal though possessed of all the books and papers on Earth.

"The Grand Secretary (Dermott) produced a very Old Manuscript, written or copied by one Bramhall of Canterbury, in the reign of King Henry the seventh, which Manuscript was presented to Br. Dermott (in 1748) by one of the descendants of the writer. On perusal it proved to contain the whole matter in the 'forementioned parchment, as well as other matters not in that parchment.

"The Grand Secretary expatiated much on the subject of this old MS. to the great satisfaction of the hearers, and on his conclusion Brother Samuel Quay made a Motion for the Thanks of the General Committee to be given to the G.S. Dermott, 'for the many pleasing instructions which he had so often administer'd to the Brethren.'

"Upon which Brother James Bradshaw, Thomas Gibbons, Robert Glave, & Evan McKenzie protested against any thanks, or even approbation of the Secretary's conduct, who instead of being useful had actually sung & lectured the Brethren out of their senses, and had then proposed to move the Grand Committee out of the House of a worthy Brother, Mr. Robert Glave, to the House of a man who was not a Mason. That the only way to promote the Society was to chuse a new Secretary, continue in the house where they then were, and not run blindly into needless expences at a Tavern, which in the end would bring ruin on them, and then what would they think of him who had Lectured and sung them out of their senses.

"As soon as the paper containing the above protest was publickly read and copied, The Secretary beg'd to be heard in answer to the Landlord and his friends. This request being granted, The Secretary said that he did not desire to continue in office longer than he should be found really useful. That if a Candidate (better qualified) offered himself, he the Secretary would for the benefit of the Craft resign in favour of such Candidate without the trouble of a General Election. And if he was so unfortunate as to sing any Brother out of his senses, he hoped the Worshipful Master in the Chair and the Grand Committee would allow him an hour's time and he would endeavour to sing them into their senses again.

" The request was granted with great good humour, the Secretary made proper use of his time, and the Worshipful Mr. John Smith Closed and Adjourned the Grand Committee to the Five Bells Tavern in the Strand, upon the 3d day of January next."

To those who are at all familiar with the history and literature of our Order, comment on the preceding episode would be superfluous; as, however, my object is not so much to instruct the well-informed as to awaken a spirit of enquiry in the minds of those who either from want of opportunity or inclination are as yet unaware of the fact that we *have* a history, and a most entertaining one, it occurs to me that a few remarks relative to the " Roll of parchment of prodigious length," formerly in the possession of Bro. Morgan, may be acceptable. No doubt this and also the old manuscript produced by Dermott were different versions of the old charges formerly used in the operative lodges, and referred to in one of our present lectures as " Constitutional Rolls."

I am happy to say there are two excellent specimens now in the archives of the Grand Lodge of England, and until I became acquainted with these curious documents I must plead guilty to considerable haziness as to what particular kind of roll had the best title to the prefix " Constitutional." Some years ago W. J. Hughan took an enormous deal of trouble in hunting up and examining all the copies of these interesting relics of our Ancient Craftsmen then known to be in existence. He published the result of his labours under the title of " Old Charges of British Freemasons," and a most valuable work it is, though now rarely to be met with. Since the period of publication (1872), several others have come to light, and R. F. Gould in *The History of Freemasonry*, Vol. 1, mentions fifty-one altogether, nearly all of which are actually located, while some few have been lost sight of, let us hope only temporarily. These old MS. Charges may fairly be regarded as connecting links between the Operative Masonry of past ages and the Speculative Masonry of to-day, the ancestors in fact of our present Book of Constitutions, and as such, I deem them of sufficient interest to the general body of the Fraternity to justify me in briefly describing one of those already mentioned as being now in the possession of Grand Lodge.

I shall select the older of the two, which is No. 4 in the list of Bro. Gould, who describes it as "First published by Hughan in his ' *Old Charges.*' " This roll of parchment (9 feet in length and 5 inches in breadth) was purchased by the "Board of General Purposes" for the Library and Museum in 1839, for the sum of £25 from Miss Siddall, the grand-daughter of Mr. Thomas Dunckerley's second wife. At the time of purchase it was declared to be "dated 25th December, 1183, in the twenty-ninth year of Henry II., and that this date is nearly correct, may be inferred from the writing, which is in the court hand of that time." After describing its character, the same writer asserts that it contains " the Ancient Charges as agreed on at the Grand Lodge held at York, A.D., about 926." This appears to have been too much even for the Rev. Dr. Oliver to accept, for on the Roll being shown to him he placed it as late as the time of Elizabeth, in this respect differing from the writer of the article.*

"A careful examination of the manuscript itself, however, reveals the fact that the date is ' Scriptum anno domini 1583, Die Decembris 25.⁰' In early days, figures were not always traced with mathematical precision, and

---

* " *Freemasons' Quarterly Review,*" 1842, p. 149.

the mistake in reading 5 for 1 may be accounted for in
many ways." On the reverse of the scroll close to the end,
is written in modern letters, probably late in the last century,
the following :—

> " In the beginning was the Word
> And the Word was with God
> And the Word was God
> Whose Sacred and universal Law
> I will endeavour to observe
> So help me God."

The article quoted by Bro. Gould from *Freemasons' Quarterly Review* is signed " Fidus," which certainly has a somewhat dogmatical sound. The writer evidently prided himself
on his knowledge of penmanship, for in addition to the assertion
as to the age of the writing in the body of the manuscript, he
further states that the verse from St. John, &c., on the back was
written by "the late Brother Thomas Dunckerly." Whether
the document ever belonged to that distinguished Mason is a
matter of opinion, but from a long familiarity with his
peculiar style, and having made a comparison, I have no
hesitation in saying that there is not the faintest resemblance
to his handwriting on this parchment; the assertion of
" Fidus " may therefore be safely relegated to the regions of
Masonic fiction. The question uppermost in my mind on
first glancing at this precious relic, was, In what language
is it written ? for the " *court writing* " seems to suggest the
idea that a whole army of spiders, after carefully marching
through an ink puddle, might have undergone a course of
severe drilling in very close order at different periods on this
long strip of parchment. Having closely examined the
document, I am of opinion that Bro. Gould is correct as to
the date being intended for 1583. From the fact of the
upper part being much soiled, and the writing partially
obliterated, while the middle is comparatively fresh and
clean, I am inclined to think that in its original use it was

rolled up from the bottom and very seldom opened at full
length, the first portion only being read or merely exhibited
on certain occasions.   In its latter days it has evidently
been used in quite a different manner, apparently having
been tightly rolled up from the top and carefully sealed,
leaving only the modern writing exposed.   I intend to give a
transcription of it, as well as a facsimile of a portion of its
contents at a future stage, and being much averse to
copying at second-hand where access to originals is possible,
I purpose devoting a portion of my time daily to hierogly-
phical study ; to this end I have concluded a bargain with
my grocer, on terms mutually advantageous, to take off his
hands for the next three months all his empty tea chests,
and if I succeed in mastering the characters thereon, as well
as those on my neighbour, the Egyptian obelisk, I may
indulge in the hope of being able, ultimately, to decipher
the outlandish figures on this parchment.

I have now to call attention to a most important epoch in
the career of the Ancients ; the election of their first Grand
Master, and their permanent assumption of the name of Grand
Lodge, for there is no reliable evidence of the use of these
distinctive titles at any previous period unless we accept as
such the statement made at the meeting of May 6th, 1752.

" Grand Committee, Decr. 5th, 1753, Bells Tavern.

" Mr. Lachlan McIntosh, Master of No. 3, in the Chair.

" The G.S. made a Motion, *i.e.*, That as the Fraternity
had not made choice of any of the Noble personages formerly
mention'd in those Transactions, and it being doubtful
whether the Antient Craft cou'd be honor'd with a Noble
G.M. at this time, he humbly beg'd that the Brethren wou'd
make choice of some worthy and skillfull Master to fill the
Chair for the space of six months successively.   Accordingly
Bro[r.] Robert Turner, Master of No. 15, was nominated, and
Unanimously Chosen to fill the G. Master's Chair for six
months, and being instal'd and saluted, &c., &c.

"His Worship chose Bro^r. William Rankin for his Deputy who was also immediately install'd, saluted, &c., &c., &c.

"Then the Lodge proceeded in the choice of Gd. Wardens when Bro^r. Samuel Quay, past Master of No. 2, was chosen Senr. Gd. Warden, and Brother Lachlan McIntosh, of No. 3, was chosen Junior Gd. Warden, who were also instal'd and saluted according to Antient Usuage, and concluded with a most agreeable harmony.

"Closed and Adjourn'd to St. John's Day next."

I have expressed an opinion that the unrecorded proceedings of the regular Grand Lodge during the first few years of its existence were probably not entirely harmonious, and no doubt I was assisted to that conclusion by being aware of the difficulties and contentions that beset the early career of its rival. It appears to have been almost a continuous struggle at the outset between Dermott with some of his personal friends, whose efforts were invariably directed towards the elevation of the Society, and a set of men of inferior intellect, some of whom exhibited a decided tendency to "kick over the traces" at every opportunity.

The following extracts will furnish a better idea of the social and mental condition of the members of the Ancient Grand Lodge at this period than any words of mine.

"Grand Lodge, &c., June 5th, 1754.

"Heard the Complaint of Brother Samuel Galbraith & others against John Hamilton, Master of No. 19, wherein it appeared beyond Hamilton's Contradiction that the said Hamilton had willfully villified every part of a Master Mason so as to render the Charge incapable of being committed to writing, &c., &c., &c.

"Agreed Unanimously (in the presence of the said J. Hamilton) that it is our opinion That John Hamilton, late Master of No. 19, is Unworthy the Name of a Freemason, and consequently unworthy of this or any other good Society.

" Ordered, That this Transaction shall be recorded in the Grand Lodge Books to inform our Worthy Successors that the foregoing Character of the said Hamilton is the well-proved and undoubted Opinion of us the Grand Officers and Officers of No. 2, 3, 5, 7, 8, 11, 13, 14, 18, 20, 27, 30, 31, 35, the whole composing a Grand Lodge of

> 4 Gd. Officers.
> 1 Gd. S.
> 14 Masters.
> 28 Wardens.
> 23 Past Masters.
> ___

" Amounting in the whole to　70 Members.
　　　　" Witness, by Order, Lau : Dermott, G.S.

" Upon which John Hamilton was turn'd down stairs, and a General Order given that he should not be admitted into any Antient Lodge directly nor indirectly." *

It will be observed that the indefatigable Dermott never did things by halves, not only were the direct or ordinary portals effectually barred against the admission of this culprit, but access by such indirect means as trap-doors, windows and chimneys was likewise denied him.

Ibid, April 2nd, 1755.

" Thomas Eastman the Master of No. 18, stood up and declared that his business to the Grand Lodge on this night was to make a formal declaration that neither he nor any of the Members of his lodge would contribute to the Grand Fund, nor attend this Grand Lodge for the future.

" Upon which the R.W.G. Master told Mr. Eastman that he was wellcome to stay away, and further that if he knew anybody of like principles in this Assembly he was also at liberty to take him or them."

---

* A Grand Ejector would have been an important personage in those days.

Some business relating to the Charity having been disposed of,

" G.W. Galbraith beg'd leave to resign his Office on acct. of the ill-usage which he had recd. at the hands of Lau. Rooke, the Master of No. 17. The Grand Warden was reconciled to his Office, and Laurence Rooke declared off the Grand Charity, and demanded two shillings which he had formerly contributed to the Fund for relief of worthy Brethren in Distress.

" The G.M. told him, ' That taking him in every sense he did realy believe him to be one of the poorest creatures in london, but wanted merit to receive a single farthing out of any Charitable fund in the Universe.' "

Ibid, March 5th, 1756.

" The Master of No. 4 made a motion that no brother of No. 4 shall be Oblidged to petition the Grand Stewards Lodge for Charity for the future, but instead thereof he or they so necessitated shall peremptorily and verbally demand the same by virtue of his or their contributing to the Grand Fund. *

" The R.W. Grand Master desired the Grand Secretary to deliver his private opinion on the affair then before the Gd. Lodge, to which the Secretary answer'd in the following manner :—

" 'Gentlemen and Brethren, I rise in Obedience to the R.W. Grand Master, tho' I Imagine it requires but little Argument to shew you that the contributions to our Grand Fund are too small to support such Absolute Demands in

---

* The functions of the Grand Stewards Lodge, or "Stewards Lodge" as it was generally called, of the " Ancients " were precisely the same as those of the Committee of Charity of the " Moderns ;" they were both composed of the Masters of lodges, and their duties were of the same character as those now relegated to the Board of Benevolence and the Board of General Purposes ; while the responsibilities of the Grand Stewards of the Moderns were limited to providing dinners and Grand Officers.

the nature of Common Money Clubs. That the small Donations paid into the fund were design'd for real Distress, and that to such (only) as wou'd petition their Brethren in writing. And I shall beg leave to remark, That in all well governed Lodges it was the usual custom to be petition'd in writing without regard to form, &c. Such petitions being attested by some Members of the Lodge, &c.'

"Then the R.W. Grand Master Order'd that the following Question be put to the vote, Whether a petitioner for Charity shall apply by verbal or by written petition?

Votes.

"For written Petitions 36
"Against 9

"Majority ... ... 27"

On the 22nd December, 1762, "Brother Davidson of No. 21 made a complaint against Richd. Gough the Pursuivant of the Grand Lodge, charging the said Gough with taking a Hat and some drinking glasses out of the Lodge No. 21 in a felonious manner," &c.

"Upon Examination it appear'd that some brother (in a jocular manner) had put the Glasses into the said Gough's pocket without his knowledge, and as to the Hat, it appear'd that some person having taken the said Gough's Hat, he (Gough) also took another Hat instead of his own," &c.

The officers of many lodges having given Gough an excellent character, it was

"Unanimously agreed that Richd. Gough is inocent of the Charge laid against him, and that the Hat now in the possession of Mr. Davidson shall be immediately deliver'd to the said Mr. Gough, which hat he the said Gough shall keep untill his own shall be return'd to him."

This weighty matter was settled at a Grand Lodge of Emergency, probably summoned for the purpose, although there were one or two minor differences of opinion adjusted at the same time. Some, at any rate, of the brethren of the present day strictly adhere to the old customs, for several similar cases have come under my own notice, but fortunately they have always been " settled out of Court,"

The first book of laws or Constitutions of the "Ancients" was published by Dermott in 1756, under the new and fanciful title of "Ahiman Rezon; or a Help to a Brother." This book bears a striking resemblance to Spratt's "Irish Constitutions," 1751, from which the greater portion of it is undoubtedly copied; the regulations being for the most part identical both in arrangement and substance, as are also the songs at the end of the book. The editor, however, introduces several pages of new matter in the place of Anderson's genealogical history of Masonry from the Creation, which forms a considerable portion of the work last named.

Some of his remarks evince so much good sense and real Masonic feeling that I am tempted to repeat them, being of opinion that our brethren even of the present enlightened age will deem them not unworthy of consideration. On page 16 he says:—

" A Mason, in Regard to himself, is carefully to avoid all Manner of Intemperance or Excess, which might obstruct him in the Performance of the necessary Duties of his laudable Profession, or lead him into any Crimes which would reflect Dishonour upon the ancient Fraternity.

" He is to treat his Inferiors as he would have his Superiors deal with him, wisely considering that the Original of Mankind is the same; and though Masonry divests no Man of his Honour, yet does the Craft admit that strictly to pursue the Paths of Virtue whereby a clear Conscience may be preserved is the only Method to make any Man noble.

" A Mason is to be so far benevolent, as never to shut

H

his Ear unkindly to the Complaints of wretched Poverty; but when a Brother is oppressed by Want, he is in a peculiar Manner to listen to his Sufferings with Attention; in Consequence of which, Pity must flow from his Breast, and Relief without Prejudice according to his Capacity.

" A Mason is to pay due Obedience to the Authority of his Master and Presiding Officers, and to behave himself meekly amongst his Brethren; neither neglecting his usual Occupation for the Sake of Company, in running from one Lodge to another, nor quarrel with the ignorant for their rediculous Aspersions concerning it: But at his leisure Hours he is required to study the Arts and Sciences with a diligent mind, that he may not only perform his Duty to his great Creator, but also to his Neighbour and himself: For to walk humbly in the Sight of God, to do Justice and love Mercy, are the certain Characteristics of a Real, Free and Accepted Ancient Mason: Which Qualifications I humbly hope they will possess to the End of Time: and I dare Venture to say, that every true Brother will join with me in, Amen."

Page 18. " Therefore to afford Succour to the Distressed, to divide our Bread with the industrious Poor, and to put the misguided Traveller in his Way, are Qualifications inherent in the Craft and suitable to its Dignity, and such as the worthy Members of that great Body have at all times strove with indefatigable pains to accomplish. These and such like Benefits, arising from a strict Observance of the Principles of the Craft (as Numbers of Brethren have lately experienced) if duly considered, will be found not only equal but to exceed any Society in Being.

" If so, the worthy Members of this great and most useful Society can never be too careful in the Election of Members; I mean a thorough knowledge of the Character and Circumstance of a Candidate that begs to be initiated into the Mystery of Free Masonry. Upon this depends the

Welfare or Destruction of the Craft ; for as Regularity, Virtue and Concord, are the only Ornaments of human Nature, (which is too often prone to act in different Capacities), so that the Happiness of Life depends in a great Measure, on our own Election and a prudent Choice of those Steps.

" For human society cannot subsist without Concord, and the Maintenance of mutual good Offices, for, like the working of an Arch of Stone it would fall to the Ground provided one Piece did not properly support another.

" In former Times every Man (at his Request) was not admitted into the Craft (tho' perhaps of a good and moral Reputation) nor allowed to share the Benefits of our ancient and noble Institution, unless he was endued with such Skill in Masonry, as he might thereby be able to improve the Art, either in Plan or Workmanship ; or had such an Affluence of Fortune as should enable him to employ, honour, and protect the Craftsmen."

Page 20, " Here I think it necessary to put in a Word of Advice to some who may have an Inclination to become members of this ancient and honourable Society ; First, they are to understand that no man can be made a regular Free-Mason, but such as are free from Bondage, of mature Age, upright in Body and Limbs, and endued with the necessary Senses of a Man. This has been the general Custom of Masons, in all Ages and Nations, throughout the Known World."

Page 21. " To this I beg leave to add a Word or two : The Persons to whom I now speak are Men of some Education and an honest Character ; but in low Circumstances : I say, let them first consider their Income and Family, and know that Free-Masonry requires Ability, Attendance, and a good Appearance, to maintain and support its ancient and honourable Grandeur.

" The next thing to be considered is the Choice of Officers to rule and govern the Lodge, according to the ancient and wholesome Laws of our Constitution ; and this is a Matter of great Concern, for the Officers of a Lodge are not only bound to advance and promote the Welfare of their own particular Lodge, but also whatsoever may tend to the good of the Fraternity in general. Therefore no Man ought to be nominated or put in such Election, but such as by his Known Skill and Merit, is deemed worthy of Performance, viz., He must be well acquainted with all the private and public Rules and Orders of the Craft, he ought to be strictly honest, humane of Nature, patient in Injuries, modest in Conversation, grave in Counsel and Advice, and (above all) constant in Amity and faithful in Secrecy. Such candidates well deserve to be chosen the Rulers and Governors of their respective Lodges, to whom the members are to be courteous and obedient ; and, by their wise and ancient Dictates may learn to dispise the over-covetous, impatient, contentious, presumptious, arrogant, and conceited Prattlers, the Bane of human Society."

The reader will please to bear in mind that the foregoing is merely a quotation from a book written a hundred and thirty years ago. I would not for one moment be thought to insinuate that such a formidable string of adjectives could possibly be applied to any of the members of our present well-regulated lodges.

It is worthy of remark, that Dermott makes no allusion whatever to the "Moderns" in the work just quoted, it is not till the appearance of the second edition, in 1764, that we are favoured with his views of the rival organization. Probably the latter had not deemed their more humble opponents worthy of notice, there being no evidence of any interference on their part until some years after the "Ancients" had firmly established themselves ; I am of opinion therefore, that the following account may be looked upon as a "return shot" from Dermott's generally well-served guns. I shall let him tell the story in his own words :—

Pp. 24 to 33 of the " Address to the Reader."

" Several eminent Craftsmen residing in Scotland, Ireland, America, and other parts both abroad and at home,
have greatly importuned me to give them some account of
what is called modern Masonry in London. I cannot be
displeased with such importunities, because I had the like
curiosity myself, about sixteen or seventeen years ago, when
I was first introduced into that Society. However, before
I proceed any further concerning the difference between
antient and modern, I think it my duty, to declare solemnly
before God and man, that I have not the least antipathy
against the gentlemen members of the modern Society,* but,
on the contrary, love and respect them, because I have
found the generality of them to be hearty cocks and good
fellows (as the bacchanalian phrase is), and many of them I
believe to be worthy of receiving every blessing that good

---

* In the third edition appears the following note :—

" Such was my declaration in the second edition of this book; nevertheless some of the modern Society have been extremely malapert of late.
Not satisfied with saying the Ancient Masons in England had no Grand
Master, some of them descended so far from truth, as to report the author
had forged the Grand Master's handwriting to masonical warrants, &c.
Upon application his Grace the most Noble Prince John Duke of Atholl,
our present Right Worshipful Grand Master, avowed his Grace's handwriting, supported the ancient Craft, and vindicated the author in public
newspapers.

" As they differ in matters of Masonry, so they did in matters of
calumny, for while some were charging me with forgery, others said that
I was so illiterate as not to know how to write my name. But what may
appear more strange is, that some insisted, that I had neither father nor
mother; but that I grew up spontaneously in the corner of a potato garden
in Ireland.

" I cannot reconcile myself to the idea of having neither father nor
mother : but am so far from contradicting the latter part of this charge
that I freely confess there is a probability of the seedling from whence I
sprung being planted in a potato garden.

" Be that as it may, as I do not find that the calumny of a few modern
masons has done me any real injury, I shall continue in the same mind as
expressed in the declaration to which this note is written."

men can ask or heaven bestow.   I hope that this declaration will acquit me of any design of giving offence, especially
if the following queries and answers be rightly considered :

"*Quere 1st. Whether free masonry, as practised in
antient lodges, is universal ?*

"*Answer.* Yes.

"*2nd. Whether what is called modern masonry is universal ?*

"*Answer.* No.

"*3rd. Whether there is any material difference between
the antient and modern ?*

"*Ans.* A great deal, because an antient mason can not
only make himself known to his brother, but in case of
necessity can discover his very thoughts to him in the presence of a modern without (his) being able to distinguish
that either of them are free masons.

"*4th. Whether a modern mason may, with safety, communicate all his secrets to an antient mason ?*

"*Ans.* Yes.

"*5th. Whether an antient mason may with the like safety
communicate all his secrets, to a modern mason without further
ceremony ?*

"*Ans.* No.   For as a Science comprehends an Art,
(though an art cannot comprehend a science) even so antient
Masonry contains everything valuable amongst the moderns,
as well as many other things that cannot be revealed without additional ceremonies.

"*6th. Whether a person made in the modern manner, and
not after the antient custom of the craft, has a right to be called
free and accepted, according to the intent and meaning of the
words ?*

"*Ans.* His being unqualified to appear in a master's
lodge, according to the universal system of masonry, renders
the appellation improper.

"*7th. Whether it is possible to initiate or introduce a
modern mason into a royal arch lodge (the very Essence of*

masonry) *without making him go through the antient cere-*
monies ?

" *Ans.* No.

" 8*th. What Art or Science has been introduced and prac-*
tised in London without receiving the least improvement ?

" *Ans.* Free Masonry.

" 9*th. Whether the present members of modern lodges are*
blameable for deviating so much from the old land marks ?

" *Ans.* No. Because the innovation was made in the
reign of King George the first, and the new form was
delivered as orthodox to the present members.

" 10*th. Therefore as it is natural for each party, to main-*
tain the orthodoxy of their masonical preceptors. How shall
we distinguish the original and most useful system ?

" *Ans.* The number of antient masons, compared with
the moderns, being as ninety-nine to one, proves the universality of the old Order, and the utility thereof appears by
the love and respect shewn to the brethren, in consequence
of their superior abilities in conversing with, and distin-
guishing the masons of all countries and denominations, a
circumstance peculiar to antient masons.

" I am so well acquainted with the truth of what I have
just now inserted, that I am not in the least apprehensive
of being contradicted. But if any person should hereafter
labour under the spirit of opposition, I shall (even then) be
contented, as I am sure of having the majority upon my
side.

"Therefore in order to satisfy the importunities of my good
Brethren (particularly the Right worshipful and very worthy
Gentlemen of America, who for their charitable disposition,
prudent choice of members and good conduct in general, deserve the unanimous thanks of the masonical world) be it
known that the innovation, already mentioned, arose upon the
fall of a Grand Master, namely, Sir Christopher Wren, who (as
Doctor Anderson says) neglected the lodges. The Doctor's

assertion is certainly true, and I will endeavour to do justice unto the memory of Sir Christopher by relating the real cause of such neglect. The famous Sir Christopher Wren, Knight, (Master of Arts formerly of Wadham college, Professor of astronomy at Gresham and Oxford, Doctor of the civil law, President of the royal Society, grand master of the most antient and honourable fraternity of free and accepted masons, architect to the crown, who built most of the churches in London, laid the first stone of the glorious cathedral of St. Paul, and lived to finish it), having served the crown upwards of fifty years, was (at the age of ninety) displaced from employment, in favour of Mr. William B—ns—n, who was made surveyor of the buildings &c. to his Majesty King George the first.* The first specimen of Mr. B—ns—n's skill in architecture was a report made to the house of Lords, that their house and the painted chamber adjoining were in immediate danger of falling ; whereupon the Lords met in a committee, to appoint some other place to sit in, while the house should be taken down. But it being proposed to cause some other builders first to inspect it, they found it in very good condition. The Lords, upon this, were going upon an address to the King against the modern architect, for such a misrepresentation, but the Earl of Sunderland, then secretary, gave them an assurance that his majesty would remove him.

" Such usage, added to Sir Christopher's great age, was more than enough to make him decline all public assemblies. And the master masons then in London were so much disgusted at the treatment of their old and excellent grand master, that they would not meet nor hold any communication under the sanction of his successor Mr. B—ns—n, in short, the brethren were struck with a Lethargy which seemed to threaten the London lodges with a final dissolution. Notwithstanding this state of inactivity in London,

---

* Mr. William Benson in subsequent editions.

the lodges in the country, particularly in Scotland and at York, kept up their antient formalities, customs and usages, without alteration, adding or diminishing, to this hour, from whence they may justly be called the most antient, &c.

"About the year 1717 some joyous companions, who had passed the degree of a Craft, (though very rusty) resolved to form a lodge for themselves, in order (by conversation) to recollect what had been formerly dictated to them, or if that should be found impracticable, to substitute something new, which might for the future pass for masonry amongst themselves. At this meeting the question was asked, whether any person in the assembly knew the Master's part, and being answered in the negative, it was resolved *nem. con.* that the deficiency should be made up with a new composition, and what fragments of the old order found amongst them should be immediately reformed and made more pliable to the humors of the people. Hence it was ordered, that every person (during the time of his initiation) should wear boots, spurs, a sword and spectacles.* That every apprentice (going and coming from work) should carry the plumb rule upon his right side, contrary to the antients. That ever fellow-craft should carry the level upon his left side and not upon his right side, as the antients did. And that every person dignified with the title of a *master mason*, should wear a square pendant to his right leg. It was also thought expedient to abolish the old custom of studying Geometry in the lodge, and some of the young brethren made it appear that a good knife and fork in the hands

---

* Foot note in third edition. "This may seem a very ludicrous description of making free-masons. But Mr. Thomas Broughton, master of the lodge No. 11, London, declared that he was present in a modern lodge not one mile from the Borough of Southwark, when two or three persons dress'd in liveries with shoulder tags, booted and spurr'd, &c. &c. were initiated into modern masonry; and upon enquiry who they were, he was told they were servants to Lord Caryfort, then Grand Master of modern masons."

of a dexterous brother (over proper materials) would give
greater satisfaction, and add more to the rotundity of
the lodge than the best scale and compass in Europe, and
farthermore added, that a line, a square, a parallelogram,
a rhombus, a rhomboides, a triangle, a trapezium, a circle,
a semicircle, a quadrant, a parabola, a cube, a parallel-
opipedon, a prism, a pyramid, a cylinder, a cone, a prismoid,
a cylindroid, a sphere, a spheroid, a parabolick, a frustrum,
segments, polygons, ellipsis and irregular figures of all
sorts might be drawn and represented upon Bread, Beef,
Mutton, Fowls, Pies, &c. as demonstratively as upon slates
or sheets of paper, and that the use of the globes might be
taught and explained as clearly and briefly upon two bottles,
as upon Mr. Senex's globes of 28 inches diameter; and we
are told that from this improvement proceeded the laudable
custom of charging to a public health at every third sentence
that is spoken in the lodge.   There was another old custom
that gave umbrage to the young architects, i.e. the wearing
of aprons, which made the gentlemen look like so many me-
chanicks, therefore it was proposed, that no brother (for the
future) should wear an apron.   This proposal was rejected
by the oldest members, who declared, that the aprons were
all the signs of masonry then remaining amongst them, and
for that reason they would keep and wear them.   It was
then proposed, that (as they were resolved to wear aprons)
they should be turned upside down in order to avoid
appearing mechanical.   This proposal took place and answered
the design, for that which was formerly the lower part, was
now fastened round the abdomen, and the bib and strings
hung downwards, dangling in such a manner as might convince the spectators, that there was not a working mason
amongst them.

   " Agreeable as this alteration might seem to the gentlemen, nevertheless it was attended with an ugly circumstance: for, in traversing the lodge, the brethren were sub-

ject to tread upon the strings, which often caused them to fall with great violence, so that it was thought necessary, to invent several methods of walking, in order to avoid treading upon the strings.* In brief, every meeting produced an addition or a palinody.†

" Amongst other things they seized on the stone masons Arms, which that good-natured Company has permitted them to wear to this day, for which reason several of the brethren have turned their aprons in the old fashion, and affect to immitate the operative masons. And it is pleasant enough to see sixty or seventy able men about a little Lewis and capstan &c. erected upon a mahogany platform (purchased at an extravagant price) all employed in raising a little square piece of marble, which the weakest man in company could take between his finger and thumb and throw it over the house.

" I have the greatest veneration for such implements as are truly emblematical or useful in refining our moral notions, and I am well convinced that the custom and use of them in lodges are both antient and instructive, but at the same time I abhor and detest the unconstitutional fopperies of cunning avaricious tradesmen, invented and introduced amongst the moderns with no other design but to extract large sums of money, which ought to be applied to more noble and charitable uses.

"There is now in my neighbourhood a large piece of iron scrole work, ornamented with foliage, &c., painted and gilt (the whole at incredible expence) and placed before the master's chair, with a gigantic sword fixed therein, during the communication of the members, a thing contrary to all

---

* The third edition contains the following foot note. " After many years observations on those ingenious methods of walking up to a brother &c. I conclude, that the first was invented by a Man grievously afflicted with the Sciatica. The second by a Sailor, much accustomed to the rolling of a Ship. And the third by a man, who for recreation or through excess of strong liquors, was wont to dance the drunken Peasant."

† A recantation.

the private and public rules of masonry: all implements of war and bloodshed being confined to the lodge door, from the day that the flaming sword was placed in the East of the garden of Eden, to the day that the sagacious modern placed his grand sword of State in the midst of his lodge. Nor is it uncommon for a tyler to receive ten or twelve shillings for drawing two sign posts with chalk, &c., and writing Jamaica rum upon one, and Barbadoes rum upon the other, and all this (I suppose) for no other use than to distinguish where these liquors are to be placed in the lodge.

" There are many other unconstitutional proceedings, which (to avoid giving offence) I pass over in silence. And I hope, that I shall live to see a general conformity and universal unity between the worthy masons of all denominations.   This is the most earnest wishes and ardent prayers of,

    " Gentlemen and Brethren,
        " Your most sincere friend,
            " Obedient servant,
                " and faithful brother,
            " LAURENCE DERMOTT, Secretary."

The foregoing is reprinted in all subsequent editions of Dermott's Constitutions with scarcely a variation, and in the third edition, 1778, the writer enters more fully into the origin of the " Moderns," criticising Anderson's account of the formation of their Grand Lodge in 1717, referring to which he says, " there were numbers of old Masons then in (and adjacent to) London, from whom the present Grand Lodge of Ancient Masons received the old system without adulteration."

Dermott asserts " that instead of a *revival*, a discontinuance of Ancient Masonry took place amongst those who organized the Grand Lodge of 1717," and on p. xv. says, " To put this matter out of the reach of contradiction, take the testimony of Mr. Spencer, one of their Grand Secretaries.

" Copy of an answer (in writing) given to Br. W. Carroll, a certified petitioner from Ireland. The original is in the author's possession. ' Your being an Ancient Mason ' you are not entitled to any of our charity. The Antient ' Masons have a lodge at the Five Bells, in the Strand, and ' their Secretary's name is Dermott. Our society is neither ' Arch, Royal Arch, or Ancient, so that you have no right ' to partake of our charity.' "

I have no doubt whatever that this answer *was* given by the Grand Secretary mentioned, for the incident is recorded in the transactions of the " Ancients," December 5th, 1759, when Carroll was relieved by private subscription with five guineas. Bro. Spencer's answer was doubtless an honest one, but whether under the circumstances it was judicious is open to question ; however, Dermott was far too astute a person not to take advantage of a blunder of this kind. He also gives his version of the Ben Jonson's Head Lodge incident already mentioned. He says, " Some of them had been abroad, and received extraordinary benefits on account of Ancient Masonry. Therefore they agreed to practise Ancient Masonry on every third lodge night. Upon one of those nights some Modern Masons attempted to visit them, but were refused admittance ; the persons so refused laid a formal complaint before the Modern Grand Lodge," &c., &c. Dermott further states that the brethren censured in this affair had no " connexion with the Ancient Grand Lodge at that time nor since." After mentioning a number of convivial clubs recently established, some of them " in imitation of the freemasons," he thus proceeds on p. 43, " From what has been said, it is evident that all unchartered societies in England are upon equal footing in respect to the legality of association. In this light we are to view the fraternities of ancient and modern free masons, who are become two great communities now in England. The ancients, under the name of free and accepted masons. The moderns, under the name of free masons of England.   And though a similiarity of names, yet they differ exceedingly in makings, ceremonies, knowledge, masonical language, and installation, so much that they always have been and still continue to be *two distinct Societies* totally independent of each other.

"As such the moderns having an undoubted right to chuse a chief from amongst themselves : accordingly they have chosen his Grace the most Noble Duke of Manchester to be their Grand Master, and have all the outward appearance of a Grand Lodge.   With equal right the Ancients have unanimously chosen his Grace the most Noble Duke of Athol (an Ancient Mason and Past Master of a regular lodge, and now Grand Master Elect for Scotland) to be their Grand Master.   And his Grace was personally installed in a general Grand Lodge, at the Half-moon tavern, Cheapside, London, in the presence, and with the concurrence and assistance of his Grace the most Noble Duke of Leinster, Grand Master of Ireland ; and the Honourable Sir James Adolphus Oughton, Grand Master of Scotland, with several others of the most eminent brethren in the three Kingdoms ; an honour never conferred on Modern Masons.

"These are sterling truths, from whence the impartial reader will draw the natural inference."

I have no intention of entering upon a lengthy analysis of the preceding extracts, but will content myself for the present, with a few observations on Dermott's somewhat comical account of the origin and customs of Modern Masonry. The writer was evidently in a lively mood during this portion of his literary labours ; probably he had just returned from a merry evening at his lodge, or what is still more likely, he may have recently recovered from the effects of a visit of his inveterate enemy, the gout, for he informs us in the records that on a particular occasion he " was so ill with the gout that he was oblidged to be carried out of his bed (when incapable to wear shoes, stockings, or even

Britches) to do his duty at the Stewards Lodge." A veritable "martyr to his duty." It is scarcely necessary therefore to hint that it would be as well not to consider Dermott's description of the rival society as literally true ; and I think I may venture to intimate that he never meant it to be so received, doubtless it was thoroughly appreciated and understood by those for whom it was written ; even at this distance of time, by making due allowance for exaggeration and playful sarcasm, we are enabled to form a pretty good idea as to the nature of some of the differences between the Ancient and Modern systems.

A disquisition on this subject is more suitable for the lodge than for these pages ; there can be no doubt, however, as to the pertinence of a portion of his insinuations, for it is evident that a good dinner was always a prominent feature in the arrangements of the higher class lodges of the opposite party, and I think it extremely probable that, had their means admitted, his own adherents would have raised no serious objections to a little geometrical exercise of a similar character.

There is one rather important point on which I am unable to agree with Dermott ; he would have us believe that the Grand Lodge of 1717 was actually a creation of the " Moderns ; " doubtless the advent of Desaguliers, Payne, Anderson, and the numerous lords, officers, and other gentlemen who joined the Order during the early days of the Grand Lodge, as a sort of fashionable pastime, resulted in the introduction of certain alterations in the working of private lodges, as well as in the government of the Craft generally ; but in my opinion the most serious innovations are to be ascribed to the year 1730, after the publication of Prichard's pamphlet.

Anderson's account of the formation of the Grand Lodge, is, to my thinking, far from complete ; but the ridiculous description given by Dermott is scarcely worth a moment's thought, notwithstanding the information he says he received from " Brother Thomas Grinsell, a man of great veracity, who often told the author that he (Grinsell) was a free mason before modern masonry was known." I am sorry to say I have some doubt as to the value of the " great veracity " of Brother Grinsell, for I learn from the register that he only joined No. 3 in 1753, and Dermott says he was apprenticed to a weaver in Dublin; unfortunately his age is not stated, neither are we told when he first came to London.

In 1754 he petitioned, and was relieved with forty shillings, on account of his great age. His name is certainly not in any list on the "Modern" register prior to 1730; and, with regard to the latter part of his statement, there is nothing extraordinary in that; similar instances of longevity are to be found in the records of the "Moderns," notably that of Jacob Lamball, J.G.W. in 1717, who was relieved with £10. 10s. in 1756. My conclusion is that Grinsell was an Irish mason, and probably not in England when the first Grand Lodge was formed, consequently he really knew as little of that event as Dermott himself.*

---

* Those who may be desirous of learning more about the career of this remarkable Mason, should read " *Notes on Dermott and his Work*," by Witham M. Bywater, P.M. No. 19. Published in London, 1884.

CHAPTER IV.

ST. JOHN'S LODGES, AND JEWISH MASONS.

"There St. John mingles with my friendly bowl,
The feast of reason and the flow of soul."—*Pope.*

N the course of my researches amongst Masonic records of the last century, I have frequently met with allusions to "Lodges of St. John," which seemed to indicate something different to the ordinary lodges; but what constituted the distinction, or why certain lodges should have been thus designated, was for a long time a source of considerable perplexity.

Bro. Gould seems to have been the first to hit the right nail on the head, for in Vol. 2 of the "History of Free-masonry," p. 384, he says the appellation in question denoted the "unattached lodge, or brother," and with this opinion I cordially agree.

The earliest use of the expression I have met with is in a petition from some masons at Gibraltar in 1728, full particulars of which have already been given in my extracts from the Grand Lodge minutes. To quote the opinions of the various Masonic writers on the derivation of the term "St. John of Jerusalem," and its application to our old lodges would far exceed the proposed limits of this treatise; I shall therefore confine myself to the articles on the subject in Peck's edition of *Mackey's Lexicon*, which, to my thinking offer a very reasonable explanation. Under the head of "Saint John of Jerusalem," the writer says, "The primitive, or mother lodge, was held at Jerusalem, and dedicated to St. John, and hence was called 'The lodge of the holy St. John of Jerusalem.' Of this first lodge all other lodges are but branches, and they therefore receive the same general name, accompanied by another local and distinctive one."*

* Very few lodges on either side had distinctive names until towards the latter part of the last century.

I

Under "Saint John the Almoner," he says, " The saint
to whom Encampments of Knights Templars are dedicated.
He was the son of the King of Cyprus and was born in that
island in the sixth century.   He was elected Patriarch of
Alexandria, and has been canonized by both the Greek and
Roman Churches—his festival among the former occurring
on the 11th of November, and among the latter on the 23rd
of January.

" Bazot, who published a Manual of Freemasonry in
1811, at Paris, thinks that it is this saint and not St. John
the Evangelist, or St. John the Baptist, who is meant as the
true patron of our Order.   "He quitted his country and
the hope of a throne," says this author, " to go to Jerusalem,
that he might generously aid and assist the knights and
pilgrims.   He founded an hospital and organized a fraternity
to attend upon sick and wounded Christians, and to bestow
pecuniary aid upon the pilgrims who visited the Holy
Sepulchre.   St. John, who was worthy to become the patron
of a society whose object is charity, exposed his life a
thousand times in the cause of virtue.   Neither war, nor
pestilence, nor the fury of the infidels, could deter him from
pursuits of benevolence.   But death, at length, arrested him
in the midst of his labours, yet he left the example of his
virtues to the brethren, who have made it their duty to
endeavour to imitate them.   Rome canonized him under the
name of St. John the Almoner, or St. John of Jerusalem ;
and the Masons, whose temples, overthrown by the bar-
barians, he had caused to be rebuilt, selected him with one
accord as their patron."

Whether the French author was right or wrong in his
assumption as to the derivation of the term is not important,
but taken in conjunction with the fact that our earliest
lodges, undoubtedly established for benevolent purposes,
selected St. John of Jerusalem as their patron seems to lend
an air of plausibility to the story.   I can give no reason

why at a later period independent or unattached lodges were so described, unless it was intended to distinguish them from the lodges that had been regularly constituted, and thereby acknowledging the authority of the Grand Master for the time being, while the others recognised no chief but their patron saint.

It is quite clear that, in the early part of the last century, these independent brethren were admitted to the regular lodges on terms of equality with the other members, for in an old private lodge minute book, commencing February 9th, 1737, scarcely a meeting is recorded that has not several St. John's Masons present.

The first item in this book is under the date last mentioned, and seems to be merely a record of the visitors present and the lodges to which they belonged, viz. :—

" Br. Edward Darvell and Wm. Barton, from yᵉ H. L. of St. J." (Holy Lodge of St. John).

" W. Caral from yᵉ Black Lyon in Jocky fields No. 77.

" John Fisher at yᵉ Read Lyon in Chandlers St.

" Thos. Roper   St. Johns.

" John Lambton   Made in this Lodge.

" William Dunmore   do.

" Peter Jolley   Bull Head in Grace Church St."

This lodge appears to have held weekly meetings, for under date February 16th, 1737, seven names of brethren are written as belonging to, or made, "att yᵉ Fountin in Katerin St., Strand," one "att yᵉ Goat in Spread Eagle court, Strand," and one "Holy Lodge, St. John's."

From the 9th of February, 1737 to the 30th of March following, sixteen different names are given against which is written " St. John's." The first clue to the identity of this old lodge is found in the following minute dated August 17th, 1738.

" Twas a greed that this Lodge should take a Book of Constitution of the New Edition of Bro : Anderson & pay

I

thirteen Shillings for the same Bound with the 2 black Posts in Maiden Lane on the Back." *

The engraved list for 1738 gives the date of Constitution of the lodge at the Two black Posts, No. 163, as 21st September, 1737 ; it is therefore evident that this lodge must have been working before it was constituted, how long it is impossible to say, for the minutes furnish no indication of a beginning, nor is the Constitution mentioned, indeed, the book itself has every appearance of being merely a continuation of earlier minutes.

The above is the only record under the date given ; the Secretary had evidently a proper appreciation of the value of time as well as paper, for this one page contains the minutes of no less than seven different meetings. This old book is exceedingly interesting, but want of space precludes my giving more than a few extracts from its pages.

It appears from the following item that ten pounds was allowed to the widow of a deceased member.

" Feb. 5th 1740.

" The Lodge being informed of the Death of Br. Bengough the Master paid the Widow five Pounds and allowed the other five Pounds for the funerall expenses.

" 20th Aug. 1741.

" A Motion was made this night that this Lodge should Meet but once a fortnight.

" Jan. 3rd 1745.

" Bro. Jones & Briggs being deficient in their payments of 2/- for the Burial of Marshall the Brethen unanimously agreed to Indemnify Bro. Dawson for paying 2/- on account of Br. Jones, he always behaving herein as a worthy member; But unanimously refused to pay any money for Bro. Briggs, for Reasons best Known to themselves.

---

* This was the lodge afterwards joined by the celebrated William Preston, of whom more hereafter.

" March 2nd 1752.

" Agreed to give a Guinea to the Charity provided we have a new Grand Master, but in case we have not, to give nothing."

It would seem from this that Grand Masters were valued at a guinea a head in those days.

I may state that the lodge did not save its guinea on this occasion : a new Grand Master being elected at the ensuing meeting of Grand Lodge.

In another old minute book, formerly belonging to the Lebeck's Head Lodge, constituted the 24th August, 1759, as No. 246, I find similar instances of recognition of St. John's Masons, but in this case a distinction is made with regard to the visiting fee.

Their first Articles or by-laws were agreed to on the 16th October, 1761, one of which is to the effect that " A Member of a Regular Lodge is to pay 1/6 for visiting and a Member of St. John's 2/-."

On the 21st March, 1766, " Br. Lownie proposed Mr. Wm. Dickey, Junr. and Mr. James Burn to be made modern masons of in this lodge, which was Firsted and seconded, and they went through the three Regular degrees." *

On the 21st November following, " It was proposed, seconded and unanimously agreed, That for the future no person calling himself a Mason but not having been regularly initiated under the English Constitution shall be made a Mason in this Lodge for less than One Guinea, conformable to the Constitutions and to the good order of the Royal Craft, and that such sum shall defray all expences attending his passing the three Degrees.

" Br. Keall proposed Mr. William Millar of Tookes Court, Castle Yard, Case Maker, *Irish York Mason* to be made a Mason of in this Lodge, and was seconded.

---

* Bro. Dickey had been initiated in June, 1765, in No. 14 of the " Ancients," and succeeded Dermott as Grand Secretary of that body.

This person was "Made, Crafted and became a Member" at the next meeting.

Considerable misconception exists as to the period when Jews first entered the ranks of Speculative Masonry, and, strange to say, the question seems to have exercised even our worthy Dr. Oliver, who broaches the subject in his *Revelations*, but in a rather uncertain way.

I shall not therefore in this instance utilise the opinions of our Rev. brother, his "about this time" being somewhat vague, but if I rightly interpret his meaning he ascribes the admission of Jews to some time between 1747 and 1760. If any reliance can be placed on names, I think he might safely have gone at least twenty years farther back. I find very few distinctly Jewish names in the earliest lists of members, only two, in fact, in the 1725 register, viz., Israel Segalas, of the Solomon's Temple Lodge, Hemmings Row, and Nicholas Abraham, of the Golden Lyon Lodge, Dean Street. The 1730-2 register contains the following names of members of No. 84, at Daniel's coffee house, Lombard Street; Solomon Mountford, Solomon Mendez, Abraham Ximinez, Jacob Alvares, Isaac Baruch, and Abraham De Medina ; as well as several others whom I have omitted as doubtful. The incomplete state of the register precludes my following up this clue, but I find in the list of Grand Stewards for 1738-9 Moses Mendez, and Samuel Lowman. Of course we cannot be certain that any of these brethren were Jews, but I think we may fairly conclude that those belonging to No. 84 were of the Hebrew faith. The earliest instance I have met with of a lodge being started by Jews, is that of the recently mentioned Lebeck's Head Lodge, for which there were 23 petitioners, 13 of whom have unmistakably Jewish names ; and the records inform us that several others were initiated at the first meeting of the lodge.

The minutes of this meeting exhibit some orthographical

variations, which might be useful in this age of "Spelling
Bees," and word puzzles, and, as they are very brief I will
endeavour to transcribe them *verbatim*, although I have some
doubt as to my ability to do justice to the original, which
should be seen, to be properly appreciated.

> " these Night Brother
> " Jacub moses.
> " Lazars Levy.
> " Edward morley.
> " Solomon Levy.

> " Jacub Arons ware made Masons and Past
felo Crafts, and pad thrare yousell Feas and became Bambers
of the Lodge.

" Abraham peleps was this night purposed to be made A
mason the Next night by mr. Lyon peleps Pad five Shillng
to Ward thee making.

> " Officers For the Hafe year Esueng.
> " Brother hopthrow, mastter.
> " Brother Senur Warden, Yoel.
> " Brother Juner Warden, Pusevall.
> " Secatary, Brother Henry Lyon.
> " Tresher, Brother Ross.
> " moses Levy, Past master.
> " Sep : the 19th, 1759."

There was evidently some little doubt as to the word
" officers," the writer had got as far as " Ofor," when he
altered his mind, and apparently wiped out these letters
with his fingers.

I hope the printer will be careful with the spelling as
this is the only specimen in the book by the same writer.
The lodge probably pensioned him off after that performance,
or he may have got a writership under the Government.

CHAPTER V.

"THE IRISH QUESTION" SOLVED WITHOUT DISTURBING THE
   BALANCE OF PARTIES, AND AN INVASION OF ENGLAND
   UNRECORDED IN HISTORY.

T has long been my opinion that some of our neighbours of the Emerald Isle figured prominently in the organization of the "Ancients" as a governing body, as well as in their ulterior proceedings, and this opinion has been recently strengthened by the discovery that they were described as Irish Masons in documents both written and printed at different periods and by different persons during the latter part of the last century. I have already given one example of this in the case of the Lebeck's Head Lodge, and will now quote a portion of a letter written by Wellins Calcott (author of a well-known work on Masonry, published in 1769), addressed to Bro. Heseltine, Grand Secretary of the "Moderns," dated 22nd June, 1776.

"As I have occasion to write to you on this Account, give me leave to mention another Circumstance to you which in Justice you ought to be Acquainted with. I have heard that you have been told, that Dr. Markham of Whitechapel, had preached for the Irish Faction (ye A.M.'s as they call themselves). I inquired of the Dr. abt. it who says he never preached a Mason's Sermon but once and then on St. John's at West Chester—nor was he ever in a Mason's Lo : in London in his Life. The Lodges he preached before, were regular Lodges held under the Constitution of the Grand Ma$^{r.}$ of England. I guess the mistake may have arisen thus—a Dr. Grant, an Irish Mason, was Dr. Markham's late Curate, this man was dubbed their Grd. Chaplain, and has stalked in their Processions, and the one has been taken for the other."[*]

---

[*] The Rev. Jas. Grant, LL.D., was the first Grand Chaplain of the "Ancients," and held that office from 1772 to 1775; he was a member of

Another letter is written by Thos. Postlethwaite, Secretary of No. 312 Workington, June 17th, 1793, and is addressed to Bro. W. White, Grand Secretary (Heseltine's successor). This is a complaint at not having received some Grand Lodge Certificates, and a book of " Constitutions," which the Secretary says he had written for in " 1791 & 92 and on the 13th April, 93," which neglect, to use his own words, " astonishes us all, and have much displeased some of the party most principally concerned, yea, in so much, that untill the Certificats do come down, and an account of their being duly registered in the Grand Lodge Books, they are resolved to visit this Lodge no more, at least very seldom, and in all probability if further neglect or omition be, they will join some Irish Lodge."

I may add that these extracts are from the original documents. A pamphlet on Ancient Masonry, published in London in 1806, which I need not describe minutely, as it is well known to most Masonic students and collectors, bears on its title-page these words, " Called the Most Ancient by the Irishmen."

Here, then, I take it, is conclusive evidence that in 1766, 1776, 1793 and 1806, the " Ancients " were generally looked upon as *Irish masons,* and their lodges were considered *Irish lodges.* It now remains to account for their being so described, and in order to do so I must again refer to their predecessors. The important question to be decided is: Who were they? Were they English Masons, who from some grievance, either real or imaginary, had, as we have been taught to believe, seceded from the regular body, and set up an opposition Grand Lodge, ultimately, by a combination of impudence and imposture, effecting an alliance

---

No. 3 in 1770, but whether initiated in that lodge is not quite clear, probably he joined it, if so his former lodge is not stated; he joined No. 9 in 1773 and declared off in 1775. I can find no trace of him in the register subsequently.

with the Grand Lodges in Scotland, Ireland, and many
parts of America, which all the efforts of their more aristocratic rivals, even when under the patronage and protection
of royalty itself, failed to disturb? Bearing in mind the
rapid extension of their influence, their unchecked career of
prosperity, and the decided and even triumphant stand made
by them when the question of an union came to the front, I
must say the "Modern" story of their origin seems most
improbable. I have already mentioned that an unusual
number of Irish names are to be found in the first register
of the "Ancients," also that the same authority gives as
their total strength at the start, *i.e.*, 17th July, 1751, five or
six lodges consisting at most of about eighty members.

I will now endeavour to show whence these original
members came. At the outset the Ancients had not a
No. 1 lodge on their list, that number being probably
reserved for a "Grand Masters Lodge," when they should
arrive at the dignity of having an official of that calibre to
preside over them. This from our present standpoint may
seem rather a strange proceeding, but as a matter of fact
they were in a manner copying the example of the Grand
Lodge of Ireland, wherein the following order had been
made on the 3rd of January, 1749, the Grand Officers having
recently formed a lodge for themselves :—

"That a Registry be opened in the Front of the Grand
Register Book for the said Lodge, and that the same shall
henceforth be distinguished and known by the Denomination
of the Grand Master's Lodge; and that all, or any of the
Members thereof, who does at any Time think proper to visit
the Grand Lodge, shall take place of every other Lodge on
the Registry, or Roll Books of this Kingdom; and that each
and every of them shall be as fully entitulled to all and
every of the Privileges and Freedoms thereof, as any other
Member or Members that this Grand Lodge is composed of." *

---

* "Spratt's Constitutions."   Dublin, 1751.

A lodge of a similar character was established by the Ancients in 1759, *and the names of its members are written on the front page, not of the register then in use, but the one that follows it, the first page of what would have been the proper volume, according to date, being already occupied by an index.*

This lodge has ever since been known as the Grand Masters Lodge No. 1, having had the good fortune to acquire, by lot, first place on the numerical list of the United Grand Lodge.

The first lodge in the "Ancients" register being No. 2, it is but natural therefore to conclude that this was their oldest, and consequently, the most important lodge, for my present purpose. The following eight names were apparently entered when the register was first opened, although the column headed, "Time of Entry" is blank so far as these names are concerned, viz., Saml. Quay, James Hagan, Wm. Taylor, Jno. Doughty, Jno. Smith, Jno. Morgan, Jno. Mitchell, and Richd. Coffey; Nale Mc Colm Fras. Mathews, Jas. Murphy, and Wm. Cowen are registered as having joined in July 1752. Others joined subsequently, but this was their first list of members, and I think the reader will agree with me that a second glance is not required to distinguish the nationality of a majority of them. The first name I need hardly say is a very uncommon one, and, although it seems to have an Irish sound, I am assured on very good authority that it cannot be considered as an Irish name; and this opinion coincides with the result of a brief examination of two Directories, one published in Dublin in 1782 (the earliest available) the other in Belfast some years later, in neither of which does the name of "Quay" appear, at all events not amongst those of the trading community, and time would not admit of a farther search, I will therefore leave the nationality of this brother an open question; but from the fact of his name being at the top of the register, and being one of the original committee and first Senr.

Grand Warden in 1753, when he was described as "Past master of No. 2," I should say he was an old mason and evidently much respected by his brethren, for the records show no opposition to his election, as was frequently the case with his successors in office. I presume he died in 1759, for the register indicates that his subscription was paid till September in that year; against his name is written "Dead, vide Grd. Mas. Lo."

With this one exception, *I found all the names of the original members* of this old lodge in the Dublin directory; the names of Taylor and Smith included, but these being rather a numerous family and common to the United Kingdom generally, I relinquish all claims to their being either of Irish nationality or extraction. There is, however, another circumstance in connexion with No. 2 which I will briefly mention. The transactions of Grand Lodge, March 2nd, 1757, contain an appeal from John Hamilton (formerly excluded) against his exclusion, &c., desiring to be admitted for a few moments in order to clear himself. After many debates he was admitted, but, according to the minutes his, defence consisted of a violent attack on the character of the Grand Secretary, alleging amongst other crimes that Dermott "had imposed on the whole Craft by saying that he was Regularly made in Ireland, &c., whereas the said Dermott was only a Clandestine Mason, made by James Hagan and others at a House in Long Acre, some years before."

* * * * * *

"Then his Worship call'd on the Accuser and told him that he must prove his assertion; the accuser then Ordered Jas. Hagan before the lodge, who being asked whether he did make Lau : Dermott a freemason, he declared that he did not, neither did he ever teach him anything relative to Masonry, nor could he devise what reason Mr. Hamilton had for saying so.

" The G.M. then asked Mr. Hamilton if he had any other person to call on this occasion, upon which Lau: Rooke arose and said that he verily believed that Bro^{r.} Hamilton's accusation was true. Being asked his reason for thinking so. He answered because Brother Hamilton told him so, and at the same time swore to it, in such a manner as to leave no doubt behind.

Dermott's reply on being " asked to make his defence" :

" By my conduct hitherto, I hope you are convinc'd that I have not done you any wrong. As to my intention of Robbing you, &c., This must be left to the great tell Tale Time, it being impossible to convince this lodge as to my present way of thinking, much less what I may think in future. And as to the other Charge of Imposing on you and being made in a Clandestine manner in London, I shall beg leave to have the Present and Past Masters of No. 2 examin'd on that head. And I humbly and earnestly beg that the said Master and Past Masters may be put to the Master Mason's Test on this Occasion.

" Then arose Bro^{r.} Thomas Allen Past Master of No. 2 and proved that Brother Dermott had faithfully served all Offices in a very Reputable Lodge held in his house in the City of Dublin which servitude was prior to the said Dermott's coming to England, and further declared that he never heard any crime (in or out of the Lodge) laid to his Charge.

" Bro^{r.} Charles Byrne (Senr.) Master of No. 2 proved that Bro. Lau: Dermott having faithfully served the Offices of Senr. and Junr. Deacon, Junr. & Senr. Wardens and Secretary, was by him Regularly Install'd Master of the good Lodge No. 26 in the Kingdom of Ireland, upon the 24th day of June, 1746, and that all these Transactions were prior to Mr. Dermott's coming to England. Lastly, Brother Dermott Produced a Certificate (signed Edwd. Spratt, G.S.) under the seal of the Grand Lodge of Ireland, of his good behaviour and servitude, &c., &c., &c., which gave intire satisfaction, upon which the G.L. came to the following Resolution, viz. :—'That John Hamilton, late of No. 19, is unworthy of being admitted into a Masons Lodge or any other good Society, and that therefore it is hereby Order'd that the said John Hamilton shall not be admitted within the door of any Antient Lodge during his life, the said John having been several times excluded for mal-practises and again reinstated, yet still continue in his vile offences, of which Clandestine makings are not the least."

The foregoing facts speak for themselves, and to my think-ing conclusively establish the nationality of the members of the first lodge on the "Ancient" roll. I will now go a step farther. Having copied the first hundred names in the register, I found no less than seventy-two similar names in the small directories or almanacks before mentioned, and this during a very hurried examination only, amongst the shop-keeping, manufacturing, and artizan classes, and I have every reason to believe that had the names all been correctly spelt by the Grand Secretary the proportion would have been still greater; also that a corresponding average would be found to exist all through the first register. It will thus be seen that there were good grounds for the "Ancients" being afterwards denominated "*Irish Masons.*" In order, if possible, to furnish a reason for this extraordinary invasion of the English Masonic territory, it will be necessary for me to go back for a period of about fifteen years anterior to the consolidation of the "Ancients" as an independent body, and briefly notice an incident recorded in the minutes of the regular Grand Lodge, December 11th, 1735.

"Notice being given to the Grand Lodge that the Master and Wardens of a Lodge from Ireland attended without, desiring to be admitted by virtue of a Deputation from the Lord Kingston, present Grand Master of Ireland. But it appearing there was no particular Recommendation from his Lordship in this affair, their Request could not be complied with unless they would accept of a new Constitution here."

Now, bearing in mind the fact that the nobleman mentioned had only a few years before (1728–9) presided over their own Grand Lodge with much *éclat*, and had also made them several valuable presents this proceeding seems as churlish, as it was certainly short-sighted, on the part of the " regulars."

Private lodges would of course take their cue from the Grand Lodge, and refuse to open their doors to these strangers whose working was different to theirs.

Does anyone at all familiar with the characteristics of an Irishman imagine that " Pat " would meekly submit to such treatment? If he does, I most decidedly do not. It seems to me much more likely that he would call some of his countrymen about him and open a lodge on his own account, or by virtue of the before mentioned Deputation or Warrant, for we must remember that " *exclusive Masonic jurisdiction* " was unknown at that period. One lodge would, of course, beget others, and so it probably went on until unconstituted Masonic lodges became the rallying points or centres of union of nearly all the Irish mechanics and labourers that came over to seek employment in the English metropolis. The migratory character of this class will, I think, sufficiently account for the comparatively small number to be found on the register at the formation of their Grand Lodge, also for the rapid growth of their provincial and military lodges. In the letter previously quoted, the Grand Secretary of the " Moderns " says that the " Ancients *first made their appearance about* 1746," leaving an impression that he was not quite certain on that point, and even if they were not known to the eminently respectable and very gentlemanly body of which he was a member, it by no means follows that they were not in existence. Indeed, considering the great dissimilarity between the members generally of the two societies it is hardly to be wondered at that they were at first comparatively unknown to each other.

Most of us are probably aware that ten years make a considerable slice in the life of an individual, but in that of a lodge or society it is quite a different matter. For my own part I firmly believe that the true origin of the " Ancients " dates from the period of the occurrence just mentioned, the end of 1735, and that they were probably countenanced and assisted by some few of the old school or poorer class of English Masons who had either dropped out from the regular lodges or had never acknowledged the authority of the Grand Lodge of 1717, but the real organizers and supporters—the head and backbone of the "Ancient" fraternity for the first twenty or thirty years of its existence—were Irish Masons. In support of this view I might call attention to the fact that it was to Ireland they first looked for a chief, and that, omitting the two Dukes of Athole and the Duke of Kent, six out of the remaining seven of their Grand Masters were Irishmen, and in all probability the seventh was also of the same nationality.

I have previously intimated that the first Constitutions of the " Ancients " as well as their by-laws for private lodges were derived from Ireland. Many other connecting links may be traced which, to my thinking, are rather difficult to account for except upon the hypothesis already advanced.

It will be seen that the seals of the two grand Lodges were nearly identical, and if the writer of the following letter is not in error, the " Ancients " undoubtedly adopted the Irish seal. Replying to an enquiry on this subject, kindly made by Col. Clerke; Br. Oldham, D.G. Secretary of Ireland, writes under date 20th April, 1887 :—

" I am afraid the information I can give you respecting the Grd. Lodge Seal will not be of much value.

SEALS.

1

"Moderns"
prior to 1813.

2

Grand Chapter.
"Moderns"
1769 – 1817.

6

"Ancients."
1760 – 1775.

3

"Ancients"
1775–1813.

4

"Ancients."
prior to 1817.

7

(B) 1781.

9

From 1813.

8

(A) 1735.

5

From 1817.

Nos 1 to 5 from Gould's History of Freemasonry.
Nos 6 to 9 Drawn from Originals by W. H. Rylands. F.S.A

" I have looked through all the Books and papers likely to afford any record and have failed to trace it, but I now enclose you seals taken from old documents, they are marked on the back.

" A. is from a paper dated 1735 and I have no reason to doubt that this Seal was in use from 1721, and I have found it on papers 1753, the only difference being that the ribbons came from top to bottom instead of from left to right of the parchments. The ribbons were blue and gold color.

" B., 1781. I cannot trace this further back than 1781, *but from marks on an old Warrant,* 1760, *it appears to have been then in use."*

The seal marked A, is in red wax, and consists of a crest only, a raised arm holding a trowel, encircled by the words "The Grand Lodge of Ireland." This seal was very common amongst the lodges of the Ancients, and is the crest given by Dermott to the Arms of the Operative or Stone Masons in the Frontispiece to the second edition of *Ahiman Rezon.* The seal marked B, is the one here depicted, and as will be seen the only difference between it and that of the " Ancients " is in the harp and inscription. The following extract will show that the seal of the latter was made in 1775, if therefore the Grand Lodge of Ireland had a similar one in 1760, it is quite clear where the idea came from.

G. L. M. (Ancients) 1st March, 1775.

" The Grand Secretary produced a Drawing of the Arms of the Fraternity and urged many weighty reasons for having them Engraved immediately, to be used in future as the Seal of the Grand Lodge, and also remarked that Mr. Kirk, a person of eminence in that branch, informed him that the expence would be about Fifteen Guineas.· After many Debates the Grand Lodge order'd that the Arms should be engraved for a Seal in a Masterly manner under the Inspection of Bros. Lau. Dermott, Wm. Tindall, Thos. Carter, Wm. Dickey, and John Ryland, and not to exceed the Sum

K

of Fifteen Pounds fifteen Shillings." It must not be imagined that this was the first seal used by the Ancients, they certainly had one, if not two, before this period. The first mention of a seal in their records is in the "Table of the Grand Secretary's Fees, A.D. 1751." "Dispensation for forming a new Lodge and making Masons under the Grand Seal, 2/6."

The next reference is in the disbursements entered June 3rd, 1761. "To the G.S. Dermott for a *new* Seal which he got Engraved in the year 1760, £1. 11. 6."

Unfortunately we have no knowledge of the kind of seal in use before the one last mentioned, for although there are in existence at least two original Warrants issued by this body prior to 1760, the old seals are missing.

The earliest complete "Ancient" Warrant which I have met with is dated 16th Nov. 1772, and has the seal of the Duke of Athole at the top and that of the Grand Lodge at the bottom, the latter being probably an impression of the seal of 1760, consisting merely of a Square and Compasses over which is a flaming sword; the legend being "Virtue and Silence, Grand Lodge, London," not "Grand Lodge OF London" as it is sometimes described. It is a significant and noteworthy fact that the mode of affixing this seal was *precisely the same as in the case of the old Seal of the Grand Lodge of Ireland, marked A, i.e. both being impressed on two pieces of narrow ribbon of the colors named by Br. Oldham,* the "Ancient" Warrant having the ribbons "from top to bottom instead of from left to right" as on the Irish Seal. The "Moderns" so far as I can learn never used ribbons for the Seals of their Warrants.

Considerable doubt seems to prevail as to the particular sex represented by that portion of the armorial bearings of our Society, technically termed *Supporters;* I will therefore put the reader in possession of what Dermott says on the subject in *Ahiman Rezon,* 1764.

" The free masons arms in the upper part of the frontis
piece of this book, was found in the collection of the famous
and learned hebrewist, architect and brother, Rabi Jacob
Jehudah Leon. This gentleman, at the request of the
States of Holland, built a model of Solomon's temple. The
design of this undertaking was to build a temple in Holland,
but upon surveying the model it was adjudged, that the
united provinces were not rich enough to pay for it ; whereupon the States generously bestowed the model upon the
builder, notwithstanding they had already paid him his
demand, which was very great. This model was exhibited to
public view (by authority) at Paris and Vienna, and afterwards
in London, by a patent under the great seal of England, and
signed Killigrew in the reign of King Charles the second.
At the same time, Jacob Judah Leon published a description of the tabernacle and the temple, and dedicated it to
his Majesty, and in the years 1759 and 1760 I had the
pleasure of perusing and examining both these curiosities.
The arms are emblazoned thus, quarterly per squares, coun-
terchanged Vert. In the first quarter Azure a lyon rampant
Or, in the second quarter Or, an ox passant sable ; in the
third quarter Or, a man with hands erect, proper robed,
crimson and ermin ; in the fourth quarter Azure an eagle
displayed, Or. Crest, the holy ark of the covenant, proper,
supported by Cherubims. Motto, Kodes la Adonai, *i.e.*
Holiness to the Lord.

" To this I beg leave to add what I have read concerning these arms. The learned Spencer says, ' the Cherubims
had the face of a man, the wings of an eagle, the back and
mane of a lion, and the feet of a calf. *De Legib. Hebr.
lib.* 3. *diss.* 5. *ch.* 2.'

" The Prophet Ezekiel says, ' they had four forms, a man,
a lion, an ox, and an eagle.'

" When the Israelites were in the wilderness, and en-
camped in four cohorts, the standard of the tribe of Judah

carried a lion, the tribe of Ephraim an ox, the tribe of
Ruben a man, and the tribe of Dan an eagle ; those four
standards composed a Cherubim, therefore God chose to sit
upon Cherubims bearing the forms of those animals, to
signify that he was the leader and king of the cohorts of the
Israelites. ' *Trad. of the Heb.*'

"Bochart says, that they represented the nature and
ministry of angels, by the lion's form is signified their
strength, generosity and majesty ; by that of the ox, their
constancy and assiduity in executing the commands of God ;
by their human shape, their humanity and kindness, and
by that of the eagle, their agility and speed.—*Bochart de
animal. sacr.* p. 1.

"As these were the arms of the masons that built the
tabernacle and the temple, there is not the least doubt of
their being the proper arms of the most antient and honourable fraternity of free and accepted masons, and the continual practice, formalities and tradition, in all regular
lodges, from the lowest degree to the most high, *i.e.* The
Holy Royal Arch, confirms the truth hereof."

It will thus be seen that although these arms were not
engraved and used as a seal by the "Ancients" till 1775, they
were known to Dermott, according to his own account, quite
fifteen years earlier. What strikes me as rather inconsistent
with this story, is the fact of his having had a *new* seal
engraved in 1760 of a totally different character. If we
could ascertain the nature of some of the " weighty reasons
or having them engraved immediately," the discovery
would be valuable. It could not have been that the seal
hen in use had become worn or disfigured, for I have
before me a capital impression of 1774. An explanation
may probably be found in the suggestion that the arms
were being used as a seal by some other branch of the
fraternity. We know that about this time the York Masons
had a seal engraved and a banner painted after the design

supplied by Dermott in the book just quoted.* A knowledge
of this fact would doubtless have had an accelerating effect,
and if the Grand Lodge of Ireland had also adopted the
arms (whether before 1764 or after) I think the hurry in
1775 is easily accounted for.

I have frequently lamented the absence of an official
register on the part of the " Moderns," indeed they never
had a proper system of registration, the earliest names being
simply entered in a book under their different lodges, without
a particle of further information, beyond an indication of the
actual Master and Wardens at the time the list was sent in;
yet meagre and incomplete as this system was, it would have
effectually settled the question of secession had it been continued. For a period of quite thirty years the register of
the " Moderns " is a perfect blank, while their rivals seem
to have considered a " General Register " as indispensable,
or Morgan would certainly not have taken the step of purchasing a book for the purpose at his own expense. I have
shown that this register was very carefully prepared; and,
with the exception of certain omissions at the commencement,
is most complete and comprehensive, and in my opinion a
copy of a similar book. Where, then, did Morgan get the
idea? It could not have been from the Moderns, for they
had no register whatever at that period; whereas we have
it in evidence that the Grand Lodge of Ireland, in the year
1749, kept a register of its members. Being determined to
neglect nothing likely to shed even the smallest ray of light
on this important question, I made a tracing of a page in
Dermott's first register, which Colonel Clerke was good
enough to forward to Bro. Oldham. I then learnt, to my
great regret, that the early records of the Grand Lodge of
Ireland had been destroyed by fire at the beginning of this
century; but, in response to the query whether my tracing

---

* Hughan's " Origin of the English Rite," and Gould's " History of
Freemasonry." Vol. II.

bore any resemblance to the original register of that body, Bro. Oldham writes on the tracing, " Previous to 1860," meaning, I presume, that Dermott's mode of registering was the same, or nearly so, as that of his countrymen in Dublin at a later period. This may fairly be taken as another link in the chain, although it must be admitted that the absence of the original Irish register preventing a proper comparison, to some extent lessens its value.

There is another point of resemblance, which although of no great weight, I think should not be passed over.

Bro. Oldham kindly sent me a sketch of the earliest existing register of the Grand Lodge of Ireland (I think about 1806), as well as one of the system of registration now in use; and in both these I notice that the members are numbered consecutively, in the margin of the book, after the manner of Morgan's register, only the latter continued from No. 1 up to the close of the register when there were over a thousand names in the book, the Secretary probably not anticipating so rapid an increase, while in the Dublin registers each lodge has a separate enumeration. The practice of giving each member a different number was not at any period in vogue by the " Moderns," and Dermott seems to have deemed it unnecessary when he began his new system of registration, which system I may add, is totally different to that adopted by the Moderns when they introduced compulsory registration in 1768 ; and if it be any satisfaction to my brethren of " Ancient descent " I may state that Dermott's system was considered worthy of being continued by the United Grand Lodge, and has been in use down to the present day, of course with a few necessary additions and improvements. This scrap of evidence will doubtless be considered of little value, but the fact remains, that the first register of the " Ancients " and the earliest existing register of the Grand Lodge of Ireland are almost identical. Considering the frequent arrivals from Ireland, I see nothing

improbable in the theory that both Morgan and his successor
derived their ideas of registration from the same source.
The following extract from the Grand Lodge minutes
(Ancients) of March 1st, 1758, will shew that Dermott was
in communication with the Grand Secretary of Ireland at a
very early period.

"Heard a Letter from Mr. John Calder (G.S.) in Dublin wherein he assured the Grand Lodge of Antient Masons
in London that the Grand Lodge of Ireland did mutually
concur in a strict Union with the Antient Grand Lodge in
London, and promised to keep a Constant Correspondence
with them.

"Order'd that the Grand Secretary shall draw up an
Answer in the most Respectful and Brotherly Terms wherein
the General thanks of this Grand Lodge shall be convey'd,
and assure them that we will to the utmost of our powers
promote the wellfare of the Craft in General."

The first mention I have met with of Grand Lodge certificates on the "Modern" side is in the minutes of Grand
Lodge of 24th July, 1755, as follows :—

"Ordered, that every Certificate granted to a brother of
his being a mason, shall, for the future, be sealed with the
seal of Masonry, and signed by the Grand Secretary, for
which five shillings shall be paid to the General Fund of
Charity."

Dermott, with his usual smartness, soon availed himself
of this incident to have a shot at his rivals, for in a foot
note added to page 59 of his Grand Lodge minutes of 27th
December, 1755, he says, "This year 1755, the Modern
Masons began to make use of Certificates, Though the
Ancient Masons had granted Certificates time immemorial."
Which, being interpreted, means that the Grand Lodge of
Ireland had issued Certificates as far back as his own know-
ledge of Masonry extended, and the Society to which he
then belonged had granted them from its commencement;

of which there is independent evidence both in Morgan's register and in the Table of fees at the end of the first minute book. In 1751 and 1755 the Grand Secretary's fee for writing a "Certificate in English" was 1/-. The first mention of "A Latin and English Certificate" is in the Table of fees for 1756, for writing which his fee was 2/-.

I may here mention that the Modern Grand Lodge never issued Certificates in Latin and English; while the Grand Lodge of Ireland and that of the "Ancients" in London invariably did so, certainly for many years prior to the Union, for I have now before me two of these documents signed by the Grand Secretary of Ireland, one in 1808, the other in 1812. * Also several issued by the Ancients during the latter part of the last century. It will thus be seen that our present form of Certificate is derived from the "Ancients."

It is well known that Warrants issued by the "Moderns" only recognized the three Craft degrees, while those of the "Ancients" virtually included, from the first, the Royal Arch.

In order to show that Warrants issued by the G.L. of Ireland allowed a similar license, I will quote a portion of a letter written in 1782, by John Thompson, of Belfast, and addressed to the Grand Secretary of the "Moderns." "Tho' personally a stranger, yet my name cannot be wholly unknown to you; as, upon a retrospect, you will find it subscribed to a Petition presented to the Grand Lodge of England, two or three years ago, from the Lodge of St. Michael, Barbadoes, in which I had the honour of being Made, passed and raised. Having now been for some months past, on a visit to this, my native place, for the recovery of my health, and having made myself known as a

---

* Both these Certificates begin : "We Chiefs of the Enlightened Men of the Most Antient and Right Worshipful Lodge of St. John do hereby Certify that Brother" &c., &c.

Master Mason to my Brethren of the Lodge in this town
No. 257 on the list of regular Irish Lodges, they have
thought me worthy of being admitted amongst them as a
Member, and have in a Royal Arch and Knights Templars
Encampment, held in and under the sanction of their said
Lodge, conferred on me the high honour of those two degrees.
Whether or no I am now addressing myself to a Brother of
either or both of those Degrees, I know not, but if I be I
am persuaded that you will not disapprove of what I am
about to add, which is, that I have much at heart, upon my
return to Barbadoes, the forming a Royal Arch and Knights
Templars Encampments, under the sanction of the Lodge to
which I belong there. I am aware that I am likely to meet
with obstruction from the Provincial Grand Lodge of that
Island ; amongst the members of which I know there pre-
vails an opinion that those Degrees are unknown to the
English Constitution, and that therefore they cannot be
legally conferred in any Lodge held under the authority of
the Grand Lodge of England. I am persuaded that the
opinion I have mentioned is without foundation, Yet as I
cannot in St. Michael's Lodge, attempt anything which may
be judged illegal by the Provincial Grand Lodge, I wish to
be favoured with your sentiments, fully on this head.

"By a Brother lately returned from a voyage to the Island
of St. Christophers I learn that in the said Island, besides
several M. M. Lodges, which as he apprehends are held
under the Authority of the Grand Lodge of England, there
is a Lodge of Knights Templars, which latter he has understood derive their Constitution from the Old Kilwynnin
Lodge, or the Grand Lodge of Scotland ; and, I am credibly
informed that in case of my applying to the Grand Lodge of
Ireland, and producing a recommendation from the aforesaid
Lodge of this town, I could immediately obtain a Warrant
for holding a Lodge in Barbadoes ; which mode would at once
remove every difficulty, as there is no other authority ever

required for holding such Encampments as I have mentioned than the Common Warrant or Constitution, which it is necessary for all regular Lodges to have."

This letter seems to indicate a similarity between the Grand Lodges of Ireland, Scotland, and of the "Ancients" in England with regard to the scope of their Warrants.

Unfortunately, we have no record of the Grand Secretary's reply. As the letter was intended for his own private perusal it is not mentioned in the minutes of Grand Lodge.

The following is from a long letter written to Wm. White by Thos. Bryden of Whitehaven, dated 4th February, 1786 :—

"If you will lay this as soon as possible before the Grand, will you please favour us immediately with your reply, at the same time giving us to know when a Warrant for us may be made out. We are the more urgent to know this, as we believe it would come at a time when many respectable youths would enter our Order, but more particularly it would arrive at a time when dissentions prevail amongst a class, who have long been cajoled, and whose eyes are now opened to view themselves under an obsolete *Irish* Warrant ; and consequently be the means of establishing more than one or two Lodges in this town under the Grand Lodge, Lincoln's Inn Fields."

CHAPTER VI.

"ANCIENT" OR "MODERN"?—"THAT IS THE QUESTION."

"Together let us beat this ample field,
Try what the open, what the covert yield."—*Pope.*

ASONIC writers generally seem to be of opinion that the terms "Ancient" and "Modern" if correctly applied should be reversed. In other words, that the persons who assumed the title of "Ancient Masons" had no more real grounds for this distinction than they had for conferring the appellation of "Modern Masons" on the descendants of those who had formed a Grand Lodge in 1717. Of course if the relative age of the two Grand Lodges were the only consideration, this view would be just and reasonable; but it being quite clear that these expressions were in use prior to the formation of the Grand Lodge of the "Ancients" the question of seniority cannot possibly affect their derivation.

Unfortunately, we have no means of ascertaining when these phrases first came into general use; as already noted they are to be found in the earliest records of the "Ancients" as a regularly organized Society, and for what we know to the contrary, they may have been common expressions in the fraternity for many years prior to 1751.

Dermott and his friends are generally credited with having invented and adopted the terms for their own purposes, whereas it seems to me that they really borrowed them from their rivals; indeed I am strongly of opinion that we have to thank Dr. Anderson for their introduction into Masonry, for on page 133 of the Constitutions of 1738, in his account of the proceedings of Grand Lodge on the 31st March, 1735, he says:—"Brother Anderson was order'd also to insert in the New Edition of the Constitutions, the Patrons of Antient Masonry that could be collected from the Beginning of

Time, with the Grand Masters and Wardens antient and modern."

The words "antient and modern" are not in the original motion as written in the Grand Lodge minute book, nor have I met with them anywhere at an earlier period, although they are repeated in every edition of the Constitutions down to the Union. The inference, therefore, is that our enthusiastic historian invented them himself, and if he chose to apply the term "modern" to the Society of which he was a most distinguished member, I fail to see any just cause of complaint for a similar application of the expression by others a few years later. I am inclined to think that undue importance is attached to these designations, and that when the "Ancients," or Irish Masons, first applied the term "Moderns" to the adherents of the regular Grand Lodge, they were actuated more by a desire of making what they doubtless considered a just and necessary distinction between the two Societies than of using the words in a derogatory sense; it was not till their prosperity and influence attracted notice, and the officials of the rival community were called upon by their own members to answer rather awkward questions, that the bitterness of strife began, and the words, "Ancient" and "Modern" became really important expressions.

It will be seen from the wording of the following document that even so late as the year 1781, at all events one of the lodges on the regular list applied the term "Modern" to the authority under which it acted :—

"Lodge of Love and Honour No. 94.

"This is to Certify to all Masters of regular Lodges and Brethren in General under the Modern Constitution whereof His Grace the Duke of Manchester is present Grand Master, that Patrick Murray late Commander of the *Retalliation* private Ship of War, was made an Entered Apprentice, past a Fellow Craft, and raised to the Third

Degree of a Master Mason in this Lodge, the Twelfth Day of July Five Thousand Seven hundred and Eighty, and hereby recommend him as a worthy Brother and a true Supporter and Contributor to the Craft in General.

"Given under our hands and Seal of our Lodge at Falmouth this Thirtieth Day of May in the Year of Masonry Five Thousand Seven hundred and Eighty one.

"Willm. Calder, Mr.

"Thos. Williams, S.W.

"George Quash, J.W.

"John Bellhouse, Tr.

"J. Philip Elliot, Secretary."

I have also a letter before me dated, 11th December, 1771, applying for a Warrant for a lodge at Evesham, in which Heseltine is addressed as the Grand Secretary under the "Modern Constitution."

The greatest difficulty I, in common with everyone who has written on this subject, have to encounter, is in ascertaining the differences that existed in the recognised forms of the two rival societies. How the one body which, in point of organisation, was undoubtedly the younger, could have firmly and successfully maintained that they were of the real old stock, and that their opponents were of comparatively recent origin, has never yet been accounted for, at any rate not to my satisfaction. The old story of Dermott having made certain alterations in the ceremonies, and then palmed them off as ancient is utterly inconsistent. He could not have suddenly spread "a species of Masonry unknown in former times "* throughout Scotland and Ireland, yet it is quite evident that there were important differences in the two systems. I have already noticed instances of brethren of the Ancient *regime* being re-made in a Modern lodge ; and, in order to show that a similar course was

---

* " Revelations of a Square," p. 91.

adopted by the other side, I will give an extract from the
first minute book of the Neptune Lodge, No. 22, kindly
lent me by Bro. L. V. Walker, the present W. Master.
Being the oldest private lodge book of the Ancients I have yet
seen, I need hardly say it is exceedingly interesting, especially
as the first minutes, as well as a code of twenty-five By-
laws, are in the handwriting of Dermott. The Transactions
of the 24th of June, 1754, are as follows :—" Lodge open'd
at two at *Noon*, being the festival of St. John, Call'd off to
Refreshment at three, Call'd on in order to make Bror.
Robert Whitehall an Antient Mason, he being a Moddren
Mason before, Made him in all the parts. Master enstall'd
& Wardens, Call'd off the Second time to Refreshment,
Call'd on to Work. Clos'd at 10 with Good Harmony."

Here is an example of brevity which might well serve
as a pattern to some of our worthy secretaries of the present
day. From the fact that the joining brethren from either
side had to pass through the three degrees over again, it is
clear that the differences were not confined to one degree ;
the problem to be solved is Why, When, and How they
came about ? If we believe Dermott, most of them date
from the formation of the Grand Lodge in 1717, although
even he seems to have admitted that there was still a vestige
of Ancient Masonry extant in the rival system up to the
period of the initiation of Frederick, Prince of Wales (1737).
While confessing the highest admiration for the pluck and
ingenuity of our distinguished brother (I mean the one first
named), I must say I have grave doubts as to the truth of
his assertion in this particular instance. It is, I think,
generally acknowledged that symbolical or Speculative
Masonry originated in England, whence it spread rapidly
to adjacent countries, our extensive commercial relations
soon carrying it to the most distant parts of the world.

The actual period of its rise is, and will probably ever
remain a mystery ; but there can be no doubt that the for-

mation of the Grand Lodge in 1717 attracted a greater number of the educated class than had hitherto been found in its ranks, probably ·leading to certain alterations and possibly improvements in the forms (although this does not always follow), as well as in the customs and regulations of the Fraternity ; but as we have no certain knowledge as to the nature of the early ceremonies, my first suggestion must be taken on its merits. One thing is quite clear to my mind, that no such radical changes as are more than hinted at by Dermott would have been permitted by the old class of Masons, nor attempted by the new ones at this period. I refer to the ordinary modes of recognition.

Bro. Gould in his third volume gives some interesting particulars of early Masonry in Ireland, naturally one of the very first places beyond sea to welcome with open arms the most deservedly popular institution that ever existed ; for I may remind my readers that the extraordinary prejudice now evinced by some of our fellow subjects of the Roman Catholic faith was then comparatively unknown.* I may also mention for the information of a certain eminent personage residing in Rome, and who takes a very warm interest in our welfare, occupying himself occasionally, animated, no doubt by the *best* of motives, in sending us a sort of " Happy Dispatch ";—that several of our most popular Grand Masters were of his own " persuasion " I will make honourable mentiono f two only, viz., Thomas Howard, Duke of Norfolk, Grand Master in 1730 (who made valuable presents to the Society, including our celebrated Sword of State, formerly the property of the renowned Gustavus Adolphus of Sweden), and Robert Edward, 9th Lord Petre, who laid the first stone of, and also dedicated to " *Universal*

---

* The earliest reliable reference to the Craft in Ireland Gould has been able to find, bears date 17th July, 1725, and as this refers to the election of a Grand Master, there can be no doubt that symbolical Masonry had been known and practised in that country for several years before.

Charity and Benevolence," the Grand Hall of which we are justly proud, and towards the expenses of which he contributed most liberally ; indeed, nearly thrice as much as any other single individual. He also presided in person at several meetings of the Committee of Charity.

I have incidentally noticed the fact of Lord Kingston being Grand Master of England in 1728–9. This nobleman was evidently an enthusiastic Mason, he attended three meetings of Grand Lodge during his term of office. In *Peck's* list of the Grand Masters of Ireland his name is given as presiding over the Craft in that kingdom in the years 1729, 1731, 1735 and 1746, although the first year mentioned does not correspond with the account given by the Irish historian, Edward Spratt, who says on p. 121 of his Constitutions : " At last the antient Fraternity of the Free and Accepted Masons in *Ireland,* being assembled in their Grand Lodge at *Dublin* chose a Noble Grand Master in Imitation of their Brethren of *England,* in the third Year of his present Majesty King *George* the Second A.D. 1730, even our Noble Brother *James King* Lord Viscount *Kingston,* the very next Year after his Lordship had, with great Reputation been the Grand-Master of England ; and he has introduced the same Constitutions and Usages."

It is more than probable that Lord Kingston was an English Mason, and apart from the significance of the concluding words of the paragraph just quoted, it is most unlikely that he should have introduced, or even tolerated any such differences as were afterwards found to exist in the Irish and "Modern" English systems of Masonry. At all events there being no evidence to the contrary we may reasonably conclude that at this period the forms and usages were the same or similar in both countries.

Hitherto I have had little occasion to refer to Scotland, but will now venture to express an opinion that the assertion of the Ancients in the year 1752, "That they found the freemasons from Ireland and Scotland had been initiated in the very same manner as themselves,"* was made in perfect good faith, and I have not a shadow of doubt as to its being literally true. D. Murray Lyon on pp. 151, 2, 3, of his *"Masonry in Scotland,"* gives a very lucid account of a visit paid by Dr. Desaguliers to Edinburgh in the year 1721, and also cogent reasons for his desiring a conference with the principal Masons in that city, leaving no room for doubt that the new or symbolical system recently formulated in London was, if not actually introduced by the Doctor into the operative Scottish lodges, then more fully explained, and the old Craft customs altered and assimilated to the new English working.

The following extract from an original letter dated 15th October, 1776, will doubtless be read with interest :—

"1. His Grace the Duke of Athol would wish to know by what Authority the G. L. of England pretends to a supremacy over the G. L. of Scotland, Instituted by Royal Charter granted by King James the sixth to the family of Roslin in the year 1589, and then acknowledged to be the new head and first L. in Europe.

"2. Why the G. L. of England has thought propper to alter the mode of Initiation; also the Word, Pas-word & Grip of the different Degrees in Masonry.

"3. Whether Dermot constitutes Lodges in his own Name or in the name and Authority of the Duke of Athol, and whether anything can be laid to his charge, inconsistent with the character of an honest man and a Mason.

"4. Whether any mode of union could be thought of, and in such a manner, that might appear probable to both parties. I have promised His Grace an answer as soon as possible."

---

* I fancy had these words been spoken or written by English Masons "Ireland" would not have had first place, it would have been "Scotland and Ireland."

L

This letter is headed " Royal Military Academy" (Wool-
wich), and was written by Captain George Smith, Inspector
of that establishment, who shortly afterwards was appointed
Provincial Grand Master of Kent. * It is endorsed on the
back "Ans^d. J. H." in the handwriting of Heseltine the
Grand Secretary, but unfortunately I can find no trace of
the answer ; it is not in the letter book of the period, and I
am of opinion that a copy of it was not kept. The first of
the series of questions will probably be sufficiently answered
by the information that His Grace was then only *twenty-one*.

The second speaks for itself, and the third and fourth
appear to partake of the nature of a reply to an attack on
the much abused Dermott, as well as of a suggestion for an
amalgamation of the two Grand Lodges. At any rate that
is my interpretation of them, and if correct, the importance
of this document will readily be understood, as showing a
desire on the part of the " Moderns " for a reconciliation at
this early period with their despised rivals.

In order of date I will now quote a letter written to
Heseltine by George Yarde Sparke, Master of a lodge at
Dartmouth in 1782 : " a foreigner apply'd to the Lodge
of Friendship in this Town (over which I have the honour
to preside), and beg'd to be admitted as a visitor, said he
was made in the G. Lodge of Dublin, and produced a Certificate to that purpose. Upon examination he appear'd to
have been made antient, in consequence of which an ob-
jection was made to his being admitted, but after considering the matter he was at last admitted, (I was not in the
Lodge at the time) therefore have to beg of you to inform

---

* " The Grand Lodge of Scotland holds, by virtue of a Royal Charter
granted by James VI., to the family of Roslin."

Free-masons' Calendar, 1776, p. 37.

Captain Smith and Wm. Preston assisted in the compilation of the
Calendar at this period. Probably the Duke of Athole was studying at
the establishment named when this letter was written.

me whether it was right to admitt him or not, and in case
he should be remade under the Constitution of the Grand
Lodge of England (which he is very willing of) what fees
he ought to pay."

This letter is endorsed " Ans^{d.} " but we have no copy
of the reply, and to avoid repetition, I may state that this
remark will apply to future letters quoted.

The next document I shall reproduce in full; it is headed
"Maidstone, Kent, March, 1791," and is addressed to Mr.
Wm. White (the then Grand Secretary of the "Moderns.")

" Sir,

" As a Brother who admires the venerable institution
of Free-masonry, I take the liberty of requesting your
opinion on a particular point, trusting that, as far as is in your
power, you will return me a satisfactory answer. I have
often lamented the distinction that has been introduced in
this Country among Masons, that of *Antient* and *Modern*—a
distinction no way favorable to the reputation of the Craft—
a distinction which by restraining its universality, strikes
deep at the root of its Philanthropic principles, and prevents
the expansion of that benign influence which is the boast
and glory of our respectable fraternity. However necessary
(as a check to the gross abuses that were making alarming
inroads into the very vitals of the institution) it may have
been to make a trivial alteration, I presume the Grand
Lodge of England does not consider Masons regularly made
under the constitutions of other countrys, as aliens to the
Craft, nor deem it unconstitutional to admit Bretheren of
France, Germany, Scotland, &c., &c., into our Modern lodges.*
A circumstance of this nature lately happened in this town,
upon which, for the satisfaction of many respectable Brothers,
I shall be glad to have your advice.

"A person who is a regular Mason under the Grand Lodge

---

* Why is Ireland not mentioned ?

L 2

of Scotland, applied for admission at the Lodge of Fortitude here, on last St. John's day—was examined and admitted—was present at a subsequent meeting, and on last lodge night objected to, as having not been made a *Modern* Mason.　He stated, that formerly residing in another country, he conceived, that by joining himself to our august Society there, he became a Mason in the most extensive and universal sense of the word, that in the place where he had the honor to be initiated, no difference of that kind was known ; that Masonry considered in its true spirit, entertained no such contracted principles, but in imitation of the Grand luminary the Sun diffused its genial rays for the welfare of the brethcren in every part of the Globe.　That also as a *Scotch* Mason, he had introduced himself to several lodges in London, to one of which he is actually at this time a subscribing member, that in the course of the many lectures he had attended, had occasion to go thro' every material part, and, of consequence, considered himself as entitled to admission into any lodge in England, within certain degrees.　To all this it was briefly answered, that he could not be admitted, unless he would submit to be *made* in a modern lodge.

" Your thoughts on this subject will honor

" Sir, your obedt. Servant,

" John Cockburn."

This letter requires very little comment.　No doubt it aptly illustrates the anomalous condition of English Masonry at the time it was written.　I may, however, mention that the words in italics are underlined in the original ; and the allusion to " gross abuses," " trivial alteration," &c., was evidently founded on the statement in the manifesto already referred to in these pages.

Notwithstanding the inconvenience of this state of things it was not without its amusing side, for the letters intended for one Society, especially when sent from abroad, not infrequently reached the camp of the enemy, and were attended

to *" in due course"* as though coming from their own
adherents. I need hardly say that these mistakes were
generally on the part of the body that kept no register of its
foreign members.

On the 12th November, 1777, the " Modern" Grand
Lodge, upon the recommendation of their Committee of
Charity, unanimously voted the sum of " One Hundred
Pounds towards the relief of many distressed Masons at
Halifax in Nova Scotia, pursuant to a representation of
their unfortunate situation at this time by the Lodge No. 1
in the said town of Halifax."

The sequel will be found in the following extracts from
a long letter written in 1783 by Wm. White, Joint Grand
Secretary with Heseltine, addressed to the " Master of the
Lodge of Free Masons, Halifax, Nova Scotia." " I have to
acknowledge the receipt of your favour of the 17th May last,
addressed to our worthy Bro. Jas. Heseltine enclosing Copies
of papers from you to the Grand Lodge of Ancient York
Masons, by which I am sorry to find a disinclination in
you to be considered as part of our Society, which we
once flattered ourselves you were, and under which idea the
remittance of £100 was made to you for the relief of distressed Brethren in your parts."

*   *   *   *   *   *

" However I would not wish to be understood as want-
ing to dissuade you from your attachment to the Ancient
York Masons, tho' at the same time I must acknowledge it
would give great pleasure to see such respectable Characters
as I now address enrolled among the Lodges under the Constitution of the Grand Lodge of England.

" As our remittance to you originated from a mistake
that you either were or wished to be a part of our Body, I
am directed to request that you will return it to Rowland
Berkeley Esqr., Gd. Treasurer, Jas. Heseltine, Esqr., G.S. or
to the undersigned, for altho' our duty & inclinations urge us

to universal Benevolence—yet the paucity of our funds & the many claims on it, makes it necessary to confine our relief to those within the circle of our own Society." *

I will now direct attention to another game of cross purposes which confirms the proverb, " Out of evil cometh good," by affording me very material assistance in this enquiry.

In order to render this incident perfectly intelligible it will be necessary to present for perusal several extracts from letters written by a Major Shirreff, who, in the year 1784, had retired upon half-pay and settled at Whitchurch. Doubtless his military service had accustomed him to writing under difficulties, for his letters frequently bear the appearance of having been written in great pain, as he himself sometimes tells us was the case ; nevertheless, they are generally very lengthy, yet so quaint and interesting, that I almost regret the necessity of curtailing them. The first is addressed:—

"To Doct.ʳ· Robert Bath, No. 399 Oxford St. London," and is dated 23rd April, 1785. After referring to some bodily ailments, he says :—

" To unfold what I have to tell you I must acquaint you that I am an Antient Mason of 27 y'rs standing & from an Enter'd Apprentice have for some years past arrived to the highest Order in that Hon'ble Society, & been Master of sev'l Lodges, & Constituted one in the Island of Jersey, there is only one Bro'r here and he is only in the 1st Degree : & I do not find either in this County or in Cheshire a Grand Lodge or Power Invested in any Body that I could obtain a Deputation to Constitute a Lodge here w'ch I mean to Establish on the Antient Plan, as sev'l Respectable Characters have already made application to me to become Members of it, & for the first setting out, I can have a Master or two from Chester to assist me, till I have strength enough here to proceed, therefore I wish to know what the expences will be for obtaining this Power from the

---

* I find no record of the return of the " Hundred Pounds."

Grand Lodge, w'th the Book of Constitutions, the Masons
Songs, three Mahogany Candlesticks, three Mallets, a han-
some Bible, Square, Compass, and other Necessary Implements for Conducting this Bussiness, and I beg you will be
particular in Informing yourself from the Sec'y of the G'd
Lodge what these Expences under the sev'l heads will
amount to, that I may have a Consultation here & determine ab't it, and also send me every requisite necessary for
me to do, when I may trouble you again on this Bussiness:
or send me the G'd Sec'y's address, should your time not
permit you to do it, & when we are fix'd here on our plan the
Expences shall be paid directly by my Agent; I wish them
to be frugal, as I am only on half-pay & cannot afford
much from it, but being willing to support the Society to the
last is the only reason that Induces me to Conduct a Lodge
in these Degrees any more, Having after the three first
Degrees full Powers Invested in me by Commission to act &
do as I think proper, for w'ch purpose I am a Deputy Inspect'r
Gen'l & arrived to the *Ne plus ultra.*

"N.B.—I am known by Letter to Wm. Dickey, Esqr.,
who was 1st May 5778 Dep'y G'd Master appointed by the
Duke of Atholl, & as you know me also in this sphere, as well
as Mr. Ruspini, no objections can be made—Please to remember that I keep up to Antient Masonry & will adhere
to none other."

The next letter is headed "Whitchurch in Shropshire,
1st May, 1785," and is addressed "To the Secretary of the
Grand Lodge of London."

"Sir,

"I beg Leave to Introduce myself to you as an
Antient Mason in its highest Degree, have been Master of
sev'l Lodges in America, & Constituted one in the Island of
Jersey of the Registery of Guernsey, & after 32 years'
service in the Military line, have made this my Residence,
& did not purpose working in the Lower Degrees of

Masonry any more, but as many Respectable persons here are willing to become Members of this Hon'ble Society, & will be a Credit to it, Causes me to Relinquish my former opinion for the good of the Craft, & to become their Master & form a Body here, and work in the Antient way as I always have done ; to accomplish which, not having the pleasure of knowing the G'd Lodge's Sec'y, I wrote to my worthy friend, Dr. Bath, fully on this head, that I might on his answer know how to proceed ; and as I am from the Rheumatism in too much pain to repeat to you here what I wrote him, I have beg'd of him either to see you in person, or else acquaint you by L'r with that part I wrote him Respecting Masonry, we'h I doubt not he will do, as many things can be done in our Society in cases of Emergency.

*   *   *   *   *   *

"I hope to have the Hon'r of a Line from you, to inform me what I wish to know, I shall on y'r Answer write you fully on this Bussiness, in the Interim I am, Sir, &c., &c.

"C. SHIRREFF.

"This will be given, or forwarded to you by Bro. Bath."

This letter, evidently intended for the "Antients," somehow went to the opposition camp, for on the 27th June following the old soldier writes another, and addresses it himself "To Mr. William White, Freemasons' Hall, Great Queen Street, Lincoln's Inn Fields, London."

"Sir,

"I had the pleasure to receive your favor in answer to mine of the first Ultimo, on the 24th inst., and am Led to think that you & I were Initiated in the same way, & I am the more confirm'd in it, as I find the Provincial G.M. for Guernsey and Jersey is in your Registery, & by a Warrant from him (T. Dobree, Esqre.) I Constituted a Lodge in Jersey in '65, No. 1, in the Town of St. Helary's, and is in my printed List of Lodges, No. 349 : I worked in that Body as I had ever been taught, & left them a very Respect-

able one in '68, & had the thanks of the G'd M'r for my
attention to the Crafft, & as I have arrived at the *Ne plus
Ultra*, or 25. Step, I am the more convinced. I was Intro-
duced into this Noble Institution according to the most
Antient manner, & that you may understand me more
clearly, when a Candidate is presented to me, my first
Instruction to him springs from the Second Le'r of the
Alphabet, & I never knew but one Lodge since I have been
a Bro'r that ever begun with the ninth Le'r I have met
several Brothers that have been Initiated so ; but all such
I was from the first told were call'd Modern Masons, and as
I have been in the Society upwards of 32 years,* I have
Represented many Bodys, & being fond of it, I never miss'd
visiting Lodges when in my power, & always found them of
my sentiments, & worked in the same manner.   Except the
one already mentioned, where I gain'd Admittance and
found them Regular in their proceedings & their method of
Making, &c., very little different from that of mine, so that
I lament there should be any dissensions in the Society, as
from its first Institution it was never intended should be any.*

" I am in hopes from what I have now related I shall
find from your Answer that we agree together, which will
give me satisfaction : I am ever open to conviction, but till
such time as I can be persuaded in my own mind, & from
good grounds, that I have not from the 1st been Introduced
as I now think I have, in the Most Antient way : none can
blame me for adhering to my present Tenets.

*   *   *   *   *   *

" Except in one Lodge in America our W't was from

---

* There is something wrong here, it is 27 in the first letter.

* Several alleged differences between the two systems are pointed out
in various Masonic pamphlets published in the latter half of the last
century, and the early part of the present, and it is but fair to mention
that they are generally in accord with the description given by the writer
of this letter.

the G'd Lodge in Scotland ; all the others I was in held by W'ts from the G'd Lodge in England, the last I belonged to was in E. Florida & in the G'd Lodge I presided in every capacity ; in '78 the Duke of Atholl was G'd M'r, & Wm. Dickey, Esq., was D.G. M'r, & transmitted to me at St. Augustine a Warrent for the 14th Regt. & in these Lodges I worked as I ever did, and in '80, when I left that Province there were three Respectable Body's besides the Grand one, so that upon the whole I think we are one and the same thing."

We may assume that mutual and satisfactory explanations were given, as a Warrant was eventually granted for the Whitchurch Lodge, No. 478, of which Shirreff was first Master, but whether he continued "to work in the Antient way," or became modernized in his old age, is not quite clear. I have carefully read his numerous letters, and they do not indicate any change in this respect, indeed I am inclined to think he was hardly the sort of person to be easily convinced that he had been wrong during the whole of his Masonic career.

There is no doubt as to the truth of his statement about the lodge at St. Helary's being Constituted in 1765, for it appears in the engraved list for the next year under the No. he mentions; nor do I see any reason for disbelieving his assertion, "I worked in that Body as I had ever been taught," for I think it very probable that many of the foreign lodges on the "Modern" roll, especially those in America, never deviated materially from the ancient customs.

On the 17th November, 1785, he writes to White as follows :—

"On the 15th Instant with the assistance of three masters from Chester, and two besides myself here, I open'd the Lodge in the usual way, & haveing one above the Number that can Constitute ; it was accordingly done, and Named the Whitchurch Lodge, No. 1, to be held at the White

Lion Inn, in said Town. Now in America Every Master you can get is generally present at Constituting Lodges, five will do it, but not four, so that you will now know what I meant by having one Master to spare.

" Agreeable to your Desire I now send you a List of the members that compose this Body, viz., C : Shirreff, Master, Rev'd Francis Henry Egerton, S.W., Wm. L. Brooks, J.W., Arthur Blaney, S.D., Wm. Turner, J.D., James Turner Meakin, Stew'd, Rev'd Godfrey Wolley, Treasurer, Rev'd John Collier, Secretary, Peter Newton, and Richard Bentley, Tylers."

A month later he writes, "I have the pleasure to acquaint you that every one seems Determined to observe the Antient Customs of Masonry."

This coupled with the appointment of Deacons,* seems to support my idea that he did not alter his mode of working.

The zeal of our military brother cannot be questioned, and he may fairly be credited with having resuscitated the Order in Shropshire. In one of his letters he intimates that he intends applying for the Provincial Grand Mastership, " Provided it is within the reach of his Finances," but having previously told the Grand Secretary that he was " on half-pay at 2/6 pr. diem," it is just possible that his " Finances" were deemed scarcely sufficient to enable him to support the office with becoming dignity. Although the honour of the highest place was unattainable, he advised his S.W. the Rev. Francis Egerton, a son of the then

---

* I have somewhere read that Deacons were unknown in the " Modern" lodges. They certainly were not considered essential, but in a list of the members of No. 263 Darlington, returned in 1770, all the officers are named, including a Deputy Master and two Deacons. This lodge is now The Restoration Lodge, No. 111. And in a list of the officers for the year 1772, of No. 243, Barnard Castle, Senr. & Junr. Deacons are mentioned. I have also met with them in other lodges on the " Modern" roll, so that I think we may take it for granted that the office, though not deemed essential, was optional with them.

Bishop of Durham, to apply for the post, who got it in
1786, and of course appointed Shirreff his Deputy.

He became very intimate with the Grand Secretary and
some of the leading London Masons, whom he innoculated
with his "*Ne Plus Ultra*" notions, warranted genuine as
imported, from Prussia, *via* America, * but the information
most desirable, viz., where he first joined the fraternity, his
letters do not give.   In 1795 he seems to have had a difference of opinion with his chief, which resulted in the D.G.
Mastership becoming vacant.

I have already noticed the sensation created by the publication of Prichard's pamphlet in 1730, when the "D.G.M.
recommended several things to the consideration of the
Grand Lodge," and I will now state, without fear of contradiction, that in no part of the records is there a passage
so capable of being interpreted as forming a prelude to an
alteration in the recognized forms as the one referred to.
A second edition of a rather curious, and now scarce, book
on Masonry was published in London in 1766, † which pro-
fesses to show the differences between the "Ancient" and
"Modern" systems. The writer states that the then E. A.'s
Word was formerly the F. C.'s " till a pretended Discovery of
Free Masonry came out wrote by Samuel Pritchard, and
still continues to be published to this time.   It is about
Three-fourths Fiction, and the Fourth *real*, though he has
been so audacious as to verify the Truth of the whole by an
oath, which is annexed to his spurious Performance in order
to propagate the sale and make a confusion amongst the
Brotherhood ; the latter of which it did, in Regard to the

---

* He writes on the 14th November, 1785, "After the three first Degrees
my Patent which gives me such extensive Powers in the Process of this
Work, proceeds from His Majesty of Prussia, through one of the Deputy
Grand Inspectors in North America, over all Lodges wherever held at
the Distance of 25 Leagues from each other round the Globe, and I have
the Honor to be one of the D : G : I : &c., &c."

† Printed for Johnson and Davenport in Pater-noster Row.

Fourth *real* part; But, in order to prevent being imposed
upon by Cowans or Impostors, who might want to gain
Admittance from his Performance, the Fraternity held a
general Council, and the E. A.'s and F. C.'s Words were
reversed, and Private Accounts transmitted to each Lodge,
tho' there are some unconstituted Lodges still retain the
former Custom." We can readily appreciate the disparaging
remarks this author applies to Prichard's pamphlet, but it
is not so easy to find a motive for his story about changing
the words.

According to his own account he knew nothing of
Masonry before 1753. It is not at all likely that he ever
had access to the Grand Lodge Minutes, and Anderson says
nothing about the Prichard incident; my inference is, that
it is a case of "from information received." Having been
able to verify other assertions of this writer, I can only come
to the conclusion that his story is reasonable, and therefore
not inconsistent with truth. There is another curious fact
which ought not to be lost sight of in considering this
question, which seems to me to be something more than "a
remarkable coincidence," it is, that wherever we have reliable
evidence of the introduction of Speculative Masonry prior to,
or in the year 1730, the particular words of the degrees are
the same as those used by the Ancient fraternity in England;
while in France and Germany where we have no definite
knowledge of the Order until after the period named, and
then from "Modern" sources, the latter system is generally
adopted.

In the regular Grand Lodge, April 12th, 1809, the
following Resolution was passed, printed in the report, and
circulated amongst the lodges under its jurisdiction :—

"That this Grand Lodge do agree in Opinion with the
Committee of Charity, that it is not necessary any longer to
continue in Force those Measures which were resorted to, in
or about the year 1739, respecting irregular Masons, and

do therefore enjoin the several Lodges to revert to the Ancient Land-Marks of the Society."

We have in this Resolution two very important admissions on the part of the body from which it emanated, namely, that they had previously departed from the " *Ancient Land-Marks* " *of the Order*, and were ignorant of the precise period when this event occurred.

At this time there was a general feeling on both sides that an union of the two Sections of the Order was within measurable distance, and the passing of the foregoing Resolution was evidently intended to smoothe the way to so desirable a consummation.

The result of this decision was the issuing of a Warrant, dated 26th October, 1809, authorising certain brethren " to hold a special lodge for the purpose of ascertaining and promulgating the Ancient Land Marks of the Craft which Warrant empowers them to add to the Lodge such discreet and intelligent Brethren as to them may seem proper."

The first meeting under this Warrant was held on the 21st November, 1809, when it was " Resolved that this Lodge be called ' The Special Lodge of Promulgation,' " and the number was increased by the election of twenty-five new members, who appear to have been selected from the most distinguished brethren of the "Modern " Society, including the Duke of Sussex and several Provincial Grand Masters. My quotations from the minutes of this lodge must of necessity be few, as well as carefully selected, and will therefore probably be deemed worthy of particular attention.

I may premise that the meetings were held once a week at Freemasons' Hall, and that nothing of sufficient interest for reproduction transpires until the fourth meeting of the lodge, on the 13th December, when it was " Resolved that Deacons (being proved on due investigation to be not only Ancient but useful and necessary officers) be recommended." After discussing certain points in the ceremonies it was also

" Resolved that the following obligations shall be conformed to by the Members of this Lodge."

"We do hereby solemnly engage and obligate ourselves not to reveal improperly any of the Secrets or Mysteries Forms or Ceremonies of Ancient Masonry which we now know, which have been, or may hereafter be communicated unto us."

At the next meeting (22nd December) Brother Charles Valentine, of the Lodge of Antiquity No. 1, was unanimously elected a member. This brother is registered as having *joined* that lodge in 1801, and R. F. Gould in *Atholl Lodges*, p. 46, mentions a Charles Valentine as having been expelled from the " Ancient " body " for various irregularities, including the taking of the Warrent of said lodge (No. 245) to a Society called ' Modern ' Masons." I have no doubt, therefore, that this Valentine of the Lodge of Promulgation was the identical person thus referred to by Gould, for from the time of his becoming a member of the last named lodge, references are to be met with in the minutes to the " Proceedings of the Athol Lodges," certain points previously discussed, were reconsidered, and decisions arrived at thereon ; he is mentioned by name on several occasions as describing the Ancient practice in the various ceremonies, and several of his suggestions were adopted for promulgation amongst the lodges.

"The near prospect of an Union with the Athol Lodges" is referred to, and during one of the adjournments for refreshment to which the Masters of lodges were invited, in order, I presume, that profit and pleasure might be the result, " the R.W.M. introduced the Toast of the Duke of Athol, with appropriate observations on the prevailing hopes and expectations attached to it."

On the 19th October, 1810, it was " Resolved that it appears to this Lodge, that the ceremony of Installation of Masters of Lodges is one of the two Landmarks of the Craft, and ought to be observed."

" Resolved that it be referred to those members of this Lodge who are Installed Masters, to Install the R.W.M. of this Lodge, and under his direction take such measures as may appear necessary for Installing Masters of the Lodges."

Sixteen members attended the next meeting, only four of whom appear to have been regularly installed, although they are, with one exception, represented as Masters of lodges on the " Modern " side ; three out of the four were members of the Lodge of Antiquity, including Valentine, the other was Thomas Carr, Master of No. 30. As an example of the laxity of the times, I may mention that this brother, although appointed by the Grand Master, one of the original members of the Lodge of Promulgation was not registered in the Grand Lodge Book as a member of the lodge of which he is described as Master ; he may have been originally an " Ancient," as might also some of the other members, as the " Modern " register, unlike that of the " Ancients," throws no light upon the antecedents of joining Members.

The following is extracted from the minutes of 16th November, 1810 :—

" The proceedings in open lodge preparatory to the cere-mony of Installation having been conducted in due form, Brothers John Bayford, Grand Treasurer (No. 1), Thomas Carr (No. 30), Charles Valentine and Charles Bonnor (No. 1), being themselves Installed Masters, retired to an adjoining chamber, formed a Board of Installed Masters according to the *Ancient Constitutions* of the Order, and forthwith Installed Bro. James Earnshaw R.W.M. of this Lodge, and of the St. Albans Lodge, No. 22."

The other members of the Lodge of Promulgation who were present were then " Installed in the same manner."

In order to give more time for the masters of the lodges to attend for the purpose of being regularly Installed, the Grand Master, at the request of the members, renewed the

powers of the Lodge of Promulgation for two months beyond
the date for which the Warrant was originally intended,
the 31st December, 1810 ; the lodge therefore continued to
act till the end of February, 1811. The Masters of all the
Lodges in London and its vicinity (Moderns) were ultimately summoned for the purpose specified, and any master
or other brother presenting himself with a certificate from
his lodge, of his having served the office of Warden and
been duly elected to that of Master, was then and there
regularly installed, as were also several Provincial Grand
Masters, as well as the Earl of Moira, the Acting Grand
Master himself, who had filled that distinguished office from
the year 1790.

It is therefore perfectly clear that the " Moderns " had,
certainly for many years, dispensed with the ceremony of
Installation, while their rivals had kept up the old custom
in this respect, as will be seen by a reference to the extracts
from their records.

On the 14th December, 1810. " It was resolved that
the members of the Lodge of Promulgation shall dine
together at their own expense on Thursday the 27th instant
being the Festival of Saint John the Evangelist." This
incident, although at first sight unimportant, is not without
its significance, as evincing a desire on the part of the
" Moderns " to revive an old custom most rigidly observed
by the " Ancients," but which they themselves had neglected
for a very long period, that of holding a festival on Saint
John's Day.

At the next meeting, on the 28th December, eighteen
members of the lodge and forty Masters of other lodges
attended, and the " R.W.M. took a retrospective view of the
proceedings of the Lodge of Promulgation." I need not
reproduce everything that was said and done on this occasion, no doubt the following extract will be sufficient for our
present purpose :—" The R.W.M. therefore proceeded to

M

point out the material parts in and between the several Degrees to which the attention of the Masters of Lodges would be requisite in preserving the Ancient Land Marks of the Order,—such as the form of the Lodge, the number and situation of the Officers—their different distinctions in the different Degrees—the restoration of the proper words to each Degree, and the making of the pass words *between* one Degree and another,—instead of *in* the Degree."

The preceding extracts afford ample proof that the "Moderns" had at last been brought to see the "error of their ways"; their readiness to revert to the Ancient forms and ceremonies is much to their credit, and speaks volumes for their intelligence and genuine Masonic spirit. The whole of the proceedings appear to have been conducted with the utmost harmony, and the alterations suggested by the lodge were received and adopted with marked unanimity; indeed, so popular had the Lodge of Promulgation become, that on the 22nd February, 1811, a petition to the Earl of Moira was drawn up and signed by seven Masters of lodges, on behalf of twenty-eight other Masters, asking for a further renewal of the Warrant for twelve months, to enable Wardens to attend the meetings, "in order that a knowledge of the Ancient Land Marks of Masonry may be more generally diffused." This petition was not, however, acceded to, as active negotiations were then proceeding with a view of uniting the two Grand Lodges.

I shall now endeavour to show that, apart from the question of form or ceremony, innovations upon the ancient usages and established customs of the Order had, at different times, been countenanced by the leaders of the regular Grand Lodge; that from the advent of the aristocratic element in such large numbers, the Society had undergone a process, of what for want of a better word, I shall call modernizing. The 24th of June and the 27th of December were literally "*red letter days*" in the old Masonic Calendar, and are still regarded by many of the fraternity with veneration. In the metropolis of England no particular importance is attached to these dates, and in the provinces their significance is being gradually lost sight of, but formerly a very different state of things existed. On these days the new officers were installed and the Annual Festival was celebrated. In the country there was the procession to church in full regalia, the Masonic sermon, the collection for the local charities, and the convivial supper "when all grave business is over." Indeed the Saints John days were generally looked upon as *the* days for all important Masonic gatherings, not only in this country but in Scotland and Ireland also. Our first Grand Master (Anthony Sayer) was elected and installed on St. John Baptist's day, 1717, and this day was adhered to by the Grand Lodge for the installation of his successors until 1725, when "being unprovided with a new noble Grand Master, the officers were continued six months longer." Lord Paisley was, however, installed on the 27th December following; Lord Inchiquin on the 27th February, 1727; Lord Coleraine on the 27th December of the same year; and Lord Kingston on the 27th December, 1728. From this time forward the "regulars" seem to have been utterly oblivious of the fact,—

> " That saints will aid if men will call."

for the eighteen installations between 1730 and 1753 appear to have taken place on a day best suited to the convenience of the noble personage most concerned, and not once on either of the popular Saint's days. Now this irreverent disregard of an old custom was not likely to strengthen their claims to antiquity when put forth at a later period. The "Ancients" from the very first seem to have been most scrupulous in selecting one or the other of these days for their Grand ceremonials.

Their first Grand officers were taken on a six months' probation at a "Grand Committee" on the 5th December,

1753, and the record states that they were installed on that day; if so, it was probably done hurriedly and without thought, for on the 27th of the same month the Grand Master gave orders for " The whole Ceremony of Grand Installation " to be repeated. They were re-elected at the end of their term for a similar period and " solemnly Installed " on the 24th June, 1754.

From this time up to the Union in 1813 their Grand Officers were invariably installed on St. John the Evangelist's Day (27th December).

In the early days of the original Grand Lodge the members undoubtedly had the privilege of electing the whole of the Grand Officers; this was also the custom observed in the Grand Lodges of Scotland and Ireland, and was still continued in their assemblies long after it had become a prerogative of the ruler of the senior body. As will have been seen the " Ancients " adopted the old and popular mode of selection from their earliest organization. I am not prepared to say it was the better method, for it certainly in no way contributed to the harmony and good-fellowship of the fraternity in London, and occasionally led to some rather lively scenes in the Grand Lodge itself, which is not a matter of surprise considering the social status of a great majority of the electors. This, however, is a question of fact rather than of superiority.

On the subject of Stewards for the Grand Festival, as well as of the social position of the brethren, a resemblance may be observed between the regular Grand Lodge in the first stage of its existence and that of the "Ancients" at a later period; no such official being recognized by the former body until several years after it was established, and then they were at first chosen at irregular intervals by the members, while on the part of the latter I find no mention of Grand Stewards until the 12th of June, 1767, when in accordance with the old custom, six were nominated, or, to be strictly correct, four were chosen "with liberty to chuse two more on St. John's Day next." The number was afterwards increased to twelve, but the old mode of selection was not altered, nor did the office confer any special privileges, as on the other side, not even that of paying a large portion of the expenses of the day.

Having, I think, conclusively proved that the "Ancients" preserved and practised more of the old customs than their rivals (and it was evidently upon this ground alone that they assumed their distinctive title), it is but fair that I should briefly notice the one feature, which seems to militate against their claim of being *bonâ fide* Ancient Masons. I allude to their adoption of and working the Royal Arch degree under the ordinary Craft Warrant. It is not my present intention to enter upon a general disquisition on this branch of our Order, the subject having been recently most ably handled by an eminent writer whose views on the question are in general accord with my own.* I will however state, for the information of the reader, that both the date and place of its origin are at present uncertain. Earlier writers credit Dermott with having concocted it and introduced it into England as a part of the "Ancient" system. I reject the first part of this theory as being contrary to evidence, and I can hardly believe that the degree was known in England, or indeed anywhere else, under its present title prior to 1740.

Dermott says he was exalted in Dublin in 1746, and as this agrees with the date given for his Installation as Master, I see no reason to doubt the truth of his statement. My own opinion is that, although not officially recognised by the "Modern" Grand Lodge, Royal Arch Masonry was practised by some of the adherents of that body in England quite as early as it was elsewhere.

The earliest reference to the Royal Arch in the Grand

---

* *"Origin of the English Rite of Freemasonry."* W. J. Hughan.

Lodge records appears in the Minutes of a Grand Committee of the "Ancients," September 2nd, 1752, when Dermott gave a lecture, "and every part of Real freemasonry was traced and explained except the Royal Arch."

The degree is not mentioned again in the minutes till the 2nd March, 1754, when it was Ordered, "The Masters of the Royal Arch shall be summoned to meet in order to regulate things relative to that most valuable branch of the Craft."

A still wider gap may be observed between the last reference and the following :—" 4th Dec., 1771, At a General Grand Chapter held on the above date it was Resolved, That no person for the future shall be made a Royal Arch Mason but the Legal Representative of the Lodge, except a brother that is going abroad who hath been twelve months a Registered Mason."

The first R. A. Register of the "Ancients" was begun in 1783 by Dermott, whose name heads the list, and I have no doubt such of my readers as may have been led to believe that this Order was originated by that personage and his associates will be surprised to learn that, including himself, only eight brethren are entered as having been exalted prior to the end of 1770. Of these, two are stated to have taken the degree in Ireland in 1746 and 1767, two in Scotland in 1768 and 1770, and one in America in the latter year.

When this register was opened a Resolution was passed "That for the better preservation of the Supreme Degree of Free Masonry (aforesaid) the names of all the Regular Royal Archmen shall be recorded (gratis) in a particular Book prepared for that purpose."

Only twenty names of brethren from all parts are registered as having been exalted between the year 1770 and 1780, so that notwithstanding the early reference to the R. A. in the minutes of the "Ancients" it is evident that the degree was not at this period extensively patronized by that body.

The earliest known R. A. records of the "Moderns"

show a striking contrast to the torpid condition of the degree
under the Ancient *regime*, being the minutes of an independent chapter in full swing in 1765, supported by some of
the most active members of the " Modern " Grand Lodge,
several of whom afterwards became Grand Officers, a distinction, which at that time, none dared aspire to save
those who were blessed with a pretty well-filled purse.
Taken generally, they were certainly not the sort of people
to be found in the ranks of the rival Society, although to
this rule there is to be found the time-honoured exception,
which in this instance is of so curious a nature that I feel
bound to notice it. It is the appearance, amongst the
original members, of our former acquaintance, and Dermott's
antagonist, the notorious " Mr. John Hamilton," who it
will be remembered was expelled from the " Ancient" Grand
Lodge in 1757. There is no doubt as to the identity of
this person, for the address and designation (Painter) are the
same in both books ; there is also another unmistakable
point of resemblance ; and that is the word " Expell'd "
written against his name in the List of Members, an explanation of which is to be found in the minutes of 13th
November, 1765 :—

" Bro^r. Potts and Bro^r. Hamilton not having conformed
to the By Laws, are ordered to be expell'd."

The first minutes recorded in this book refer to a meet-
ing held on the 22nd March, 1765, and are as follows :—
" The most Excellent Grands and Brethren met at Mr.
Inge's. Br. Bourcard, Br. Paken, & Br. Vander Upwich
pass'd the Arch and paid the fine of one Guinea £3 3 0
Bro^r. Williamson pass'd the Arch & pd. a fine of 0 5 0
Rec^d. of Br. Inge the Balance in his hands ... 0 12 0

					4	0	0
Expences this Night ...	...	...	...	...	1	14	2
Balance in hand	...	...	...		2	5	10

It will thus be seen that the Chapter must have met before or there would have been no balance to be brought forward. Who the "Most Excellent Grands" were is not stated, but they were evidently appointed at a previous meeting or they would have been referred to in a different manner. From the 22nd of March to the 12th June (inclusive), ten brethren are named as having "pass'd the Arch," and on the day last mentioned, which was election day, 34 members were actually present.

It is impossible to say, with anything like certainty, how long this Chapter had been working prior to the meeting of the 22nd March. The remark previously made with reference to lodges will apply with equal force to Chapters, viz., that the mere absence of written records is no proof of non-existence. I am inclined to think that this particular Chapter was formed but a short time before, say about one year, for I fancy I can trace, by the aid of a glass, "Feby., 1764" on the cover of the minute book; but that there were other and probably older Chapters known and acknowledged by the "Moderns" at this time, I have not the least doubt. By-Law 6, passed on the 12th June, 1765, is to this effect :—" That none but Members shall be admitted to sit in the Chapter unless on very particular occasions; and then such Visitors shall pay Half a Guinea each to the current expence."

On the 12th February, 1766, it was "Resolved (unanimously) That from henceforth no Brother be admitted a member of this Chapter, for less than Two Guineas, including the sum he has already paid at his admission, unless he can give satisfactory Proof that he received his Exaltation before the Twelfth Day of June last, or in the Caledonian Chapter, or some Chapter in the Country, or beyond the Seas; in which cases he may be admitted on Payment of One Guinea to the General Fund.

"Likewise Resolved. That the Companions belonging

to, & having been Exalted in the Caledonian Chapter, or any
Chapter in the Country, or Abroad being properly vouched
for, shall be admitted Visitors in this Chapter on payment
of Two Shillings & sixpence each."

On the 8th of January, 1766, Thomas Dunckerley was
proposed to become a member, and on the same night
elected to the third Chair; it is clear, therefore, that he
must have been exalted in some other lodge or Chapter.
Dunckerley was a natural son of George II., and one
of the most enthusiastic Masons of his time; until recently the lodge in which he was initiated was unknown,
and I was inclined to the opinion, held by several others,
that he was originally an "Antient," and was in some
measure responsible for the introduction of the R.A. amongst
the "Moderns;" but in the early part of last year I had
the good fortune to come across a letter in his own handwriting, in which he mentions his "Mother Lodge," then
No. 20, at Portsmouth,* and from what I have since learnt
of his antipathy to Dermott and his party, I should say
he would have been about the last person to have attended
their lodges, or adopted any of their customs.

On the 12th March, 1766, two visitors were present,
where they came from is not stated, but on the 11th June
following, a "Br. Power of Plymouth" visited the Chapter.
I gather from the Register of the "Ancients" that they had
no lodge at Plymouth at this period. A London Warrant
was re-issued to some brethren there in 1763, but they
never returned any names after that year, and there is not
a "Power" amongst the members recorded.

The "Modern" list gives four lodges at Plymouth in
1766, and it seems to me highly probable that the person
in question was a member of one of these lodges; and for
all we know to the contrary, he may have also belonged to

---

* See the *Freemason*, 24th April, 1886.

a Chapter in that town, unless the R.A. was at that time worked in the lodges.

Apropos of Plymouth Masonry, I have before me a certificate to the purport " that our loving Brother, *Wm. McKenzie* was made a Mason, *Past, Rose to a Master & made a R : Arch* at our regularly constituted Lodge, *Fortitude, No.* 160, *now held at the sign of the Half Moon, Liberty Street, Plymouth Dock, Devon.*"* There is no mistake as to the genuineness of this document, it was signed by the Master and the rest of the Officers, sealed with the lodge seal, and forwarded with the following letter to Wm. White, Grand Secretary of the " Moderns " :—

" Plymouth Dock,
" 14th May, 1793.

" Sir & Br.,

"We beg leave to acquaint you that we have received a Letter from our Worthy Brother William McKenzie laying forth his Distressful Situation, being a Prisoner in the King's Bench Prison, and praying for Relief, We therefore, the Master, Wardens and Brethren of the Lodge of Fortitude, No. 160, Do heartily Recommend the said Distress'd Brother to the Grand Lodge's favourable notice and attention, praying they will be pleas'd to Relieve him in his present Distress, as we think he is very deserving, we have enclosed his Certificate by his desire for satisfaction that he was really made a Mason, &c. by us and in our Lodge."

Unfortunately the dates of making, passing, &c., are not stated, but there is no doubt this certificate was obtained for the purpose indicated in the letter. The Committee of Charity voted five pounds towards the relief of the applicant at the next meeting after the Petition was received.

Here we have conclusive evidence that the R.A. was

---

* The words in Italic are written in the Certificate, the rest being printed.

worked by one lodge under the "Modern" Constitution, and if by one, why not others? But to return to the minute book of the London Chapter. On the 16th May, 1766, twenty-one members were present, "The Chapter being open'd in due form, the M.E. Gd. proceeded to give the different Sections." This does not look like an entirely new organisation. At the next meeting the Grand Master, Lord Blaney, passed the Arch, and became a member of the Chapter. On the 2nd July Br. Berkeley the Grand Treasurer was a visitor; he came again on the 30th with the Grand Secretary, when they both joined the Chapter, but where they were exalted is not stated.

At the Anniversary Feast held at the Turk's Head, 26th December, 1766, "The Thanks of the Chapter was given by Z. in an Address to Bro^r. John Maclean, as Father & Promoter, who for his Instructions and careful Attendance was requested to accept a Gold Plate."

In my opinion Maclean was one of the most active in the promulgation of the R.A. amongst the "Moderns" in London, at any rate. He was evidently highly respected by the members of the Chapter, but unfortunately we are almost in the dark as to his early masonic life.

All that I have hitherto been able to learn, is that a person answering to his description joined the Lodge of Concord, No. 228, on the "Modern" list* in 1771, when he is described as an "Upholder," made a Mason at the age of 21, in the year 1740; and from the fact of his having been ordered by the Chapter in 1765, "to provide a Stool & Bench 6½ foot long, stuff'd and covered with Crimson Moreen & Brass Nails," I concluded he was the same person. I can find no trace of him in the records of the "Ancients," and I have reasons which I need not here explain, for thinking that he always belonged to the other side.

---

* Now the Old Concord Lodge, No. 172.

In 1767 this private Chapter, by a Charter of Compact*
between Lord Blaney and the principal members, was formed
into a Grand Chapter, with power to grant Charters, &c.,
which was no doubt a capital thing for the Order generally,
but I am of opinion that it was in a great measure the
cause of the downfall of poor old Maclean, for we afterwards find him mentioned as going about in different parts
of the country on R.A. affairs, probably to the neglect of
his legitimate business. However that may be, he fell into
poverty in his latter days, and was several times relieved
from the funds of Grand Chapter, the last occasion being in
1793, when the sum of two guineas was voted to him,
but he died before he could receive the money.

An esteemed friend, who I fancy must have been forgotten
when bumps of "*veneration*" were served out, and was com-
pensated by a double share of "*combativeness*," and who has
a world-wide reputation for his hatred of fictions (I need
scarcely say I allude to Jacob Norton, of Boston, U.S.A.), is,
or was, of opinion that the Caledonian Lodge† was the medium
of the introduction of the R.A. amongst the "Moderns."
Possibly others may be of the same way of thinking. I will
therefore briefly give the result of a search for evidence in
support of this view. Twenty-nine members of this lodge
were registered while it was under the "Ancients," not one

---

* This important and most interesting document, which had been lost
and recovered at various periods, last came to the surface during the re-
building of the Grand Lodge premises about twenty years ago. Having
made a copy I deposited the original where it could be found if wanted.
Shortly after the appointment of the present Grand Secretary I handed
it to him, and he, in order to ensure that it should not be again lost sight
of, gave directions to have it framed and hung in the then Grand Chapter-
room at Freemasons' Hall, London. Hughan's *Origin of the English
Rite, &c.*, contains a verbatim copy of the Charter of Compact.

† Constituted by the "Moderns" in 1764; formerly No. 111 "Ancients."
See Gould's *Atholl Lodges*, p. 22.

of whose names are to be found in their R.A. register; neither are any of their names to be found in the lists of members of the "Modern" Chapter recently under examination.

I presume Br. Norton bases his theory on a reference to "the Caledonian Chapter" previously quoted, if so I may mention that there was a Caledonian Lodge, No. 260, on the "Modern" list in 1765, as well as the one referred to, as No. 325. The register does not contain a list of the members of the former lodge; so that nothing can be gleaned from that source.

In my opinion the Chapter in question is quite as likely to have taken its name from one lodge as from the other, but I think it much more probable that it had no particular connexion with either; that, in fact it was an independent Chapter got up by Maclean, whose name certainly savours of

"Caledonia stern and wild,"

and the reservations referred to were intended as complimentary to him. Another point worthy of notice is the fact that William Preston, the celebrated Masonic historian, was a member of No. 325, while it was under the "Ancients," and was instrumental in getting a "Constitution" from the "Moderns," but I do not find his name in the early R.A. records of either Society.

I have previously referred to visitors from the country being present at the meetings of this Old Chapter, and I may state that those mentioned were not the only ones, but for reasons already given it is impossible to identify them. After the year 1768, however, the identification is much easier. The minutes of the Grand Chapter, 13th January, 1769, inform us that "Br. Galloway moved, That a Constitution be granted to the R.A.M.'s residing at Portsmouth which they requested by letter to Br. Dunckerley; Unanimously agreed to."

This Chapter was duly constituted as No. 3 by a charter

bearing date 11th August, 1769, issued to Wm. Cook, Samuel Palmer, and Thomas Scanville.

At this period there were but two lodges on the "Modern" roll at Portsmouth, viz., No. 20, constituted 1724, and No. 234, constituted in 1762; the former was evidently in a bad way, being very mutinous and most irregular in making returns, and was only kept on the list by the personal influence and private contributions of Dunckerley himself, out of the respect he had for his "Mother Lodge," although he was not then a member of it; the latter never returned any names at all, and was erased in 1773. In a list of members of No. 20 sent in for registration, probably about 1785, I find the name of Saml. Palmer, stated to have been made "before 1769." The other two persons named in the Charter I cannot trace anywhere; however, I think we may fairly take it for granted that at the time the application was made to Dunckerley for a Charter the petitioners were members of his old Lodge, for I find in the list referred to (doubtless the first return that was made from that lodge), five out of the first ten names sent in as members of the Chapter; the date of their exaltation is not given, but it was prior to February, 1788.

The "Ancients" had two lodges on their list in the same neighbourhood, but both were in abeyance in 1769, viz., No. 79, at Gosport, constituted 1759, last names returned in 1764; and No. 101, Portsmouth Common, constituted 1762, the latter never returned a list of its members, and probably came to grief soon after it was started. Charter No. 4 was dated 12th May, 1769, and was granted to "John Dean, Richd. Sagar, & Wm. Towers, at Burnley in Lancashire." The first two are registered as members of No. 247 in 1769, now No. 126 Burnley, as are also the first two names on the list of members; the date of exaltation given for the two latter is 12th June, 1769. Wm. Towers

I cannot trace, he probably belonged to another lodge. No. 5 was also dated 12th May, 1769, and granted to Thos. Hargreaves, James Lansdale and James Varley at Colne, in Lancashire. These names are registered as members of No. 216 in 1769, now the Royal Lancashire Lodge, No. 116.

The petitioning Principals for Chapter No. 6, Manchester, constituted in 1769, (originally No. 2) were Joseph Carter, John Hawcourt and John Clegg. Carter was a member of No. 319 in 1768, now No. 163, and the last two names are in the list of members of No. 154, now No. 89, both lodges then meeting in Manchester. No. 7 Chapter was constituted at Bury, 11th November, 1769, and here we have proof positive of the existence of R. A. Masonry in that neighbourhood certainly one year before the Charter was applied for. In this instance the date of exaltation of two of the principals named in the Charter is given as 1768, while in the cases previously mentioned no date of exaltation of the Petitioners is recorded. The Petitioners for this Chapter were all members of No. 61, present No. 42, Bury.

" I have not restricted my researches with regard to the antecedents of these early members of the Royal Arch degree, to the " Modern " records, but only in one instance have I found a similar name on the register of the " Ancients," which, as I have before stated, is much more complete than that of the former body.

As will be seen Joseph Carter was the first Z. of No. 6 Chapter and was then a member of No. 319 of the "Moderns;" and a Joseph Carter was returned in 1756 as a member of No. 56 (Manchester) on the roll of the "Ancients." This lodge registered no members after 1764, and as I find six of its former members on the register of No. 319 Constituted by the Moderns in 1766, it seems highly probable that No. 56 went over to the enemy.

I have not deemed it necessary to continue my examination on these lines beyond No. 7 Chapter, for I am pretty sure the result would have been the same had I taken every Chapter on the list. It will thus be seen that notwithstanding that the R.A. was first mentioned by Dermott in the records of the "Ancients" it was not generally adopted by them until some years after it had become exceedingly popular with the "Moderns." The "glorious Union" of the two Grand Lodges took place on 27th December, 1813, when it was "declared and pronounced, that pure Ancient Masonry consists of three degrees and no more; *viz.* those of the Entered Apprentice, the Fellow Craft, and the Master Mason, including the Supreme Order of the Holy Royal Arch."

At the Union of the two Grand Chapters in 1817 it was resolved "That such regular Chapters as have existed prior to the 27th Decr., 1813, without being attached to any regular Lodge, shall unite themselves to some Lodge."

I will close this chapter by briefly enumerating some of the other customs of the "Ancients," adopted by the United Grand Lodge in 1813, and still in practice.

The stated meetings of the "Ancient" Grand Lodge were on the first Wednesdays in March, June, September, and December, whereas the "Moderns" seem to have been very irregular in this respect, meeting on almost every day in the week except Sunday. Towards the latter part of the last century, they appear to have adopted Wednesday as their favorite day, and generally had what they called a "Quarterly Communication" three times a year, viz., on either the first or second Wednesday in February and April, and the fourth Wednesday in November.

Our present Grand Lodge Seal includes the whole of the Armorial bearings of the "Ancients" except the legend; the mottoes of both "Ancients and "Moderns" having been discarded in 1813 for the one now in use.

Grand Lodge Certificates written in Latin and English as before noted.

The system of registering members and their contributions to the Fund of Benevolence.

Past Masters were not members of Grand Lodge according to the regulations of the " Moderns," but they were by those of the " Ancients," and it was this custom that retarded the Union for several years.

The ceremony of Installation of Master is derived from the "Ancients" as well as certain portions of the other ceremonies.

Offices in Grand Lodge not restricted to those who had served the office of Grand Steward, as was formerly the case with the " Moderns."

Grand Pursuivants not recognized by the " Moderns " prior to the Union, but always appointed by the " Ancients."

Deacons adopted generally, not previously appointed in either of the Grand Lodges, but always in the private lodges of the " Ancients."

So far as I can learn, the only old customs of the " Moderns " which survived the Union were the privilege of the Grand Stewards to nominate their successors, and the Grand Master's prerogative of appointing the Grand officers.

CHAPTER VII.

THE ORIGIN OF THE "SECESSION" FICTION.

" O, what a goodly outside falsehood hath."—Shakespeare.

 SHALL now endeavour to show how and when this very plausible story of a most improbable secession originated, and, I would first ask the reader to peruse carefully the following copy of a rather lengthy, but I hope not uninteresting letter written by the Grand Secretary of the " Moderns," and which may fairly be taken as an official expression of opinion at that period on the character and origin of the rival association :—

" D'rs Commons.

" Mr. Geo. Stable,   " 8th Aug., 1769.
         " Whitehaven.

"Sir & Bro'r,

    " Agreeable to my promise that if the papers you men-
tioned in your last Letter should come into my hands you
might depend upon hearing from me fully on the several
matters therein, I now take the liberty to inform you that
I have found these papers, & with respect to the persons
you inquire after under the Denomination of Ancient Masons,
they are a set of men who first made their appearance about
the year 1746, and the same taken notice of in the Book of
Const'ns in the Marquess of Carnarvon's reign. Among
the ring-leaders of this combination were, as I am from good
authority informed, one Turner, a degraded Serjeant of the
Guards, who acted as their first Grand Master, one Bowman or Bowden a Beadle of St. James' Workhouse, who
acted as D.G.M., & 'tis said was received and entertained as
such in the City of Bristol at the time he was conveying
thither vagrants from the above parish, one Morgan, a jour-

neyman shoemaker in Pall Mall, was their first G.S., Ja's
Hagen, a Penny Barber, one of their first Masters. With
Mr. Lawrence Dermott, then a Brewer's Servant, & Geo.
Mittins, Painter, lately, if not at present, Under Turnkey of
Newgate, in Bristol, of whom it is said Mr. D. first learned
the use of ye Brush, and several others of the same stamp,
not worth notice, were Grand Officers, &c. Mr. Dermott
therefore said very true when he told Mr. Elliot in his L'r
that none of the Brethren of our G.L. had ever thought
proper to Question him or any of his officers. For the G.L.
of real Masons in England disclaiming all manner of connection with these men, disdain to enter into any arguments
or disputes with 'em, indeed they are in general beneath the
least notice of any Person of Credit, & as such we leave
them to enjoy their own sentiments & proceedings. It is
true applications have been & still are frequently made to
the G.L. for Warrants to be granted to persons who have
been first made, as it is Termed, by them, but then these
persons, tho' they had been trepanned by this sett of men,
disliking the connection, & discovering the deceit, yet still
retained a desire of becoming members of the respectable
body of real Masons, & being found worthy & afterwards
properly made, Warrants have been granted them. This
self-important body I find places its Consequence in the
G.M.'s Throne, 5 Candlesticks, Emblems, &c., Baubles well
enough to Captivate weak minds and impose on shallow
understandings, & will serve to catch the vulgar, as Worms
do Gudgeons, for a very small part of what goes to their net
would be acceptable at our Table.

" The Society of Ancient York Masons, under Direction
of the G.L. was Transferred many years ago to London (as
that of Killwinning in Scotland has been to Edinb'h),
and has ever been governed by a succession of the most
eminent & noble Brethren, as appears from the Book of
Const'ns &c. Whereas this rebellious Combination is only

N 2

the growth of a Mushroom when compared to the true
body, and notwithstanding their Benevolence extended to
all sorts who would list under their banner for the meanest
and most Despicable Consideration, yet their Progress was
very slow, & the reason is obvious, they could only look for
an increase among people of their own rank & condition, &
such being accustomed to Benefit Clubs, had little relish for
an association where nothing was to be hoped for either at
the present or in the future ; for tho' it was ordered that at
every meeting they should collect from each member 6d.,
spend 4d., and put bye 2d. for the G.L. as they called it,
out of which every sick member was to be allowed a weekly
stipend, Yet, unfortunately for the Scheme, they died at so
great a pace, that whatever Petitions were Transmitted to
London for such allowance, were seldom answered, as was
often the case likewise at Bristol & other places.   This was
the plan they set out upon, & pursued for many years ; how
far they have raised themselves in the Esteem of the public
may be gathered from the number of Persons of Eminence
who have headed 'em being at the most, to allow their
reckoning, but 3, vizt., Lord Blessington, some Lord Kelly,
and a present Mr. Matthews, whose names they have
made use of, but with what authority I shall not pretend to
say, this much I can say, that the late Mr. Revis, who
had been an Officer of our G.L. for upwards of 30 years,
declared about the year '60 that Lord Blessington being
informed of such circumstance, forbid the use of his name
any longer, under pain of prosecution ; they were long
& frequently without any Name as G.M., during which
Interregnums an old man, a Taylor, their S.G.W., acted as
G.M., whose son Mr. D. calls his Deputy.   But to proceed
as to his L'r, Mr. D. has taken much pains, but to very
little purpose, to insinuate a cause of Distinction between
what he calls Ancient & Modern Masonry.   Ancient
Masonry, he says, received the finishing stroke at the

making the late P. of W. sitting. Wonderful! I could
wish there had not been a stool or chair in the Universe
rather than the magnificent & noble structure of Ancient
Masonry should by the use of them in this Instance have
received that mortal wound. He also laments it as a woeful
circumstance that Dr. Anderson was obliged thro' his con-
nections with the Craft to represent that proceeding in the
best light he could. Mr. D. does not venture to say it was
in a false light; and if in a true one, how does he gather
any impropriety in the proceeding, or how dare he arraign
the fidelity, judgement and prudence of so many respectable
persons? But suppose (which is far from being allowed)
that there was any impropriety in the proceeding, how could
one irregular Transaction, & that in a private & very
particular Lodge, destroy the Fundamentals of the whole
Society, & metamorphose an Ancient Institution of more
than 2,000 years standing into one of a new name and
nature, of fresh existence. I shall pass over the curious
Anecdote that the Woman who bore him was nearly related
to one of the Gentlemen present at the above Transactions,
as it is not clear to me whether he ever acknowledged any
such relations as Mother or Son, or that he was not like
Moses, found in the bulrushes.

"With regard to your future conduct, I need say little
more than refer you to the Constitutions Book and other
particulars extracted from the G.L. Book herewith enclosed,
which, for the information of such Brethren as may be
Ignorant in these matters, you'll please to communicate,
and with respect to the distinction of Ancient and Modern,
it must appear too ridiculous to be regarded by any intelligent
Mason.

"Upon the whole, Sir, your Lodge will no doubt discover
the total fallacy of Mr. Law. Dermott's account, & that
ours is the real Ancient Grand Lodge of York, the Great
Mr. D.'s, a spurious upstart race of fanatics; & therefore

that you will treat all those pretending to be Masons under
this man's authority as rebels to the Craft, & no Masons
at all.

" Your, &c.,
" J. H."

The writer of this document evidently stood high in the
estimation of those with whom he was associated, not only
in Masonry, but judging from his correspondence, in his
profession also. He is described as "Proctor," and was
initiated in the Philanthropic Lodge, London, in 1764, and
shortly afterwards joined the Globe Lodge (now No. 23),
of which he was Master in 1768; he also joined the
Emulation Lodge (now No. 21) in 1772, the London Lodge
(now 108) in 1773, and continued an active member for
many years. He served as Grand Steward in 1767, Grand
Secretary from 1769 to 1784, Senior Grand Warden in
1785, and was elected Grand Treasurer every year from 1786
till his decease in 1804.

Taking him all round I should say he was a clever and
methodical man of business, as well as one of the most
deservedly respected Masons of his time.

I mention these facts in order that my readers may judge
for themselves whether this was the sort of man to neglect
anything likely to tell against the people of whom he was
writing, and yet it will be observed that the words *seceders*,
or *schismatics*, are not to be found in this long and carefully
written document, nor does the writer even insinuate that
these terms might with propriety be applied to them.

He says they "*first made their appearance about the year*
1746," but as he was not a member of the Order until
nearly twenty years after that period, this assertion is about
as valuable as the one that follows it, that they were " taken
notice of in the Book of Constitutions in the Marquess of
Carnarvon's reign." This nobleman was Grand Master in
1754–56, and I have previously shown that the persons

No 1. FIRST GRAND SECRETARY OF THE "ANCIENTS".

„ 2. SECOND G. S., AFTERWARDS DEP. G. M. OF THE "ANCIENTS"

„ 3. FIRST GRAND MASTER OF THE ANCIENTS

„ 4. "THE FATHER OF THE SOCIETY" (R. A." MODERNS" 1766.)

„ 5. CELEBRATED MASONIC HISTORIAN, AUTHOR OF THE SECESSION FICTION

„ 6 DEP. PROVˡ GRAND MASTER OF SHROPSHIRE. (1786).

then complained of by the " Moderns " were some of their own members and totally unconnected with the Ancient Grand Lodge.

Further on he says " the late Br. Revis " told him the Blessington story, and very likely he did ; but how is it that Revis, who was Grand Secretary from 1734 to 1756, did not at the same time tell him about the Secession ?

Heseltine is most decidedly wrong with regard to the first D.G.M., who, as I have already stated, was a Br. Rankin, no such name as Bowman or Bowden is to be found in the early register of the Ancients, indeed he evinces so much uncertainty as to the names of the originators of the body which he condemns that I am pretty certain his information was hurriedly obtained for the purpose of his letter, and is therefore not entirely reliable. For instance, he describes James Hagan as a penny barber, the register says he was a peruke maker in Pall Mall. Robert Turner, whose christian name he is evidently unacquainted with, is described as " Gentn." George Mittens was not an original member, according to the register he was only made in October, 1752. Dermott's first appearance in the register is in the character of a " Painter," and no mention of his being a " Brewer's Servant " is to be found in any part of the " Ancient " records. He describes Morgan as " a journeyman shoemaker in Pall Mall," while the register gives no information on that point, but his handwriting is certainly not what one might expect from a person of that calling a hundred and thirty years ago. The notion of a " journeyman shoemaker " being " appointed to an office on board a stationed ship " at some foreign port seems to me rather peculiar, and I fancy if he depended entirely upon the patronage of the ship's company, it would have been a very long time before he would be able to retire from business with a competency.

The Grand Secretary probably got a little mixed over

these descriptions, for the only person designated as "a shoemaker in Pall Mall" is John Doughty, Master of No. 2. The reference to a throne and candlesticks is rather rich, coming from an official whose predecessor had, about a year before, sent out circulars to all the lodges under his jurisdiction, asking for donations towards purchasing similar articles for the use of his own Grand Lodge.

The assertion that the York Grand Lodge had been transferred to London was a tremendous stretch of the imagination. Lane's Records will show that during the year (1769), when this letter was written, two lodges were chartered by that body; equally unreliable is the fanciful description of the mode of collecting and disposing of the members' dues. The 10th rule of the original laws enacts that "one shilling each member pr. Quarter" shall be paid to the Grand Lodge "for the use of Indigent Brethren," the same amount, in fact, as at present. I am fully convinced that at this period the leaders of the rival Grand Lodges really knew very little of each other's origin and antecedents, or they would have been less reckless in their assertions.

The foregoing document appears in the letter book in Heseltine's own handwriting, but another letter was written on the 1st April, 1775, substantially to the same purport, although with a few variations which seem to indicate that some other person had assisted in framing it; the copy before me bearing a strong resemblance to the style of the celebrated William Preston, then Deputy Grand Secretary. As this second letter is the real source of the "secession fiction" it will be necessary to notice certain passages wherein it differs materially from the former, which for the sake of brevity I shall hereafter distinguish as No. 1. The writer is still in doubt as to the precise period when "these pretended Ancient Masons first made their appearance," but he goes a year further back, and says "*about the year* 1745 *or* 1746 *a few of the very lowest class of People admitted Masons in some of our lodges were the promoters of this Schism."*

The old story of Lord Blessington having refused the use of his name, is repeated, but not as in the former case, at second-hand; for having insinuated that it is doubtful whether they ever had a right to use the names of certain noblemen as Grand Masters of their Order; he continues *" but this is certain that Lord Blessington, &c."*

Full particulars of the *" Ben Johnson's Head "* Lodge incident are given, and it is unwarrantably asserted that the members had " been prevailed upon to unite themselves with these people." Here is another choice bit. " I can assure your Lordship that the members of their Lodges are in general the very lowest people we have in London, such as Chairmen, Brewers' Draymen, and others of the same Class, so very contemptible that I have heard a Gentleman of their Body say—he was ashamed to be seen among them, and that in one of their best Lodges a stranger would be alarmed & suppose his Purse and even his life in danger from the appearance of its members." The name of the nobleman to whom this letter was written is omitted, but, whoever he was, the last paragraph appears to have been designed to frighten him from visiting any of the " Ancient" lodges. An explanation of the differences between letters Nos. 1 and 2 may be found in the appearance of Preston on the "Modern " stage, and I have no hesitation in saying that he was the real author of this secession story, and further, that there is no evidence in existence to justify the conclusion that prior to 1775, the Ancients were considered " Seceders or Schismatics ; " neither can I accept the statement made by Dermott in 1752, " that so many of them withdrew from Lodges under the Modern Sanction," as other than, what in the simple and expressive vernacular of Yankee land, would be termed " *bunkum.*"

We learn from Preston's biography published during his

lifetime in the *Freemasons' Magazine*, 1795, that he was
apprenticed to a printer in Edinburgh, and in 1760 he did
what many of his countrymen had done before, and have
done since, *i.e.*, came to London in the hope of bettering
himself; I need not say, he never went back, at all events,
not to stay. His biographer says " Soon after his arrival in
London, a number of Brethren from Edinburgh resolved to
institute a Freemasons' Lodge in this city under sanction of
a Constitution from Scotland; but not having succeeded in
their application, they were recommended by the Grand
Lodge at Edinburgh to the Antient Grand Lodge in London,
who immediately granted them a dispensation to form a
Lodge. They accordingly met at the White Hart, in the
Strand, and Mr. Preston was the second person initiated
under that dispensation. The Lodge was soon after regularly constituted by the Officers of the Antient Grand Lodge
in person. Having increased considerably in numbers, it
was found necessary to remove to the Horn Tavern, in Fleet-
street, where it continued some time, till that house being
unable to furnish proper accommodations, it was removed to
Scots Hall, Blackfriars. Here it continued to flourish about
two years, when the decayed state of that building obliged
them to remove to the Half Moon Tavern, Cheapside, where
it continued to meet for a considerable time. At length Mr.
Preston and some others of the members, having joined a
Lodge under the regular English Constitution, at the Talbot
Inn, in the Strand, they prevailed on the rest of the Lodge
at the Half Moon Tavern to petition for a Constitution.*

   " Lord Blaney, at that time Grand Master, readily ac-
quiesced with the desire of the Brethren, and *the Lodge* was
soon after constituted a second time in *ample form*, by the
name of ' *The Caledonian Lodge.*' The ceremonies observed,
and the numerous assembly of respectable Brethren who

---

* The writer should have said " some of the members."

attended the Grand Officers on this occasion, must long be remembered to the honour of that Lodge."

Taken as it stands, the foregoing extract seems calculated to mislead, by creating an impression that Preston had been several years a member of the Order before he went over to the "Moderns." As a matter of fact, the dispensation from the "Ancients" was granted on the 2nd March, 1763, and the *Caledonian Lodge* was constituted by the "Moderns" on the 15th November, 1764, but this lodge was represented by the Master and Wardens in Grand Lodge on the 31st of October previously, and the fee for the Constitution was paid on or before that date, leaving Preston a membership of about eighteen months before he finally severed his connection with the "Ancients." Scarcely long enough it seems to me, to entitle him to be considered an authority with regard to their origin and antecedents. The character of Preston must be patent to every one familiar with his career. His chief failings appear to have been a love of notoriety, and excess of Masonic zeal. His educational and literary attainments were in some respects superior to those of his great rival the journeyman Painter, than whom he was not a whit less enthusiastic as a Mason. He was probably not long in arriving at the conclusion that he had made a mistake in entering the Order under the auspices of the humbler branch of the fraternity, and no doubt his coming over from the enemy was looked upon as a great gain by the "Moderns" who accordingly made much of him ; he joined several lodges and soon attracted the notice of the Grand Secretary, who engaged him as an assistant, or, as his biographer says, "Deputy." Without going into details, I may safely assert that Preston became a most energetic and enthusiastic supporter of the cause he had adopted, and, as is frequently the case, proportionately bitter against that which he had deserted. He was chiefly responsible for the publication of the *Free-Masons' Calendar* which first appeared in 1775, and for which he wrote a History of Masonry, which may not inaptly be described as *compressed Anderson and Entick* with a little "Modern" spice to freshen it up and render it more palatable.

It was in this history in the year 1776 that the "secession fable" first appeared boldly in the light of day, in the very plausible form in which it was afterwards printed in the book of Constitutions, and while the calendar was passing through the press the sheet which contained the story of the schism was sent about the country on the slightest provocation. If anyone asked a question about the "Ancients" and a good many questions *were* asked at this period, the reply he got was a sheet of Preston's history. I have no doubt Preston himself believed in a greater portion of his assertions, but it is not at all likely that during his brief connection with the Ancients he ever had access to their records; and in writing a history of Masonry he had to account for their existence. This he did in the only way that seemed feasible, and at the same time well calculated to damage them in the eyes of the Masonic world, by taking the "Complaints of Irregular Makings," &c., and out of these very flimsy materials building up a story which evidently suited his employers, as well as his customers, whereas I have shown pretty clearly clearly that these complaints had no reference to the "Ancients."

It is a great pity he did not act upon the maxim of a wise writer of some three hundred years ago, who says, "Historians ought to be precise, truthful, and quite unprejudiced, and neither interest nor fear, hatred nor affection, should cause them to swerve from the path of truth, whose mother is history, the rival of time, the depository of great actions, the witness of what is past, the example and instruction to the present, and monitor to the future."*

---

* Cervantes.

There is one statement of Preston's which seems to invite further comment. He says, "Under the fictitious sanction of the antient York constitution, which was entirely dropt at the revival of the Grand Lodge in 1717, they presumed to claim the right of Constituting Lodges." Now as far as I can learn the "Ancients" never pretended that they were acting under any such sanction, consequently they laid no claim to any rights in connection with it.

What they really did was this. They found Anderson's York tradition, where it was of no particular use to anyone ; either in his Constitutions of 1738, or in the Irish book of 1751 (for Spratt copied Anderson's history verbatim), and, with their usual foresight, they probably conjectured that identifying *their* Institution with the Grand Lodge said to have been held at York in the year 926, would give them an advantage over their "Modern" rivals, especially amongst the Masons abroad ; they annexed the story accordingly, and embellished their Warrants with it. But this was undoubtedly an afterthought, for I have before me two original Warrants of the "Ancients," one granted in 1757, the other in 1759, and they contain no mention of "*Prince Edwin,*" nor even the "Old Constitutions." This is Anderson's version on p. 63 of the Constitutions, 1738 :—
"That Prince Edwin, the King's Brother, being taught Geometry and Masonry, for the Love he had to the said Craft, and to the honourable principles whereon it is grounded, purchased a Free Charter of King Athelstan his Brother, for the Free Masons having among themselves, a Correction or a Power and Freedom to regulate themselves, to amend what might happen amiss, and to hold an yearly Communication in a General Assembly.

" That accordingly Prince Edwin summon'd all the Free and Accepted Masons in the Realm to meet him in a Congregation at York, who came and form'd the Grand Lodge under him as their Grand Master, A.D. 926. That they brought with them many old Writings and Records of the Craft, some in Greek, some in Latin, some in French, and other Languages ; and from the contents thereof, they fram'd the Constitutions of the English Lodges, and made a Law for Themselves, to preserve and observe the same in all Time coming, &c., &c., &c.

"But good Prince Edwin died before the King (A.D. 938) without Issue, to the great Grief of the Fraternity ; though his Memory is fragrant in the Lodges, and honourably mention'd in all the old Constitutions."

It seems to me somewhat inconsistent for the successor and imitator, as an historian, of the writer of the foregoing, to make it a cause of complaint, that a certain section of the fraternity should endeavour in the most effective and simple manner possible, to preserve in their lodges the fragrance of the memory of this eminent individual, by making honourable mention of him in connection with the "Old Constitutions," for that is really all they did in the matter.

Their Warrants begin as follows :—

"To all whom it may concern.

"We the Grand Lodge of the most Ancient and Honourable Fraternity of Free and Accepted Masons (according to the Old Constitutions granted by his Royal Highness Prince Edwin at York, Anno Domini Nine hundred twenty and six, and in the year of Masonry, Four thousand Nine hundred twenty and six) in ample Form assembled," &c.

Whoever conceived the idea of utilizing this bit of Masonic history in the manner indicated, deserved well of his fellows, if not "of his country," for there is no doubt it did wonders for the Ancients, especially in America, where to this day we find a vast number of the brethren labouring under the delusion that they are descended from the real "Ancient York Masons," whereas their early lodges were constituted by a Society that never had the

remotest connection with the Grand Lodge at York,* and
as a matter of fact that old lodge was in abeyance and
almost defunct when the " Ancients " started as an independent body. I have only to add that as this interesting
story of Prince Edwin has appeared every year in the
"Freemasons' Calendar," among the " Remarkable Occur-
rences of Masonry," from the time it was first inserted by
Preston, down to the last issue, there can be no doubt as to
its authenticity.

In the Calendar for 1776, Preston's name appears along
with those of the Grand Officers for the year as " Printer to
the Society," and I have no doubt that had he kept his
ambitious propensities within reasonable bounds he would
have, sooner or later, occupied a prominent position in the
Grand Lodge itself, although perhaps not quite so high an
office as he might have reached amongst the " Ancients "
had he retained his allegiance to that body.

Amongst other lodges on the " Modern " side of which
he was a member was the " Time Immemorial " Lodge of
Antiquity, then as now, one of the most celebrated Lodges
in the Craft. In the year 1778, a difference of opinion arose
amongst the members of this lodge which eventually assumed
a serious aspect and was brought before the regular Grand
Lodge for adjudication. In the course of the dispute, Preston and some of his friends comported themselves in a very
high-handed manner, treating the Grand Lodge with contempt, and refusing to obey its mandates. For this rebellious conduct they were very properly expelled the Society
in 1779. They then acted in what at this distance of time
seems a most idiotic manner ; by endeavouring to start an
independent Grand Lodge, being probably under the impression that as one set of seceders whose character and

---

* T. B. Whytehead, of York, has published some interesting particulars of this old lodge ; see also Hughan's " Masonic Sketches and
Reprints."

conduct were so utterly contemptible in *their* eyes, had, less than thirty years before, successfully established a Grand Lodge of their own, there could not possibly be the least obstacle in the way of such eminently respectable and exceedingly clever people as themselves doing a similar thing. They soon found that to *imagine* a secession was much easier than to carry one out, for their failure was most decided, notwithstanding that they chartered two lodges and made Preston the first Master of one of them. After a precarious existence of ten years the whole affair collapsed. " Little Solomon," as Preston was called, by some of his opponents, held out as long as it suited him to do so, but finding that the Grand Lodge maintained its firm demeanour, he tendered an apology, and on he and his supporters promising to conform to the laws in future, they were restored to their masonic rank and privileges on the 25th November, 1789. Full particulars of this affair are given in Gould's " History of Freemasonry," but I think I have stated enough to show that the author of the pretended Secession of the "Ancients" was also one of the authors of the only real secession which has occurred in the history of Masonry in England.

As may be imagined, after this unhappy incident, Preston did not resume his former activity in the executive affairs of the Grand Lodge. I shall, however, only be doing strict justice to his memory, by stating that his regard for the Order was most strikingly evinced at his decease in 1818, by having bequeathed the munificent sum of £1,300 in various legacies, for the benefit of the fraternity.

Having to the best of my belief placed on record every available item of reliable intelligence relative to the subject on hand, I will now invite the reader to bear me company in a brief retrospect of the principal points of the evidence on which my new theory of the origin of the " Ancients " is founded.

I would first direct attention to the fact that the records

of the regular Grand Lodge furnish no indication of a
secession except during the years 1722 and 1779. In the
former year there was evidently a division in the fraternity,
but it was of so short and insignificant a nature as scarcely
to justify the use of the word secession, nor is it quite clear
which of the two parties concerned best merited the title of
seceders. According to Anderson it would be the supporters
of the Duke of Wharton, but if we draw our conclusions
from an independent view of the evidence, it would be the
party described by our historian as " the better sort," that
" healed the breach," or as I prefer to put it, the party that
surrendered ; however, there can be no mistake as to the
failure of the attempt then made to create disunion in the
ranks, nor can there be any doubt as to the collapse of the
Prestonian affair in 1779. Now it seems to me most incredible that we should find ample evidence in the records of
these two comparatively insignificant events, and not a
word to enlighten us with regard to a much more important
secession which we have been taught to believe took place
at some indefinite period between the years mentioned, and
which, so far from being a failure, succeeded beyond the
most sanguine expectations of those who are supposed to
have promoted it, resulting indeed in an organization of such
magnitude that its members were enabled to dictate terms,
nearly akin to *unconditional surrender* to the body from
which it is said to have emanated. When a section of any
particular class or community detaches itself and starts on
its own account we invariably find in its customs and proceedings some affinity to those of the original stock, whereas
between the two Societies implicated, there was very little
in common, except the wearing of aprons and the cultivation
and practice of charity.

A comparison of the social condition of the members of
the rival bodies in 1751, will, I think, show that for a
secession to have occurred and succeeded under the circum-

stances would have been almost an impossibility, and to believe in it, little less than absurdity. On one side, we have a Grand Lodge with an unbroken existence from the year 1717, and a roll of about 200 subordinate lodges whose members and adherents included many who had distinguished themselves in their country's service on sea and land, others who had attained eminence in the pursuits of Art, Science and Literature, and a large proportion distinguished by nobility of birth ; in short, I may say it was in a measure supported by the wealth, wit, and wisdom of England. On the other side, we have a comparatively few mechanics, journeymen painters, shoemakers, and tailors, a majority of whose constituents were even lower in the social scale than themselves ; of a similar character indeed to those who had established the earlier Grand Lodge, and whom they also resembled in their Masonic practices and general procedure. By means of the records I have been able to show, that at different periods during the first half of the last century, there were lodges in existence that acknowledged no central authority, and in my opinion it was by means of these St. John's, or unconstituted lodges, whose members were probably of the humbler classes and did not recognize the alterations I assume to have been made in 1730, that the so-called seceders derived their knowledge of the old customs of the English fraternity. I think it not at all unlikely that the first Grand Secretary, although probably of Irish birth, was an English Mason, for it will be remembered that his code of laws for private lodges were entirely superseded by Dermott's, " the latter being deemed the most correct," and that it is in the original rules written by Morgan, that we first meet with the title " Ancient Masons ;" but from their ready acquiescence in Dermott's suggestions, and the extent of his influence generally, I am of opinion that there were very few Englishmen amongst the founders of the " Ancient " Grand Lodge.

Had the early records of the Grand Lodge of Ireland been now available, I make no doubt that they would have greatly facilitated identification and rendered my task comparatively an easy one ; but even without their aid a fairly strong chain of circumstantial evidence may be adduced in support of the Irish theory. In my opinion the most important link is the fact of nearly all the members of the first lodge on the "Ancient" roll being Irishmen, several of whom had formerly belonged to Dermott's mother lodge in Dublin.

It will doubtless suffice if I merely mention the chief remaining points of connexion and similarity without further comment : The Book of Constitutions, and the By-Laws for private lodges; Craft Warrant recognizing the Royal Arch degree ; Grand Lodge Seals, and the method of affixing them *with the same coloured ribbons, which so far as I know were not used by any other Grand Lodge;* Certificates in Latin and English ; Constitution of a lodge for Grand Officers only, and the names of the members entered in the front of the register ; System of registration in the books of the Grand Lodge ; the *fact* that the " Ancients " were designated " *Irish Masons,*" their lodges, " *Irish Lodges,*" and their Warrants " *Irish Warrants,*" by independent and unofficial writers at various periods, from about fifteen years after their organization up to the end of the last century.

When " Great Kings, Dukes and Lords " became imbued with the idea that the proper thing to do was to be made a " Free and an Accepted Mason," we can readily understand that there should have grown up a tendency to disregard the " Ancient usages and established customs," and to adopt such as were most likely to suit the habits and inclinations of the aristocratic recruits. A critical examination of the Andersonian records, and the written minutes of the Grand Lodge, will I think enable us to infer that from the time of the election of the Duke of Montagu, there were frequent struggles between the older and more humble members, for the retention of their rights and privileges, and the "*Society*" element, which generally resulted in the former going to the wall. First we have the abortive attempt to continue the Grand Mastership of the before-named nobleman beyond the usual period, no former Grand Master having occupied the Chair longer than one year. From Anderson's description of the Wharton incident, and his frequent use of the words, "now the Master of a lodge," I am inclined to think that Past Masters were considered members of Grand Lodge by the pre-1723 Masons, as they certainly were by the "Ancients" of 1751. Then we have the abrogation of the popular mode of selecting the Grand Officers and the extraordinary privileges granted at different periods to the Grand Stewards, on no other ground than that of having a longer purse than some of their brethren. The old minute book of 1737, previously quoted, shows that the duties of Stewards in the early days were similar to those performed by the Stewards of the "Ancients," viz., to visit and relieve the "poor and distressed." The Constitutions of 1723 strictly enjoin the registration of members in the Grand Lodge book, and the observance of the Saints John days, both of which orders, I have elsewhere shown, were utterly disregarded from about the year 1730.

If in addition to the foregoing we take into account the abolition of the ceremony of Installation (also enjoined and partly described in the Constitutions of 1723), and the important alterations made in the other ceremonies, I think we must admit, that after the year last-mentioned the adherents of the regular Grand Lodge had done much to merit the distinctive title of "Modern Masons," the justice of which they tacitly acknowledged as the records of the Lodge of Promulgation testify. Whereas the rival body having kept alive and continued to observe so many of the old customs of the Order, had a stronger title to the appellation of "Ancients" than has generally been accorded them.

After the year 1739, there was an unmistakable falling off in the attendances of members, as well as in the receipts of the regular Grand Lodge, and it is not unlikely that the knowlege of this fact contributed in some measure to the idea that at this period a separation had taken place, it is also probable that this subsidence has been looked upon as confirmatory of the secession theory ; if so, its fallacy will be apparent when I state that the prospects of the "Regulars" began to brighten in the very year the "Ancients" came into notice, and from that time they continued steadily to improve, although, notwithstanding the social advantages of the former body, they found it no easy matter to hold their own until the energetic and clever Heseltine and Preston came to the front ; the three previous Grand Secretaries being evidently mere pigmies in comparison with the daring and astute "journeyman painter."

In my opinion the most feasible explanation of this falling off is, that the former injudicious proceedings were then beginning to bear fruit, and it may be, that the unsettled condition of political affairs was not without influence, for ruinous wars abroad and rebellion at home can hardly be expected to conduce to the prosperity of an Order whose watchwords are " Brotherly love, Relief, and Truth." By way of conclusion I cannot resist the temptation to " point a moral," although it may not in this instance, " adorn a tale."

One of the greatest charms and strongest props of genuine Masonry is its universality and unsectarian principles, and it is perfectly clear to my mind that the decadence of the regular Grand Lodge was the result of endeavours on the part of some of its shortsighted leaders to restrict to a particular class what was originally intended for the benefit of the community at large, and that these mistaken efforts were the cause of the ancient land-marks being neglected, the alterations made in the ceremonies, and the door shut in the face of poor Pat from over the " say." No doubt the elevating process went on to the perfect satisfaction of those who designed it, and in all probability that particular section of the Order would in the course of a few years have been elevated and improved " off the face of the earth," had not the appearance of a young and vigorous rival whose doors were open to all " good men and true," brought them to a sense of their danger, prompting them to lower their standard, and exert themselves in order to avoid total extinction. From this point of view the event of 1751 was the very best thing that could have happened, second only in importance and permanent advantages to the happy union of the two great Fraternities sixty years afterwards.

In the terse but expressive language of the law, "That is my case." If I have not proved it to the entire satisfaction of all my readers, I shall at any rate have the gratification of knowing that by a little patience and labour I have been enabled to shed a few additional rays of light on a most important epoch in the history of our Order, and in the words of a celebrated legal luminary * I now appeal " to an enlightened, a high-minded, a right-feeling, a conscientious, a dispassionate, a sympathising, a contemplative jury," for a verdict.

* Mr. Sergeant Buzfuz.   *Bardell v. Pickwick.*

APPENDIX A.

TRANSCRIPT OF A "CONSTITUTIONAL ROLL" OR THE ANCIENT CHARGES
AND HISTORY OF MASONRY; THE PROPERTY OF THE GRAND LODGE OF
ENGLAND, WITH COMMENTS THEREON BY HENRY JENNER, F.S.A.

The mighte of the ffather of heaven and the wysedome
of the glorious soonne through the grace & the goodnes of
the holly ghoste y^t been three p'sons & one god be wth vs at
o^r beginning and give vs grace so to gou'ne vs here in
o^r lyving that wee maye come to his blisse that neu' shall
have ending. **Amen.**

Good bretheren and fellowes our purpose is to tell yow
howe & in what mann' wise this woorthy crafte of massonrie
was begoñ & afterwards howe yt was kept by woorthy kings
& Prynces & by many other woorshipfull men & also to
those that been heire we will chardge by the chardge that
longith to eu'y trewe masson to keepe, for in good faithe and
they take good heed to yt, yt is woorthy to be well kepte,
ffor yt is a woorthy crafte & a curious science, for their
been seaven liberall Sciences of the wch seaven yt is one of
them and the names of the seaven sciences been these. ffirst
is Gramm' and that teacheth a man to speake trewly and to
wryte trewly. The second is Rethoricque and that teacheth
a man to speake faier in suttle tearmes. And the third is
Dialecticke and that teacheth a man to decerne or know
trought from false. And the fourth is Arsemetricke and
that teacheth a mann to recken & to coumpt all mann' of
numbers. And the fyfte is Geometrye and that teacheth a
man the mett & measure of earth and all other things, the
which Science is called geometrey. And the vith Science is
called Musicke & that teacheth a man the crafte of song and
vice of tonge and orgaine, harpe & trompe. And the vijth
Science is called Astronomie and that teacheth a mann to

knowe the course the Soonne & the Mone and of the Starrs. These be the vij liberall Sciences, the wch vij be all found by one Scyence that is to saye geometrey, and this maye a manne prove that the Science of the worlde is found by Geometrey. ffor geometrey teacheth a man to measure ponderacōn & weight of all mann' thing on earthe, for there is no man that woorketh any crafte, but he woorketh by some mett or by some measure, nor no man buyeth or sellith but by some measure or some weight and all this is geometrey. And these martchants and all Craftsmen and all other of the vi Sciencs and especially the ploweman and the Tillers of all mann' of graine and seeds vyne planters and setters of other fruets, ffor by Gramm' nor Arsemetricke nor Astronomy nor none of all the other vi can no man fynde mett nor measure w^thout Geometrey. Wherfore we thinketh that the Science of geometrey is moste woorthey that fyndith all other &c.

how that this Woorthye Science was fyrste begon I shall you tell. Before Noes ffludd their was a man that was called Lameth as yt was wrytten in the Byble in the fourth chapt' of genesis. And this Lameth had twoe wyves, & the one wyfe heighte Adaa and the other height Sella, by this first wyfe Adaa he gat twoe soonnes and the one heighte Jabell and other heighte Juball—and by the other wyfe Sella he begat a soonne & a daughter and theis iiij children found the beginning of all the Crafte in the worlde and this eldest soonne Jabell found the Crafte of Geometry and he dep'ted flockes of sheepe and lands in the feild & firste wraught a house of stone and tree as yt is noted in the Chapter above said And his broother Juball founde the Crafte of Musicke, song of toonge, harp and orgain And the third Broother Tubalcain found Smight crafte of golde Sylu' and copper yron & steele. And there Daughter founde the crafte of weaving And these children knewe well that god woulde take vengeance for synne ether by fyer or water. Wherfore they wrytten their Science y^t they had found in ij pyllers of stone that they might be found after Noes ffludd And the one stone was marble for that will not burne wth any fyer And the other stone was called Laterno for that woulde not drown in any water Our Intent is to tell yo^u treuly howe & in what mann' these Stones weare found that these sciencs were wrytten in the greate Hermarines that was Cubyes soonne the wch Cubye was Semms soonne that was Noes soonne This same Hermarines was aft'ward called Hermes the father of wysdome, he found one of the ij pyllers of stone and found the sciencs wrytten therein And he taught yt to other men, and at the making of the Tower of Babilon their was massonrey made muche of And the kyng of Babylon that heighte Nemroth was a masson himself and loved well the Crafte as yt said wth maistrs of stories And when the cittie of Nynyvie & other Cities of the Est shoulde be made Nembroth the Kyng of Babylon sent thith^r fortie massons at the Rogacōn of the Kyng of Nynyvie his cossen And when he sent them forth he gaue them a chardge on this manner that they should be true one to another & that they should love truely togither and that they should s'ue their Lorde truely for their paie so that their m^r maye have woorship and all y^t long to him and other moe chardges he gaue them And this was the first tyme that eu' any masson had any chardge of his crafte.

Moreover when Abraham and Sara his wyfe went into Egipt and there he taught the vij Sciencs unto the Egiptians & he had a woorthy scholler that height Ewcled & he learned right well and was a m^r of all the vij Sciencs & in his daies yt befell that the Lords and the Estats of the Realme had so many soonnes that they had gotten some by their wyves and some by other ladies of thee Realme for that land ys a hott land & plenteous of gen'acōn & they had no competent lyvelehod to fynd their children wherefore they made muche care, and then the Kyng of the land made a greate counsell and a parleament to wytt howe they maye fynde their children honestly as gentlemē, and they could fynd no mann' godd waye And then did they through all the Realme that yf there weare any man that could enforme thē that he should come vnto them and he shoulde be so rewarded for his travell that he shoulde holde him well pleased After that this crye was made then came this woorthy clarke Ewklad and said to the kyng and to all his greate Lords if ye will take me yor children to gou'ne and to teache them one of vij sciencs wherewth they may lyve honestly as gentlemē should under a condicōn that ye will grant me and them that I maye haue power to rule thē after the mann' that the scyence ought to be ruled. And that the kynge and all his coūsell graunted anon, and asseyled the comission. And then this woorthy tooke to him these Lordes soonnes and taught them this science of geometrey, in prackticke for to woorke in stones all mann' of woorthy woorke that longith to buylding Churches, Temples, Castles, Towers, and Mannors, and all other mann' of buylding and he gave them a chardge on this mann'.

𝕿𝖍𝖊 𝖋𝖋𝖎𝖗𝖘𝖙 𝖞𝖘 𝖙𝖍𝖆𝖙 𝖙𝖍𝖊𝖞 𝖘𝖍𝖔𝖚𝖑𝖉𝖊 Be trewe to the King and to the Lorde that they serve and that they should love well togither & be trewe eche one to other and that they should calle eache other his ffellowe or els his broother and not his servant nor his knave nor none other foule name and that thei shoulde trwly deserue their paye of the Lorde or the m^r that they serve and they shoulde ordeinge the wysest of them to be m^r of the woorke and nether for love nor lynadge ne ryches nor ffavour to sett another that hath litle conning to be m^r of the Lords woorke wherby the Lorde should be evill served and they asshamed And also that they should call ye gov'nor of the woorke m^r in the Tyme that they woorke wth him, and other many mo chardgs that are long to tell And to all theis chardgs he made them sweare a greate othe that men used in that tyme and ordeyned for them reasonable paye that they might lyve honestly by. And also that they should come and assemble togither eu'y yere once howe they might woorke best to serve their Lorde for his proffitt and to their owen woorship and to correct wth in themselves him that had trespassed against the Crafte and thus was the crafte grownded there And that woorthy Clarke Ewklod gaue yt the name of geometrie and nowe it is called throughe all this land Massonrey sythen longe after when the childrē of Israell weare come into the land of Behest that is nowe called emong us the countrie of Jerusalem King David began the Temple that is called Templū Domī and is named w[th] us the Temple of Jerusalem And this same King David loved well massons and churisshed muche and gave them good paye and he gave the Chardges and the mann's as he had learned in Eagipt given by Ewckled And other Chardges moe that ye shall heare aft[r]ward. And after the decease of the King David Salomō that was King Davids soonne p'formed out the Temple that his ffath[r] had begon And he sent for massons into dyu's countries and dyu's lands and gath'd them togither so that he had iiii[xx] thousand of woorkemen that weare woorkers of stone and weare all named massons And he chose of them iij thousand that weare ordeyned to be maisters and gou'ners of his woorke.

And further more theare was a kyng of another reigne that me called Iram and he loved well King Salomon and he gave him tymber to his woorke and had a soonne that height Aynone and he was a m[r] of geometrey and was cheife maist[r] of all his massons and was m[r] of all his graving & carving and all other mann' of massonrye that belongith to the Temple and this Is wytnessed in the Byble in the iiij booke of the kyngs the iij[de] Chapter and the Sallomon confirmed both Chardges and the mann's that his ffath[r] had given to massons And thus was that woorthy Crafte of Massonry confirmed in the countrey of Jerusalem And in many other kyngdomes. Curious craftes men walked aboute full wyde in dyu's countries soome to learne more Crafte and conning & some to teache them that had but litle conning and so yt befell that their was on curious masson that height Naymus grecus that had byn at the making of Sallomons Temple & he came into ffraunce and there he taught the Science of Massonrey to men of ffraunce And there was one of the Royall lyne of ffraunce that height Charles Martell and he was a man that loved well suche a Crafte and drewe to this Naymus grecus and learned of him the Crafte And to uppon him the chardges & ye mann's And afterwards by the grace of God he was elect to be kyng of ffraunce. And when he was in his Estate he tooke massons and did healp to make men Massons y^t weare none & sett them to woorke and gave them bothe the Chardgs & mann's and good paye that he had learned of other massons and confirmed them a Charter from yere to yeare to holde their assembly wheare they woulde, And churishd them right muche And thus came the Crafte into ffraunce.

𝔈𝔫𝔤𝔩𝔞𝔫𝔡𝔢 in all this season stode voyde of any chardge of massonrie untill St Albon's tyme and in his dayes the Kyng of Ingland that was a paynym he did wall thee towne aboute that is called St Albons And St Albon was a woorthy knyght & stewarde of the kyngs householde and had the gou'ment of thee realme & also of thee towne walls and loved massons well and chirished them muche and he made their paye right good (standing as the realme did) for gave them ij^s vj^d a weeke & three pence to their cheire for before that tyme throwe the land a masson toke but a peny a daye and his meate untill St Albone amended yt and gave them a charter of thee kynge & his counsell for to houlde a gen'all counsell And gaue it the name of an Assemblye and was thereat himself and healped for to make massons and gave the chardges as yee shall heare afterwarde righte sone.

𝔄fter the decease of 𝔖aynte there came diu's warres into England of dyu's nacōns so that the good rule of

massory was destroyed vntill the time of knigte Athelston
that was a woorthy Kyng of England, & brought all this
land into rest and peace and buylded many greate workes of
Abyes and Toweres and many other buyldings and loved
well massons And had a soonne that height Edwin and he
loved massons muche more then his ffather did And he was a
greate practyzer of Geometrey and he drewe him muche to
taulke & comen wth massons to learne of them the Crafte And
afterwards for love that he had to Massons and to the Crafte
he was made a masson. And he gat of the kyng his ffather
a Charter and a Comission to houlde eu'y yere asembly once a
yere where they woulde within thee realme of England And
to correct w^{th}in them self faults and Trespasses that weare
done w^{th}in the Crafte And he held himself an assembly at
Yorke & there he made Massons and gave them chargs and
taught them manners and comaunded that rule to be kept
for eu' after And gave them the Charter and the comission
to keepe, and made an ordynaunce that yt should be renewed
from Kyng to Kyng. And when the assembly was gathered
togither he made a crye that all olde massons & yoong that
had any wryting or understanding of the chardges and the
mann's that weare made before in this land or in any other
y^{t} they should bring and shewe them forth, And when yt was
prooved their were founde some in ffreanche, some in Greeke
and some in english and some in other langags and they
weare found all to one intent And he made a booke thereof
howe the Crafte was founded, And he himself bade and
commaunded that yt should be redd or told when any masson
should be made And for to give his chardge and from that
daie vntill this tyme mann's of massons haue byn kept in that
forme as well as men might gou'ne yt &c. ffurthermore at dyu's
assemblies certain chardges have byn made and ordeyned by
the best advise of m^{rs} & fellowes. *Tunc unus ex Senioribus
tenerit librum et ille vel illi apposuerunt manus sub librum tūc
præcepta deberent legi &c.*

𝔈𝔳𝔢𝔯𝔶 𝔪𝔞𝔫 𝔱𝔥𝔞𝔱 𝔦𝔰 𝔞 𝔪𝔞𝔰𝔬𝔫 take right good heede to these chardgs yf that any mann fynde himself gyltye in any of these chardgs that he amend himself agaynste god and especially ye that are to be charged take good heede that ye maye keepe these chargs right well for yt is great p'rill a mann to forsweare himself upon a booke. The fyrst Chardge ys this That ye shall bee trewe men to god and holly churche and you use no Errour nor heresye by yor vnd^{r}standing or discreacion, but be yee discreet men or wyse men in eache thing, And also that ye should be true leage men to the King of England w^{t}houte treason or any other falshoode and that ye knowe no treason nor treachery but yf ye amend yt preevylie if ye maye or els warne the kyng or his counsell thereof And also ye shall be true eache on to another, That is to say to eu'y masson of the crafte of massonry that be massons allowed, ye shall do vnto them as ye would that they shoulde doe vnto yo^u And also that ye kepe all the counsells of yor ffellowes truely be yt in Lodge or in Chamber and all other counsells that ought to be kept by the waye of masson hoode And also that no masson shall be a theefe or theevise as far fourth as ye maye wytt or knowe, And also that ye shall be true eache one to oth^r, and to the Lord or m^r that ye serve, And truly to see to his p'ffits & his vantadge, And also yo^u shall call massons yor ffellowes or brythren and none other foule names And also ye shall not take yor ffellowes weif in vyllany, nor desyre vngodly his daughter nor his servant nor put him to no diswoorship And also that ye paye trewly for his meate and drynke there wheare you goe to boorde, And also ye shall doe no vyllany in that place where yo^u goe to borde wherby the Crafte might be slaundred. These be thee Chardges in gen'all that longith to eu'y true masson to keepe both m^{rs} and ffellowes,

ℜ𝔢𝔥𝔢𝔞𝔯𝔰𝔢 I will other Chardges singular for m^{rs} & ffellowes, ffirst that no m^r or ffellowe shall take vpon him any Lordes woorke nor any other mans woorke vnles he knowes himself able and sufficient of conning to p'forme the same so that their Crafte haue no slaunder or diswoorship therby, but y^t the Lorde maye be well & truely served. Also that no m^r take no woorke but y^t he take yt reasonably so that the Lorde maye be well served wth his owne good and the m^r to lyve honestly and to paye his fellowes truely their paye as the mann' is, Also that no m^r nor fellowe shall not supplant any other of theire woorke, that is to saye, yf he have taken a woorke in hand, or els stand m^r of the Lordes woorke he shall put him out, except he shall be vnable of conning to end the woorke. **And also** that no m^{rs} or ffellowes take no prentice but for thee terme of vij yeres, and the prentice be able of byrthe, that is to saye free borne, & hole of lymes as a man ought to be. And also that no m^{rs} nor ffellowes take no allouaunc to be made masson wth assent & counsell of his fellowes. And that he take him for no lesse tyme then vj or vij yeres and that he wch shall be made a masson be able in all mann' degrees, that is to saye free borne, come of good kyndred, true and no bondman And also that he have his right lyms, as a mā ought to haue, Also that no mason take any prentice vnles he have sufficient occupacōn for to sett him on, or to sett iij of his fellowes or ij at the least on woorke And also that no m^r nor ffellowe shall take no mans woorke to Taske that was woont to goe to jorney, Also that every m^r shall give paye to his fellowes but as they deserve, so that hee be not deceived by false woorkemen.

Also that noe Mason sclander another behynde his backe to make him lose his godd name or his worldly goods, also that no fellowe wthin the lodge or wthout mysc answer another vngodly nor reprochefully without some reasonable cause Also that eu'y mason shall reu'nce his elder and put him to woorship. And also that no mason shall be no comon player at hassard or at dyce nor at none other vnlawfull playes wherby the Crafte might be slaundred And also that no mason shall use no leachery nor be no baude

wherby the Crafte might be slandred And also that no
ffellowe goe into the Towne a nights tyme there as is a
lodge of ffellowe wthout that he have a fellowe wth him that
might beare him wyttnesse that he was in honest placs Also
that eu'y m^r and fellowe shall come to the assembly if that it
be wthin fyftie myles aboute him, yf he haue any warning,
And if he haue trespassed againste the crafte then for to
abyde the awarde of the m^{rs} & fellowes Also that eu'y m^r &
fellowe that haue trespassed againste the crafte shall stand
there at the award of the m^{rs} and ffellowes to make him
accorded if they can   And if they maye not accorde them to
goe to the comon lawe. **Also that no m^r** nor fellowe
make no moulde nor Squayer nor rule to no lay' nor sett no
lay' wthin the logge nor wthout to hewe no moulde stones
And also that eu'y mason receive & chirrishe staying ffellowes
when they come ou' the countryes And sett them aworke
if they will as the mann' is that is to saye if they haue
mould stones in his place, or els hee shall refreshe him wth
moony vnto the next logging.

Also that every mason shall truely serve the Lorde for
his paye, and eu'y m^r truly to make an end of his woorke, be
yt Taske or Jorney, if he have yor commands and that they
ought for to haue.

These Charges that wee haue nowe rehearsed vnto
you all and all others that belong to masons yee shall keepe
so healpe you god and your hallydome, And by this booke in
yor hande vnto yor power.

Amen So be it

Scriptum Anno Domini 1585°
Die Decembrie 25°

BRITISH MUSEUM.
St. Michael's Day, 1887.

MY DEAR MR. SADLER,

I have carefully examined the Roll of Masonic Charges, and have compared the revise of your printed copy with it, and I can fairly say that a completely accurate transcript has now been made.

The handwriting of the Roll is certainly of the date appended to it, 1583 or thereabouts, but the language of the Charges is considerably earlier, as may easily be seen by a comparison of the expressions used with those of Shakespere or of the Authorised Version of the Bible. I am of opinion that, making allowance for traditional corruption of the text, one may date the composition of the document some century earlier than the copy.

A good many abbreviations occur in the Roll. The greater number of these represent the letters *er* or *ar*, and have been written in the transcript either as an apostrophe or as a small *r* above the line. Thus, s'ue = *serve*, gou'ne = *governe*, eu'y = *every*, mann' or mann$^{r.}$ = *manner*, p'rill = *peril*, dyu's = *divers*, dep'ted = departed. A line above the preceding letter generally signifies an omitted *n* or *m*. Thus mē = men, thē = them. In words ending in *tion* or *cion*, this syllable is abbreviated cōn. A case also occurs in which a numeral is abbreviated in a curious, though not uncommon manner viz., iiii$^{xx.}$ *i.e.* fourscore. Keeping in mind these rules of abbreviation, no one will have any difficulty in reading the transcript, and a comparison with the excellent facsimile will show the system on which the copy has been made. I see that you have given the Latin with all its confusion of mood and tense. It is probable that the ancient masons had very little knowledge of the language.

Believe me,
Yours very truly,
HENRY JENNER.

APPENDIX B.

No. 1	No. 57	No. 121	No. 177	No. 215
,, 3	,, 62	,, 125	,, 178	., 216
,, 5	,, 63	,, 128	,, 180	,, 217
,, 7	,, 65	,, 130	,, 184	., 218
,, 9	,, 68	,, 131	,, 185	,, 220
,, 11	,, 70	,, 134*	,, 186	,, 221
,, 13	,, 72	,, 141	,, 188	,, 222
,, 15	,, 73	,, 142	,, 190	,, 223
., 19	,, 74	,, 143	,, 192	,, 224
,, 22	,, 76	,, 145	,, 193	,, 225
,, 24	,, 79	,, 146	,, 194	,, 226
,, 25	,, 80	,, 147	,, 196	,, 227
,, 27	,, 81	,, 149	,, 198	,, 228
,, 30	,, 84	,, 151	,, 199	,, 229
,, 31	,, 87	,, 152	,, 200	,, 230
,, 32	,, 90	,, 153	,, 201	,, 231*
,, 34	,, 95	,, 155	,, 203	,, 232
,, 36	,, 98	,, 156	,, 204	,, 233
,, 38	,, 101	,, 158	,, 205	,, 234
,, 40	,, 104	,, 159	,, 207	,, 239
,, 44	,, 107	,, 164	,, 209	,, 243
:, 47	,, 110	,, 168	,, 210	,, 244
,, 49	,, 113	,, 169	,, 211	,, 245
,, 50	,, 115	,, 171	,, 212	,, 246
,, 53	,, 117	,, 173	,, 213	,, 247
,, 54	,, 119	,, 175	,, 214	

> Nos. 134 and 231 were originally constituted by the "Ancients," but
afterwards applied for Warrants under the "Moderns."

INDEX.